Dangerous by Degrees

DANGEROUS
by DEGREES

Women at Oxford
and the Somerville College Novelists

Susan J. Leonardi

 Rutgers University Press • New Brunswick and London

Library of Congress Cataloging-in-Publication Data

Leonardi, Susan J., 1946–
    Dangerous by degrees.

    Bibliography: p.
    Includes index.
        1. English fiction—Women authors—History and
criticism.   2. Women and literature—England—
Oxford (Oxfordshire)—History—20th century.   3. English
fiction—20th century—History and criticism.
        4. English fiction—England—Oxford (Oxfordshire)—
History and criticism.   5. Somerville College
(University of Oxford)—History—20th century.
        6. Higher education of women—England—Oxford
(Oxfordshire)—History—20th century.   7. Novelists,
English—Education (Higher)—England—Oxford
(Oxfordshire)—History—20th century.   8. University
of Oxford in literature.   9. Higher education of
women in literature.   I. Title.
    PR888.W6L46   1988   823'.91'099287   88-15831
    ISBN 0-8135-1365-0
    ISBN 0-8135-1366-9 (pbk.)

British Cataloging-in-Publication information available

To the women of Somerville College, past and present

Contents

Illustrations follow page 108

Acknowledgments

I wrote much of this work as a Fellow of the American Association of University Women and am grateful not only for their financial support but also for their enthusiastic response to my work-in-progress. I hope they enjoy the finished product. Sandra M. Gilbert and Diane Johnson have encouraged me in this project from its inception and have conscientiously read drafts and made numerous suggestions from which this study has benefited.

I am grateful to many people from the University of California at Davis for personal support and constructive criticism; a few of these are Robert Hopkins, Joyce Wade, Anmarie Wagstaff, Marean Jordan, Patricia Tollefson, Linda Morris, members of the English Department Women's Group, and participants in the Biography Seminar. The Women's Center, the Graduate Division, and the English Department—all of the University of California at Davis— have been generous with financial support.

I am indebted to Julia Birley and Sarah Frankland (Margaret Kennedy's daughters) for generous correspondence and a photograph; to Doreen Wallace, who in spite of arthritis kindly answered my letters; to The William Ready Division of Archives and Research Collection, McMasters University Library for the photographs of Vera Brittain and Winifred Holtby; to the helpful guardians of the

Marion E. Wade Collection at Wheaton College; and to the library staffs of Somerville College, Lady Margaret Hall, and the Bodleian, in particular to the Somerville librarian, Pauline Adams. I am also grateful to Somerville College for providing me with a place to stay and work and with congenial, intelligent, and stimulating colleagues, especially Nigella Hillgarth and Rebecca A. Pope. Rebecca has spent many hours with this manuscript and has been my most tireless and trenchant critic. The Pope family has, besides, generously provided me with quiet places to write and revise.

My agent, Frances Goldin, and my editor, Leslie Mitchner, have supported me in many ways, as have my new colleagues at the University of Maryland, College Park. I thank Michael W. Foley of Texas A. & M. University for unflagging encouragement and endless practical help. Special recognition to Jakob, Allegra, Benedicta, and Julian for adapting so cheerfully to life with (and without) mother.

Introduction

The heroine of Doreen Wallace's first novel, A Little Learning, discovers in the course of the three years she spends at a women's
college in Oxford that a little learning is, indeed, at least for a naive
country girl, a dangerous thing. It separates her from her family,
from the young man who loves her, from childhood friends. It leads
her into situations she cannot handle—a handsome but careless
artist's attention confuses her, a fellow student's ardent devotion
disconcerts her. Nothing, in fact, works out well for poor Olive.
Her education only gives her a taste of something she is not ready
for, something unreachable and perhaps not even desirable, and
that taste will make her dissatisfied, the text implies, with her ordinary marriage and the ordinary life she is destined to lead.

Doreen Wallace, like Olive, spent three years at Oxford, at
Somerville College, one of the first two women's colleges there.
With a hundred other Somerville women, she learned not only her
subject, which was literature, but also the excitement of heady talk,
the pride of publication, and, most dangerous of all, the male way
of being in the world with its attendant power and privileges, sorts
of learning that, for better or for worse, make one's life irrevocably
different.

Several studies of women's education—its theory, its history, its

incarnation in women's college, the terms of its current concerns—
have appeared in the last few years and illuminate experiences like
Olive's, like Doreen Wallace's. One amazingly consistent theme
emerges from these works, a theme which suggests that it is just
these sorts of learning which have occasioned such heated debate
about higher education for women. In *Reclaiming a Conversation:
The Ideal of the Educated Woman,* for example, Jane Roland Martin
discusses Rousseau's fear that young women, if not properly re-
strained, might develop characteristics "not by nature" theirs (41);
Barbara Miller Solomon's *In the Company of Educated Women* points
out that proponents of women's education, "knowing well that men
feared that a woman of learning would get out of hand," promised
that women students would not be "spoiled for family duties" (25);
Helen Lefkowitz Horowitz in *Alma Mater* suggests that the massive
central building characteristic of early American women's colleges,
which "once suggested hope," soon became "a structure representing fear" (32). It is this "fear," which appears constantly both in
these studies and in my own research on Somerville, that gives the
debate about degrees for women its intensity. If one assumes that
women's nature or purpose is wife- and motherhood, that is, a purpose supportive and reproductive, any education which resembles
that of men runs the risk of subverting this nature or purpose.
Women's learning becomes a dangerous thing, dangerous to the
learned women because it will either make them dissatisfied with
their limited role or unfit them for that role altogether, and dangerous to men because it questions their monopoly on production,
threatens to undermine their support system, and, worst of all, casts
doubt on their necessity. If, that is, women can become producers,
then men, with their more limited role in reproduction, become
almost superfluous. The scenario is, of course, most unlikely, but the
discourse of the debate makes clear that some such fear, some such
sense of the danger of women rising up and taking over, is never
far from the surface. It is a male fear, seldom explicit and seldom,
one suspects, acknowledged. Women who want to be educated,
therefore, have often been bewildered by the intensity of the opposition. Wanting only to have a place in the world beside men,
they unwittingly challenge men's place. With their education they
absorb the sense of danger and confusion along with the conviction
of their competence and strength. This study explores this con-
gruence of fear and power in two concrete ways. First, it looks at the

experience of the women at Somerville college during the crucial years just before Oxford granted degrees to women. With the emergence of the degree debate, the concerns that surrounded the founding of these colleges decades earlier—concerns defused by and diffused with assurances that education would make better wives, mothers, and teachers of the young, that education for Somerville women would not, of course, be so rigorous and demanding as that of Oxford men—resurfaced with renewed vigor. The rhetoric surrounding these issues, I hope to show, points to the deeper concerns from which the seemingly formless and nameless fears arise.

Second, this study looks at six novelists, all students at Somerville during this time, and the figure in their fiction of the educated woman. Without assuming that these figures are portraits of either themselves or their friends, I acknowledge, nonetheless, the special investment that educated women must have in weaving stories about educated women. The vexing question of the relationship between biography and text, though relevant to my study, is not one I have tried to answer. In fact, the chapters on these women's years at Somerville are less biographical than cultural and contextual. I am here concerned less with what effect their Oxford education had on their fiction than with the similarity and overlap between the variations on cultural assumptions generated by the issue of degrees for women and the variations on novelistic assumptions generated by the figure of the educated woman.

It is because these variations become clear only in their concrete manifestations that I describe in some detail the situation of Somerville College during the years these women lived and worked there and that I describe, more briefly, their respective responses to that situation. This situation and those responses constitute one possible context from which to read the story of the educated woman. I see the chapters which follow this context as providing important readings of these texts but not definitive readings. Like Annette Kolodny, I am "turning the lens" on the texts, though for several of them, my lens is the first. This "turning," as she suggests, allows the critic to report "meanings which reflect not so much the *text qua text* but the *text as shaped by* the particular questions or analyses applied to it" (329).

Not only do I not claim definitive readings, I refrain as well from the reductive move of positing a direct causal relationship, conscious or unconscious, intentional or unintentional, between this context and the texts themselves. It is interesting to note, for example, that Winifred Holtby—who never married and lived mostly with her college friend, Vera Brittain—alone of these writers explores seriously in her fiction the possibilities of the single life for the educated woman and is, of the women discussed here, most adamant about the importance of relationships between women and least suspicious of those relationships. Although that correlation makes sense and is not particularly surprising, the endlessly complicated interplay between life and art warns against asserting cause and effect or generalizing from this instance about single writers and the concerns of their fiction.

I come to this study from the enviable and relatively easy position of building on others' foundations and under others' well-constructed roofs. I have learned from feminist critics of all sorts what questions to ask these texts. I make free use of their insights, sometimes without proper acknowledgment, because their questions have become so much a part of my own thinking that I think they are, after all, my questions. I appreciate reminders that they are not. I appreciate, for example, Toril Moi's suggestion in *Sexual/Textual Politics* that we look again at pioneer feminist critics like Mary Ellmann, whose *Thinking About Women* so carefully and cagily probes male diction and exposes and explodes assumptions about women implicit there. I have tried to do something similar in my analysis of the rhetoric of the controversy over degrees for women.

I have applied Nina Auerbach's analysis of the community of women as a literary image to my analysis of the Oxford women's colleges as visual images. Both are, as Auerbach sees, "emblems of female self-sufficiency which create their own corporate reality evoking both wishes and fears" (5). I have heeded the just complaint of American lesbian critics that we do not take the relationships among women in literary texts, even when they are prominent and obvious, as seriously as we take the heterosexual romantic relationships. The strategy of taking these relationships among women seriously seems simple and obvious, but our own acceptance of the heterosexual romance plot continues to blind us to them and to the important meanings they reveal.

I have played extensively with Rachel Blau Du Plessis' "couple-based romance" as narrative structure and ideology, so clearly elaborated in the introduction to *Writing Beyond the Ending*. Rachel Brownstein in *Becoming a Heroine* watches this ideology at work on

the readers of the "self-reflexive heroine-centered novel (xxv)."
The six Somerville novelists were, of course, readers of this novel as
well as writers of it, and they read the romance not only in fiction
but in the narrative of the struggle for degrees as well. I am indebted
to Brownstein, too, for reminding us that traditional endings not
only reinforce the romance ideology but question it; it is "undercut
as transcendence and closure are characterized as romantic, as
proper to Art, not Life" (xxvi). I assume this about all the texts
discussed here and seek to discover in what other ways these writers
undercut that ideology.

As women educated at one of the two most prestigious universities in Great Britain, these six Somerville novelists were exceptions among women, yet they shared, to one degree or another,
consciously or unconsciously, contemporary assumptions about gender, about men's and women's nature, purpose, and roles. They argued along with the founders of their college, their dons, and their
principal that educated women make good, in fact better, wives and
mothers, but they had eventually to confront their own restlessness
in these roles or defend their own refusal to play them. They sometimes saw themselves, educated women, as exceptions to woman-
kind at the expense of their less advantaged sisters. Most important
for their readers, they shared, to one degree or another, the contemporary assumptions not only of gender but of genre. They were
not experimenters in form: for the most part they wrote novels which
incorporate the romantic plot, that idealized version of the lives of
women, that rhetorical masterplot embedded so securely in story-
telling of every sort from the novel to the fairy tale, to the emerging
cinema, to advertising copy.

With, however, the introduction of a new character, the educated
woman, the plot had to change. The second part of this study traces
the figure of the educated woman in the novels of Dorothy L.
Sayers, Muriel Jaeger, Doreen Wallace, Margaret Kennedy, Winifred
Holtby, and Vera Brittain. It follows the twists and turns which the
introduction of the educated woman occasions in the heterosexual
romance. For the most part, despite their adherence to many of the
traditions of the romantic novel, these fictions end up telling quite
a different story, a story, for example, devoid of the romantic hero,
as if such a type cannot survive the presence of the educated woman;
a story as much about female community and relations between
women as about heterosexual attachments; or a story which, even

when it accepts the heterosexual romance as the plot for women's lives, does so with bewilderment that this should be the case. These novels are by no means paeans to the educated woman. They are, rather, complex, multivalent fictions, themselves imbued with the fears of the educated woman that colored their authors' Somerville experiences. In these texts educated women do the very things that Oxford men feared they would do. They "get out of hand," they take over, they reject and even attack men—attack both their position and their persons, attack both physically and verbally. Educated women threaten family life, destroy "womanly women," refuse marriage, and seize power. They also become the women promised by propagandists for women's education: super-women, the best and most self-sacrificing of wives and mothers, dedicated public servants, selfless idealists, saviors of humankind. They are, besides, victims—of men, of familial demands, of their own, in Winifred Holtby's phrase, "nasty little inferiority complexes." They suffer, that is, from the ideological plot for women's lives which has become inextricable from the very structure of the genre in which it appears.

What this study reveals, then, are some of the pitfalls of assuming, as these writers have done, that the educated woman—a figure more revolutionary than they perhaps realized—could be simply inserted into the traditional novel. In rejecting, for the most part, the formal innovation and experimentation of their modernist contemporaries, they ended up reproducing, rehearsing, in one way or another what Carolyn Heilbrun calls the "fictive scripts which control the lives of women" (Intro. TF, xxiii), scripts both accepted and subverted by their own education. Even Sayers' detective fiction, a genre she uses and deliberately misuses, and Jaeger's odd parable-like text, *The Man with Six Senses,* must do battle with the romantic plot, and even these achievements in alternative fiction cannot rival Virginia Woolf's eventual success in telling radically other stories. The reason is perhaps that these writers did not consciously confront what Gilbert and Gubar in *The Madwoman in the Attic* describe as the "infected sentence" (Chap. 2). That is, though these women questioned—directly in their non-fiction, indirectly in their novels—many of the masculinist assumptions of the world in which they lived and wrote, they did not directly question their own access to language itself or the masculinist bias in that language. By assuming the enormous improvement of their own lives as women, and more particularly as writers, over those of their nineteenth-century sisters, they failed to take sufficient account of the still-effective ideology which made those lives so difficult.

The Somerville experience, in its simultaneous embrace and rejection of this ideology, becomes itself a prototype of the ambivalent and confusing stories these six women tell. The Somerville experience performed as well the double-edged service of assuring its students that they were the intellectual equals of men, that they, like their brothers, could master the tools of power and authority, especially the tool of authorship. While this assurance on the one hand made possible the self-confidence and optimism the Somerville writers had when they "went down"[1] from college (and therefore perhaps made possible the amazingly productive literary careers these women enjoyed), it also obscured for them the important question Gilbert and Gubar ask: "What does it mean to be a woman writer in a culture whose fundamental definitions of literary authority are . . . both overtly and covertly patriarchal?" (46) That is, the optimism engendered by a female educational community of (almost) the same status as the male communities both enabled these women to write with less anxiety and fewer scruples than did their female predecessors and made the examination of those anxieties and scruples, an examination so creatively productive in someone like Woolf, less necessary, less urgent.

This lack of self-consciousness, however, and the novelists' fairly straightforward narratives introduced the educated woman to a wide audience. All these women were popular writers and produced widely read nonfiction as well as novels. Sayers' mysteries have remained in print and continue to appear in new editions; Brittain's *Testament of Youth*'s third printing sold out after three weeks. Both the mysteries and *Testament* have been televised; Margaret Kennedy's best-selling novel, *The Constant Nymph*, was made into a film. In an unpublished manuscript called "The Importance of Being Vulgar," Sayers explains that she has chosen to write in such a popular and 'vulgar' genre because there is danger that "the common man will be left entirely to the bad writers." The project does not patronize; she includes Shakespeare and Dante among the vulgar writers with whom she identifies.

This emphasis on popularity and my suggestion of the incongruity between the plot of the popular novel and the difference occasioned by the introduction of the figure of the educated woman is by

no means meant to disparage the texts or to relegate them to a shelf
of historically interesting oddities, so often the fate of popular literature. They are, for the most part, excellent novels, well-deserving
of the republication some of them have achieved and others, I
hope, will soon achieve. The incongruity, in fact, adds tension,
texture, and pathos to these works. What I am suggesting is that
this incongruity perhaps explains why the novels often seem to be
bursting out—plots at odds with the characters, characters at odds
with themselves. The incongruity points again to the predicament
of the Oxbridge-educated woman, herself relegated by gender to the
familiar heterosexual romance, a plot at odds with the message of
the female educational community that women have alternatives.

This confusion of plots, both ideological and literary, and how
this confusion works to undermine the coherence of and therefore
the hegemony of the heterosexual romance is the subject of this
inquiry.

The plot least explored here, as I have already suggested, is the
ideological-as-embodied-in-biography plot. In addition to the numerous theoretical difficulties which loom large, for me at least, in
any attempt to weave literary plots with biographical ones, there
are practical difficulties as well. While the publication of Vera Brittain's journals—a project not yet completed—adds significantly to
the biographical material in her "testaments" (material that includes Winifred Holtby as well as Brittain herself) and while there
are several biographies of Dorothy L. Sayers and a biographical
sketch of Margaret Kennedy, biographical material on Wallace is
scant and on Jaeger almost nonexistent. In the interests of balance,
focus, sanity, and a reluctance to write six short, and thus inadequate, literary biographies, I decided to leave alone, save when
temptation overpowered me, even the more readily accessible lives,
except insofar as they impinge directly on the Somerville experience. I am confident that the several scholars now working on
projects such as the friendship between Holtby and Brittain will
provide biographical material that complements the work on socio-
historical context and the readings of the novels presented here. I
am hopeful, too, that renewed interest in the novels of Jaeger, Wallace, and Kennedy will stimulate biographical research on this
whole generation of prolific women writers. (Doreen Wallace wrote,
she has informed me, forty-five novels and, altogether, fifty-four
books.) The riveting story of the brief and intense friendship be-

tween Vera Brittain and Phyllis Bentley, for example, told obliquely in Brittain's journals, should send us back to Bentley's own life and work.

I had to make other choices of focus and approach as well, of course. I chose to examine the novels and novelists considered here in the context of Somerville College and the debate over educated women—for reasons that will become clear. I could have chosen other contexts in which to place them and other vantage points from which to view them—the literary context, for example. The Somerville novelists were, of course, by no means the only women writing in Britain in the twenties and thirties. Besides such well-known modernists as Woolf, Mansfield, and Richardson, many others—May Sinclair, I. Compton-Burnett, Bryher, Rosamund Lehmann, Stella Benson, E. M. Delafield, Sheila Kaye-Smith, Storm Jameson, and Ruth Adam among them—were routinely reviewed and widely read. And these are only some of the Englanders. There were, besides, writers from the colonies, like Susannah Prichard, Jean Rhys, and Isak Dinesen. While most of these women concentrated on characters from a traditionally educated and upper- or middle-class background, novelists such as Rebecca West and Phyllis Bentley took on a wider range of characters and with them broader social causes.

Agatha Christie, Sylvia Shale, Patricia Wentworth, and Gladys Mitchell were writing detective fiction and creating female detectives of more competence at detecting than Sayers' Harriet Vane. Radclyffe Hall's celebrated lesbian novel, *The Well of Loneliness*, came out in 1928, only a year after *The Unlit Lamp*, which has a Cambridge-educated woman as one of its protagonists.

All these novelists concern themselves, often in major ways, with the "new woman." Sheila Kaye-Smith's eponymous heroine Joanna Godden, for example, so rebels at the limitations forced upon her that she scandalizes neighboring farmers with the self-promoting extravagance of her gondola-shaped wagons, decorated with scroll designs and "her name in large ornate letters" (30). She thinks of "taking a husband as she thought of taking a farm hand" (74), and when her younger sister marries, Joanna insists on appropriating that male privilege of giving the bride away—which she does in a shockingly "marvelous gown of brown and orange shot silk" (162). E. M. Delafield's gently wicked comedies poke fun at the conditions which make an aspiring new woman's life so difficult.

Mrs. Ingram, unfortunate mother of five daughters in *A Good Man's Love*, announces firmly that "when all's said and done, there's only one job for any woman, whether she's stupid or clever, and that is to be a good wife for some man, and the mother of his children" (220). Delafield's more enlightened women, however, have more sympathy with the doctor who suggests that the "one job" is at the root of the myriad of troubles—"insomnia and indigestion and other things"— for which women contantly consult him. The real "matter," he diagnoses, "is that they're unhappy" (232).

Delafield's "provincial lady," who maintains her sanity by writing in a diary, must steal minutes from sleep to do so, and even then she irritates her husband, who pronounces "kindly but quite definitely, that in his opinion, that is Waste of Time" (*Diary*, 387). Women struggling in a man's world, a woman's "proper job," and the plight of the woman writer are all concerns the Somerville novelists and their contemporaries share, but the Somervillians link these concerns much more explicitly with women's education.

Phyllis Bentley's *Inheritance*—the novel that precipitated the Brittain-Bentley relationship—explores several generations of class and gender conflict. Late in the novel a mother congratulates her son because with his grandmother's money he will be able to finish his education. She adds, "Of course there's poor Fan coming along— but then it doesn't matter so much for a girl" (565). Vita Sackville-West's Viola in *The Edwardians* has parents with a similar outlook. A member of an aristocratic and thoroughly conventional family, Viola articulates her rebellion with a bitter allusion to the education denied her: "You prevented me from going to Cambridge, Mother, but you can't prevent me from doing this [going, alone, to live in London]. I'm of age" (281).

Passing references like these to women's formal higher education abound, but to almost none of their contemporaries, even those who were themselves college-educated or who wrote explicitly about education, are these concerns of such centrality as they are to the Somerville novelists. Only at the end, for example, of *Company Parade* by Storm Jameson—who had a master's degree from Leeds and whose first ambition was, according to Elaine Feinstein (viii), to be a don—do we discover that the "new woman" heroine, Hervey Russell, has a university degree, and then only by passing reference to her "scholarship and her First" (303).[2] Like Holtby's *South Riding*, Ruth Adam's *I'm Not Complaining* portrays a school-teacher who decides to remain single. Throughout most of the novel Madge believes that all women should marry, but confronted with a proposal she decides that to accept would be to believe "that the old, tinsel-trimmed fairy tale could come true. And I should find myself . . . with the shoddy wreck of it left on my hands in the gray light of day" (343). But for Madge, teaching is not, as it is for Holtby's Sarah, a way of making the world a better place for women; neither is Madge's own education of any particular interest to her or to her readers.

What my six subjects have in common, then, is not only three years at Somerville between 1912 and 1922 but a fascination with the figure of the educated woman rivaled only, I suspect, by that of Virginia Woolf, who was fascinated with her in part because Woolf herself so consciously felt excluded from Oxbridge. One Somerville novelist who shares those years but not the fascination is Hilda Reid, whose historical novels, like *Phillida,* can explore "the woman question" but cannot directly address the university-educated woman, who emerges only in the late nineteenth-century. In *Ashley Hamel,* however, set in the early nineteenth century, Reid does lay the groundwork for the educated woman. Mr. Hastings contends that his daughter-in-law "joins to her freedom from the common prejudices a range of accomplishments not common in her sex. Greek, German, trigonometry, hydrostatics—these, united, are seldom found within the reaches of the female mind." The daughter-in-law's self-confidently laconic response—"*Or* of the male mind" (53)—reflects, as we will see, the Oxford debate on women's degrees, but Reid's fiction centers much less on these issues than do the novels, in more contemporary settings, of some of her fellow Somervillians. Rose Macauley, an earlier Somervillian who liberally sprinkles her novels with Oxford-educated women, treats them more lightly and tangentially than her literary daughters who were in residence during the debate-and-war years. Not every Oxbridge woman who writes fiction, that is, uses the educated woman to the extent that these six do.

It is, then, this conjunction of the time at Somerville with extensive use of the figure of the educated woman that makes them, for me, a group. Their friendships with and observations about one another add interest, but, more important, the Somerville experience, as I hope to show, creates a context from which to unravel their plots and examine the reweaving necessitated by that odd heroine, the educated woman.

A final concern, this one organizational, in writing this study has been the relative unavailability of some of the texts. I have been unable, for example, to find Brittain's *Dark Tide* (a book that Brittain paid to publish and that was not reissued) outside the Bodleian Library. Muriel Jaeger's *The Man with Six Senses*, published by Leonard and Virginia Woolf and available only in their edition, is considered a rare book, and I had to read it under supervision. Doreen Wallace's novels have long been out of print, though some of them can still be found on the shelves of large libraries. While, then, I have tried not to clutter this study with details of plot, the details I include vary greatly in number between the readily available Sayers novels and Jaeger's difficult-to-obtain book. Even in the discussion of the less readily available novels, however, the details form not plot summaries—though they might appear so to readers unfamiliar with the books—so much as the isolation of those plot strains which make my analysis comprehensible. Someone might argue, for example, that I have skewed Kennedy's *Heroes of Clone* (not one of the several Kennedy novels currently in Virago editions) by my emphasis on the significance of the contrast between Dorothea and her Cambridge-bound niece. In *The Man with Six Senses* Michael and Ralph's stories dominate the novel, while Hilda's story dominates my analysis—though, of course, one cannot easily disentangle them. Part of the point here is to lay bare what seems to me the story underlying the more conventional, often more male-centered plot, but a reader who searches out this text in order to read about the educated woman might be disconcerted by the rather small part she plays. I hope, however, that readers will be neither bored with the plot details of several of the novels nor confused by the lack of such details in the discussion of others but will be tempted, because to know the plot threads I isolate here is not to know the whole novel, to go directly to these texts I have so promiscuously appropriated and so inevitably truncated. I promise pleasure.

1 "Done by Cheeseparing":
Somerville College
and the Degrees-for-Women Debate

In Dorothy L. Sayers' novel *Gaudy Night*, when Lord Peter Wimsey's nephew runs—quite literally—into Harriet Vane at Christ Church College, he invites her to the college kitchen to replace the meringues he had destroyed in their encounter. The Christ Church cook produces the meringues for Harriet from the "ancient and famous College oven" and overwhelms her with statistics "of the number of joints roasted and the quantity of fuel consumed per week in term-time" (145). A few days later, though Harriet has little interest in Saint-George, she accepts his invitation to have lunch at Christ Church because "there are worse meals than those that come out of the House kitchen" (151). Since Harriet is staying at the time at Shrewsbury College the reader may infer that she finds the food there somewhat less than elegant and plentiful.

Later in the novel, Lord Peter discusses college architecture with the Shrewsbury warden. She tells him that the college has had "to make what we can out of very little—and that, you know, is typical of our position here." Practically without endowments, the college, she informs him, has been "done by cheeseparing" (275). Though the events at the imaginary Shrewsbury take place in 1935, sources confirm that the contrast between Christ Church and Shrewsbury—between, that is, the men's colleges and the women's colleges—was even greater in Sayers' own days at Somerville College twenty years before. Vera Brittain, in her history *The Women at Oxford*, maintains that during the years she and Sayers were there "poor cooking and graceless serving rivalled Virginia Woolf's description of Newnham College suppers in *A Room of One's Own*" (119). Woolf had enumerated the courses: first soup, "a plain gravy," then "beef with its attendant greens and potatoes, . . . suggesting rumps of cattle in a muddy market, and sprouts curled and yellowed at the edge, and bargaining and cheapening." Next came custard and prunes, that "uncharitable vegetable (fruit they are not), stringy as a miser's heart and exuding a fluid such as might run in misers' veins who have denied themselves wine and warmth for eighty years." The final course was biscuits, with which "the water jug was liberally passed round, for it is the nature of biscuits to be dry, and these were biscuits to the core" (17–18).

In a 1931 novel by Christine Longford, *Making Conversation*, the protagonist, Martha, describes her first "Springfield" College supper: "Dinner started with clear soup, which was clear enough, but hardly soup; next came minced mutton, boiled potatoes which had been put through a mincing machine and had come out in flakes like rice, but black in places (which showed they were potatoes still); and mashed yellow turnips; and a hot chocolate sweet, which could not be expected to be very sweet, and revealed the familiar taste of cocoa-butter" (150). The men at Christ Church, one is sure, would have tolerated such meals as badly as did Margaret Thomas (later Viscontess Rhondda),[1] a young upper-class woman who left Somerville shortly after arriving because, she explains in her memoirs, she "disliked the ugliness of most of the public rooms and . . . the glass and the crockery and the way in which the tables were set. I disliked the food, and more still, the way in which it was served" (Morris, 360). The Oxford men, in fact, had a long tradition, hinted at in the phrase "ancient and famous college oven," of comfortable quarters and plentiful food. An 1888 *Murray's Magazine* carries a piece called "A Day of His Life at Oxford" by an anonymous and possibly spurious undergraduate, but the lunch scene is real enough and contrasts sharply with the accounts, both real and fictional, of women students' meals. First of all, the undergraduate orders lunch brought to his sitting room (which is, he has already explained, nicer than his bedroom) for himself and his friends. He asks the servant what is available and the servant replies,

"Usual meats, sir—roast beef, boiled beef, chicken, ham, lamb, and tongue."

"No salmon, George?"

"Yes, sir—salmon."

"Well, I'll take some salmon and salad, roll and butter, and half a pint of cider." The friends each order a different lunch and one asks about dessert. George answers, "Gooseberry tart, plum pudding, and sandwich pastry." This opulence is confirmed by Christopher Hobhouse in his *Oxford*, written fifty years later than this account, in which he criticizes the women's "repellent" way of life: "Instead of claret and port, they drink cocoa and Kia-Ora. Instead of the lordly breakfasts and lunches which a man can command in his own rooms, they are fed on warm cutlets and gravy off cold plates at a long table." (102). Like the undergraduate's feast, Hobhouse's disdain emphasizes the difference between the situations of men and women at Oxford.[2]

Poor food and general inelegance were not the only inconveniences at the Oxford women's colleges in the first quarter of the century. Brittain, who "came up" to Somerville College when Sayers was a third-year student there, recalled that "Bathrooms were still scanty, and the 'hot' water was invariably tepid; the poor quality coal which after a struggle warmed the students' small studies was quite inadequate for large public rooms and long draughty corridors; and anyone unlucky enough to fall ill was usually left to the mercy of domestic ministrations as inexpert as they were casual" (*WO*, 119). In the autobiography of the first part of her life, *Testament of Youth*, Brittain recounts her own experience with illness at Somerville: "After several days of existing for meal after meal upon the monotonous slops which constituted 'invalid diet' and getting up to wash in a chilly room with a temperature of 103 degrees, I began to feel very weak" (127).

While each Oxford man occupied a suite cared for by servants, the women, from the earliest days of their colleges, vied for a single room. When Somerville Hall opened in 1879, its seven students shared the ground-floor bath with the scout (college servant), who used it as a bedroom. Such arrangements had been somewhat ameliorated by Sayers' and Brittain's time, but they had by no means reached the standard of the men's colleges. As Woolf points out in *A Room of One's Own*, women's lack of economic resources perpetuated the disparity between women's institutions and men's

institutions. In 1920, during a period of University-wide concern
for economy, *Oxford Magazine* reminded its readers "that one economy is already practiced universally by the women's Halls and Colleges—the bed-sitting room. Many women students undoubtedly
dislike the arrangement, but manage to lead a full and enjoyable
existence in spite of it. . . . Very few would be prepared to recom-
mend that all men undergraduates should be *compelled* to live in a
single room, or to share two rooms with another" (March 12).
Nevertheless, the editor felt that a brave man or two might consider
the deprivation in deference to the war-induced need for a lower
standard of living, a standard already adhered to, of necessity, in all
the women's colleges.

Some women did "undoubtedly dislike the situation," but serious
complaints seem to have been minimal. One of Martha's friends in
Making Conversation notes "What a lovely time men have com-
pared with women . . . lovely sitting rooms and bedrooms and
lunch-parties [in their rooms]" (196–197), but the women were too
cognizant of their good fortune in being at Oxford at all to object
seriously to their living conditions. They accepted with a sense of
humor and even of pride the "cheeseparing" and the constant lack
of funds. In a college play written by Winifred Holtby, "Bolshevism
in Bagdad," the women sing, "When a meeting's declared I will tidy
the hall,/When subscriptions are wanted I'll answer the call." Later
in the play they answer the call for money in a piece called "Finance Song," whose chorus is "Will you, won't you, will you, won't
you, won't you give a grant?" Supporters of women's education like
Professor Gilbert Murray admired this tolerance and good humor.
He points out in his preface to a short college history that Somerville is

> like the better of the men's colleges in most respects, but un-
> like in one. They all have large endowments or foundations,
> while Somerville . . . has none. It has long seemed to the
> present writer that at Somerville, as at other colleges, many
> women of high ability have been, year in and year out, giving
> invaluable services to the University and the country under
> conditions only made tolerable by their own generosity and
> enthusiasm. (Byrne, preface)

That Somerville women and the students at other women's colleges
did manage "to lead a full and enjoyable existence in spite of it," as

Murray continues, and to be good-humored, generous, and enthusiastic is all the more remarkable in that from the inception of the
women's colleges in 1879 until 1920, no woman at Oxford was given
a degree; the women's colleges were not considered part of the University; no woman, not even the college dons and principals, was
a University member.[3] When Gilbert Murray declared that Somerville was unlike the men's colleges in only one respect, he was reflecting the very new situation of 1921 in which Somerville "is now
a College in the University with full rights" (Byrne, preface). For
more than forty years Oxford authorities had at best ignored the
presence of women and their growing institutions, but more often
had objected strenuously to this presence. The issues involved,
though numerous, stemmed from two main concerns—the general
advisability of higher education for women and the effects of the
female presence on male Oxford. These concerns, of course, overlap at many points; both were regularly aired in committees, debates, and journals and became especially prominent whenever the
women raised the further question of granting degrees and University membership.

In *Reclaiming a Conversation: The Ideal of the Educated Woman*,
Jane Roland Martin compares and contrasts the theories of female
education of Plato, Rousseau, Wollstonecraft, Beecher, and Gilman,
which range from the identical curriculum proposed for the prospective guardians of the *Republic* to the education, completely different from Emile's, that Rousseau advocates for Sophie, Emile's
future wife. Martin admits at the end of her study that "some of the
most interesting and significant theories of female education may
have been authored not by single individuals but by groups of individuals—for instance those founding and running schools" (181)
and, she might have added, those opposing such foundings. Differ-
ing assumptions about the "nature" of women and about their
capabilities underlie, of course, all proposals and foundings, both
concrete and theoretical. The late nineteenth-century advocates of
higher education for women had themselves no unified assumptions, but the strength of their society's commitment to the view
that male and female were, indeed, quite different creatures with
quite different functions forced even the most outspoken agitators
to concede the importance of this difference in fashioning a wom-
en's college. Like Rousseau, opponents questioned the wisdom,
given the difference, of higher education for women at all. They
feared that higher education would unfit women, both mentally and

physically, for their task as wives and homemakers; they opined that women were too frail to undertake rigorous study or that women's minds were too irrational and undisciplined for such study; and finally they feared that these same women—unfit, frail, and irrational—would outdo and replace men.

These arguments and fears, of course, surface as well in similar debates about female franchise and women working outside the home; but for male Oxford the debate over degrees was intensified by the presence not only of the women themselves in Oxford's heretofore exclusively male midst, but also by the buildings taken over or erected for the purpose of educating women, buildings so visible and so powerfully symbolic of women's ambitions and aspirations. In *Alma Mater: Design and Experience in the Women's Colleges from their 19th-Century Beginnings to the 1930s* Helen Horowitz discusses the significance of the specific architectural features of the first American women's colleges, which avoided the male precedent of "a growing number of separate buildings for different purposes grouped together in a common" and chose instead "a single gigantic building" in which the women could be carefully guarded. Faced, however, with these close-knit female communities which began to assert themselves socially and politically, the next generation of colleges built cottages "to simulate family life within a New England town" (6).

Oxbridge women's colleges, housed at first in buildings appropriated rather than built for the purpose, owed their importance less to design than to the mere physical fact of their existence. Unlike American women's colleges, which until the founding of the Harvard Annex (later Radcliffe) saw themselves as independent institutions, the Oxford women's colleges were at first merely boarding, chaperoning, and logistic arrangements—evidenced by the names Somerville Hall and Lady Margaret Hall—for women who wished to take advantage of Oxford lectures open to non-members of the University and tutorials with resident scholars arranged by the halls. Only gradually did they take on the functions and characteristics of colleges. As a woman reader of *Oxford Magazine* several decades later writes, "The position of our women teachers and students in this University is one of those delightful anomalies which flourish in England and in all English institutions; we let things grow and never plan them logically" (15 May 1913). The presence of the buildings and their inhabitants was, however unplanned, however unrecognized, a constant reminder to the university that eventually some decisions would have to be made about women at Oxford and with those decisions a whole host of others about women themselves and about the nature of the relationship between the sexes.

In 1871, A.M.A.H. Rogers received the highest results on the Senior Local examinations, and Worcester College offered the successful student a scholarship. The discovery that A.M.A.H. was not Andrew or Arthur but Annie both greatly embarrassed Oxford officials (who sent Annie Marie Anne Henley Rogers some books to compensate for the withdrawn offer) and called into question the assumptions behind, for example, Ruskin's refusal that same year to allow any women to attend his lectures: "I cannot let the bonnets in, on any conditions this term. The three public lectures will be chiefly on angles, degrees of colour, prisms (without any prunes) and other such things of no use to the female mind, and they would occupy the seats in mere disappointed puzzlement" (Brittain, *WO*, 39). The brilliant Miss Rogers, whom one cannot imagine sitting in mere disappointed puzzlement, in *Degrees by Degrees* quotes an 1884 Oxford sermon by Dean Burgon, who, addressing "the other sex," reminded them that "inferior to us God made you, and inferior to the end of time you will remain" (90). Though Ruskin and Burgon perhaps represented an extreme within a community of educated men, they were by no means unrepresentative of society at large, which believed with Burgon and Ruskin that women's minds were inferior and that higher education might be physically harmful. According to a former school head, Joseph Wick, for example, "far more than is recognized, the higher education of women . . . has been responsible for physical and nervous damage scarcely less cruel than the premature sex life, or the relentless frequent motherhood of savage and barbarous peoples" (quoted in Spender and Sarah, 188).

More prevalent at Oxford, however, than such concern for the frail minds and bodies of young women—which concern must have been mitigated by their intelligent and healthy presence in its midst—was something stronger, less concrete, and more difficult to counter. As Annie Rogers recognized, "The real strength of the opposition lay, not in any alleged care for the education or health of women, but in a dislike and fear of their presence in the University" (Brittain, *WO*, 109). The women could easily answer attacks on their intellectual and physical capabilities by pointing to examination results and athletic achievements. The first year, for example, that the Arnold Essay prize, the most prestigious of the University essay contests, was open to women, it was won by a student at Lady Margaret Hall—a fact that one of the editors of *The Fritillary*, the publication of the women's colleges, was quick to note (4 May 1922). The "dislike and fear," however, were much more difficult to deal with and often much more virulent than the attacks. Ruskin and Burgon seem tolerant in comparison to Dr. Pusey, who opined that the establishment of women's halls was "one of the greatest misfortunes that have happened even in our own time in Oxford" (Brittain, *WO*, 69).

Expressions of this great misfortune fell into two groups: first and more particular, fears that the character of Oxford as a haven for the intellectual life and a ground for the establishment of male relationships would be diluted by the presence of women; second, fears that women themselves would change in various ways to the detriment of men and society. Occasions for voicing the first of these concerns were amusingly diverse. *The Fritillary* reports in March 1912 on the first debate between a men's college and a women's college, Balliol and Somerville. One of the men welcomed the women and reminded them of the story of a Senior Fellow who took to his bed upon the appearance of a woman student in Balliol. The anonymous Fellow may have worried that his students would be distracted by such a presence, a common concern evidenced by the "tiresome complaint" which Mrs. Johnson, Principal of the Home Students, related to her Senior Student "that the men examinees are disturbed by the way our students sit in their tight skirts and show off their legs" (Brittain, *WO*, 135).[4] Photographs of the women at this time and the acknowledged industry of the women students make the grounds for this grouse seem particularly unlikely, but the incident was not an isolated one. *The Isis*, an Oxford student paper, published in its 28 May 1919 issue a list of "Don'ts for Women Students Who Live Laborious Days at the Bodleian," which includes "stooping ungracefully over the Catalogues for long periods of time" and leaving on hats so that men have to look at "fuzzy hair." The male students seem to have been easily disturbed and distracted. Warnings such as "Don't glance more than once in five minutes at the being you adore," "Don't pay more than two visits a morning to the Cadena," and "Don't drop notes on to desks as you are carelessly

walking up towards the Catalogues" (all from the *Isis* list) imply
that the women are frivolous and not serious about their work as
well as distracting and disturbing to their male counterparts.
Further suggestions of intolerable female frivolity include a cartoon in the 27 October 1920 *Isis*, which shows the Junior Common
Room full of women, babies, women's magazines, embroidery projects, and toys, implying that this place of intellectual exchange had
been given over to trivial concerns (Fig.3). The November 17 issue
facetiously maintains that a woman student "has written to ask
whether we would mind changing the colour of our cover, as it
clashes with her new jumper." These complaints, both explicit and
implied, suggest that the women are lowering the tone of this place
of learning, but novels, autobiographies, and memoirs which re-
count Oxford life at this time make clear that frivolity was by no
means limited to the women students. Stephen Spender reports
that he "was sitting in a chair reading Blake when about a dozen of
them [fellow students] traipsed in, equipped with buckets and other
clanking instruments of room-breakers and throwers-into-rivers"
(Morris, 373) and that these young men made his Oxford life miserable. The undergraduate describing his day in *Murray's* eats breakfast out, then goes back to bed instead of going to his lecture. After
lunch, he and his friends play pool long past the allowed time and
accept cheerfully and unconcernedly the fact that they will be fined
for this infraction. Such male frivolities as hard drinking, pranks,
and all-consuming sports, far from being censured, were commonly
accepted and even condoned as aids to the establishment of male
friendship, one of the acknowledged aims of an Oxford education.
   Jan Morris in *The Oxford Book of Oxford* notes the "barely concealed nostalgia" of many accounts of days before women received
degrees and University membership. She quotes Harold Macmillan:
"There were no women. Ours was an entirely masculine, almost
monastic society. We knew of course that there were women's colleges with women students. But . . . for practical purposes they
did not exist" (361). L. F. Jones, Morris suggests, felt the same:
"Women-free were our lives. . . Let them come, less as fellow-
creatures than as a distant species, lightly touched by mysteries, to
Eights Week or to Commemorative Balls, but never to disturb our
brave masculine preoccupations!" (361) The all-male ambience
of Oxford evoked nostalgia when recalled, but male students and
dons who partook of this ambience often expressed a much stronger

feeling—a sort of horror that the ambience might change with the giving of degrees to women. The anonymous author of an *Isis* editorial (20 Oct. 1920) predicted:

> What is inevitably bound to happen is that the women members of the University will outnumber and swamp the men! And the logical outcome of such a certainty is that men will go to Cambridge and give woman-ridden Oxford a miss! . . . Men come up to the University for a variety of reasons, but underlying the ulterior objective is the very potent if unconscious desire of making new friends with and having a good time amongst other men.

He concludes by lamenting "how Cambridge must be laughing at us." Cambridge continued to refuse membership and degrees to women until 1947.

When Somerville College was converted to an infirmary during World War I and the women were moved to an empty hall at a men's college, *London Opinion* carried some verses which express the panic that, once allowed to occupy a small part of the sacred grounds of Oriel which was "centuries ago/ To flowing-vested monks devoted," women would never give it back: "And when thy gallant sons return,/ Of whom the cruel wars bereave thee/ Will not thy fair alumnae spurn/ Suggestions that it's time to leave thee?" (Brittain, *TY*, 150). An *Isis* article (27 Oct. 1920) quotes fears that the "Fresher of 1930 will come into the J.C.R. one morning with a nervous headache and will find a dozen [women] . . . 'chatting round the fire and knitting jumpers.' He'll wish he had gone to Cambridge. The Fresher of 1940 certainly will go there." These visions of the replacement of men by women, of male pursuits and concerns by female pursuits and concerns were pervasive and ranged from the eccentric to the official. A favorite Somerville anecdote from the WWI years when the women were housed in Oriel concerns an Oriel alumnus who had returned one day to wander the grounds of his alma mater. A Somerville woman hurried past him at the gate and "disgusted, he peered close into her face muttering: 'O *hateful sight! hateful* sight!'" (Farnell, 41) More serious, however, was a proposed amendment to the statute admitting women to matriculation and degrees "the effect of which would have been to exclude women . . . from serving on . . . committees and from acting as

University examiners." Dr. B. W. Henderson, who seconded the motion, "expressed his fear that women would come to be predominant in the University" (*Log*, March 1919). Although the motion was defeated, ten years later "a University statute, narrowly approved, limited women students at Oxford to 840, about one-sixth the number of men students" (Berry, 356).

Such fears of take-over seem, in retrospect at least, out of all proportion, in view, for example, of the low profile that Miss Emily Penrose, Principal of Somerville from 1907 to 1926, insisted upon and that *Oxford Magazine*, generally more sympathetic to women than *The Isis*, acknowledges in a 29 January 1915 editoral: "the women's Colleges in Oxford have always deserved the Thucydidean compliment of being as little talked of as possible." The women students did, of course, become more visible during the war, when the proportion of women to men was so much greater, and afterward, when they mingled more freely with their male counterparts; nevertheless, women, even with degrees, by no means took over Oxford. Indeed, women students were still bound by numerous restrictions on such mingling. They were not allowed to visit men's rooms without permission of the Principal, and even with such permission they were required to have a chaperone. Nor could women be out anywhere in the evening without permission or be a part of mixed gatherings other than those held between 2 P.M. and 5:30 P.M., and even these required permission and at least two women in the party. (Rules quoted in Morris, 358.) Such rules, comments Holtby, suggest that "women are dangerous. Especially after 10 o'clock at night" (Berry, 69).

Besides being hemmed in by numerous rules, the women lived at some distance from the center of Oxford. Their colleges were farthest from the oldest men's establishments and on the outskirts of the city. The Somerville women who were moved to Oriel during the war remarked often on the novel sensation of being, for the first time, in the midst of University life. Their physical separation, their small numbers, and their effective regulation make women's threat to male ambience and male friendship seem minimal. Furthermore, romantic attachments, widely regarded as disturbing to male students' intellectual lives, were usually formed with young women *not* a part of the university; female undergraduates had the reputation of being too dowdy, too prudish, and, worst of all, too serious, for any such involvements.

On the one hand, then, the males excoriated female frivolity, and on the other scorned and feared female industry. The "Lady Undergraduate" who described her day in *Murray's* companion piece to "A Day of His Life at Oxford" spends the hours discussing politics, attending, besides lectures and tutorials, a meeting of the Shakespeare society, and sewing for recreation. The next morning, she explains, "I am called soon after seven, and I get up feeling myself to be but an unworthy member of this learned body, as I know that several of the very hard-working students have been at their books for an hour already." Mr. Hobhouse, for one, resented such diligence:

> Though their numbers are so small, a casual visitor to Oxford might well gain the impression that the women form an actual majority. They are perpetually awheel. They bicycle in droves from lecture to lecture, capped and gowned, handle-bars laden with note-books, and note-books crammed with notes. Relatively few men go to lectures, the usefulness of which was superseded . . . by the invention of the printing press. The women, docile and literal, continue to flock to every lecture with medieval zeal and record in an hour of longhand scribbling what could have been assimilated in ten-minutes in an armchair. The assiduity of the women undergraduates is stupefying (101).

Medieval zeal and notetaking were common complaints about the women, especially Somervillians, who had the reputation of being the most intellectual of the female students. An anonymous *Isis* parody of 1920 asks:

> Oh, why do you never stop scribbling notes—
> Missing so much and so much?
> You pale, pink women in Somerville coats,
> Why do you never stop scribbling notes?

Such recognition and resentment of women's industry was not limited to the undergraduates. *Oxford Magazine* marveled at an official report issued by the University of London in which the Deans of the Medical Schools admitted that there would be no serious difficulties in teaching men and women students together but objected, nonetheless, "that the women students are so keen that they monopolize all the best places" (1 Dec. 1916). Women, because they were eager students and grateful for the opportunity to receive an education comparable to that of their brothers, threatened, by their very eagerness and by the greater visibility this eagerness entailed, to seem the majority rather than the minority, that place assigned to them by even the most liberal male advocates of higher education for women. Men feared that women would surpass them academically, that women would change the atmosphere of male Oxford so much that young men would prefer to attend Cambridge. They feared, too, the leveling of class which, to a certain extent, the women's colleges represented. "Not only," reported the Royal Commission in 1922, "are the actual fees lower [in the women's colleges], but the incidental expenses of college life are also extremely moderate; the average J.C.R. terminal subscription, including admission to boating and games clubs, is £1" (*Oxford Mag.* 15 June 1922). The Commission notes the women's colleges' concern about "the danger of making the University inaccessible to poorer students." Class privileges and consciousness, so clearly assumed and valued in the *Murray's* male undergraduate's frivolity, in Hobhouse and Macmillan's scorn, and in Lord Saint-George's easy graciousness, threatened to erode, thanks in part to the ascetic lives and egalitarian concerns of women students.[5]

In spite of women students' "keenness" in the midst of relative poverty and in spite of their recognized accomplishments, University members like Dr. Godley were still arguing in 1921 that "the difficulty of maintaining severe intellectual tests, in a University where women are members of educational boards, is known to many" (*Oxford Mag.* 8 Dec.). The worries, as we have seen, were many and contradictory. Women are not intellectually vigorous, but they threaten to surpass men's achievements; women are frivolous, but they go to lectures too assiduously, study too much, and are too intellectual; women encroach upon male bonding, but their social lives are too severely curtailed by stringent rules to which they are absurd enough to adhere. (Hobhouse complained, "They are tremendous sticklers for tradition and routine. Every rule and regulation of college or university is literally observed" [101]); women distract men with their provocative ways, but they are too dowdy and prudish to make agreeable dates. Women students are, in the end, an outrage and a blight on male Oxford, according to someone like Hobhouse, who regarded even their living arrangements as an affront to refinement and their personal habits an insult to male taste: "Fifty years have not mellowed them; they still care nothing for appearance; . . . but deck themselves in hairy woollens and shapeless tweeds. Germer's luxurious hairdressing salons are unknown to them; their hair is braided into stringy buns" (102). Although Hobhouse's rhetoric may be extreme, the content and tone of his tirades indicate an important concern which underlies almost all these attacks: the women at Oxford are not particularly interested in the men, not interested enough to attend to their clothes and hair, not interested enough to break chaperone regulations, not interested enough to refrain from competing. And without this interest to coerce them into submission, they may take over entirely.

Here the distinction between complaints about women's effects on Oxford life and Oxford's effects on the women themselves breaks down. Both have to do with the "nature" of women and the potentially disruptive effect on Oxford in particular, and society in general, of any tampering with traditional notions about that nature. It is important, however, to examine the expression of the two kinds of complaint separately, because speculation about the effects of Oxford on women is an activity by no means contained within the boundaries of Oxford, and, further, it parades, most often, as sympathetic concern for women's well-being and as a desire to give women what they really need and want.

A verse which appeared in the 30 March 1920 issue of *The Isis*, part of an advertisement for Abdulla cigarettes, contends uncharacteristically that an Oxford education is simply a veneer which has little real effect on women's nature. The violence of its diction, however, suggests the fear that Oxford women are ceasing to be interested in men and suggests further the necessity of violence to remedy the situation.

> Pretty Phyllis with a vote
> And a Varsity degree,
> Greek and Latin you may quote
> But you can't bamboozle me!
> Brilliant, up-to-date and smart,
> You're a savage squaw at heart.
> Phyllis, when I come to woo,
> Disregarding sneer and snub

I shall act as cave-men do—
Knock you senseless with a club!
Courtships of a higher grade
Simply bore a savage maid.

The versifier, one Mr. R. H., purports to know what women really want but what he reveals is an intense misogyny and fear that he cannot control pretty Phyllis in any other way than by knocking her senseless. What he proposes is to *undo* the effects of her Oxford education, to, that is, render her imbecilic in order to regain the upper hand in the relationship between the sexes. Her name, that of Virgil's country maiden, suggests that the natural woman has been tampered with by education and that the suitor does her a favor by restoring her to her pristine state. Although her education is presented as mere patina, the proposed solution suggests something much more deeply rooted: only depriving pretty Phyllis of her brain will make her consent to his advances. The institutional equivalent to knocking Phyllis senseless was the crowded college debate in 1926 at which the House decided by a majority of twenty-five votes that "the women's Colleges should be levelled to the ground" (Brittain WO, 171).

More civilized and moderate critics of women's higher education sought to obviate such violent extremes by keeping vote and degree away from pretty Phyllis in the first place. In support of their position they too point out the unfortunate effects of Oxford on its Phyllisses, of higher education in general on women in general. A 28 May 1920 letter to the editor of *Oxford Magazine*, for example, acknowledges that some women can make it through the course both physically and intellectually, but deplores the price: "Who really thinks that for women between seventeen and twenty-two, long and hard intellectual training, with the examinations which the Oxford course entails, is the right way to develop their best faculties and feelings? Some can stand the strain, but few can get through the full Oxford training without developing unfeminine traits both of character and appearance." He concludes with the cryptic, "Just what they want, the women have obtained. That is the Nemesis." The implication, of course, is that "what they want"—education, power, independence—cannot be what they *really* want, because these things rob them of all their best qualities, those vague feminine traits of character and appearance which make them what they are. Education, then, distorts women's nature; it makes them like men.

This writer's concession to the fact that "some women can make it through" was not universally acknowledged. Christopher Hobhouse, for example, asserts without evidence that "Many of the women suffer actual nervous breakdowns; others become stupid and mechanical" (102). But, as implied above, supporters of women's education could easily disprove assertions that women were too physically or mentally delicate to endure the rigors of gaining an Oxford degree. Difficult to counter, however, because often true, were complaints about Oxford's bad effects on the appearance of women students. Hobhouse's scorn that "they run no tailors' bills in the High street" (102) and other comments on the dowdiness of the women seem trivial considerations, and the women themselves interpreted them in this light. What, after all, had their clothes and hair to do with anything at all? But, of course, they are more serious concerns than the women acknowledged. A common rationale for simple dressing was that fashion breeds jealousy, but a male undergraduate pointed out in a 1913 *Isis* what the women who made such arguments did not see: "They dress in a superlatively simple manner—there is no jealousy—men never enter the gates of their hostel. They are combined. There is union. They do not want us." The edge of hysteria in this argument does not negate its logic. Women, men assume, dress to please men. If they do not dress well, they must not be interested in attracting men. Furthermore, clothes breed jealousy. Jealousy is a good thing among women because the object of women's jealousy is men. Without jealousy women enjoy their own company and "they do not want us." The plaintive, adolescent cry is only one manifestation of a pervasive fear that educated women will not follow the prescribed plot for the female of the species. For the male undergraduate, the fear may find expression in this nearly inarticulate and pouty "They do not want us," but educational theorists, university members, writers, and politicians had the same concern, even if they sometimes expressed it in a more sophisticated way. The argument is a commonplace, that women's role is to be a wife and mother and she should therefore be educated to that end. To follow the same course of studies as men, to receive the same degrees as men, makes women more like men and therefore less feminine, less able to play their proper role. The parents of young women, too, acquiesced in this logic and feared that their daughters would be unmarriageable with a degree. Margery Fry, after whom the present Somerville graduate residence is named, "studied mathematics but had not been allowed by her parents to take an examination" (Farnell, 52). Fry was fortunate; most parents drew the line at sending their daughters to the University at all. A concerned friend of Vera Brittain's mother asked, "How can you send your daughter to college, Mrs. Brittain? . . . Don't you want her ever to get married?" (Bailey, 9) Vera Brittain had to fight for her parents' consent.

Ideas about women's roles and what might threaten them have always been, of course, in various guises, a focus of feminist activity. The inherent differences between men and women—what they were and how to preserve them—became, in the argument for degrees and in the argument for the vote or any other political right, the subject for passionate debate, the terms of which have been amply described in the numerous histories of women's struggles for equality.[6] The particular form the argument takes in the debate over higher education for women often centered on degrees rather than on the education itself, because the rhetoric of the early, degreeless days of women's colleges was in line with Rousseau's conviction that "Once it is demonstrated that man and woman are not and ought not to be constituted in the same way in either character or temperament, it follows that they ought not to have the same education" (Martin, 40).

In the late nineteenth century, advocates of higher education for women believed, for the most part, that the claims of domestic life had priority for women. Miss Wordsworth, the first Principal of Lady Margaret Hall, repeated firmly, "We want to turn out girls so that they will be capable of making homes happy" (Brittain, WO, 36). Miss Shaw Lefevre, the first Principal of Somerville, an admiring student wrote, "was not principally interested in education . . . she was perhaps more of a . . . social influence than anything else" (Farnell, 9). Vera Farnell notes that "Her charm and distinction were invaluable in disarming the hostile criticism with which the foundation of a women's college in Oxford was greeted in many quarters" (8). Miss Lefevre even disarmed Ruskin, that implacable foe of women's colleges, who declared himself glad, after a day as her guest, "to be let come and have tea at Somerville and to watch the girlies play at ball" (9). The reason, however, that she could thus disarm was that the women's colleges ostensibly carried out Rousseau's edict that "they ought not to have the same education." When the question of degrees arose, however, opponents of higher education for women were not so easily deflected from their hostility. An Oxford degree implies "the same education" and although by World War I most of the women students were taking the same courses and the same examinations as the men, the fact that the women did not actually receive degrees made it possible to continue to believe that women's education was different, was less rigorous and more suited to female frailty of mind and body. Miss Penrose, the Somerville Principal at the time, realized that "the strongest argument [for degrees] would be the number of women qualified to receive them" (Brittain, WO, 121).[7] She therefore refused to admit women who would not take the degree course. Though Somerville women had, as a result, been receiving more or less the same education as their brothers for many years, without the public recognition of a degree, adversaries could consider them "honored guests" and not real students. (Arthur Sedgwick, an advocate of degrees for women, wrote as early as 1896 that "It is not my idea of honouring a guest to make her do all the work and refuse her due recognition and rewards" [Brittain, WO, 107]). Brittain notes the women's "magic cloak of invisibility" (WO, 132) at the turn of the century, but no magic cloak could make them invisible if they had degrees, and degrees meant that they were being educated, for all the world to see, like men.

The consequences of this, believed the opponents, could only be that, given the differences between men and women, women with degrees would be unhappy and ultimately unsuited for their roles as wives and mothers. In an early polemic against women's pursuing degrees, Dr. Godley, in *Oxford Magazine*, warned women: "Doomed to a course that's narrow (i.e. like the men's), your recklessness you'll rue/The toad beneath a harrow will be happier than you" (Brittain WO, 107). Again, the objection rests on assumptions about woman's nature and what she really wants. The fear is that what she really wants may not be what is most advantageous for men. But that fear, except for the occasional spontaneous outburst like "they don't want us," is cloaked in concern for women's adherence to their natural position in society and assumptions that this will be best for everyone. Degrees acknowledge that women's position might, in theory at least, differ little from men's, that wife- and motherhood might not be the universal desire of women. And if it is not the universal desire of women, it might turn out to be not the desire of women at all.

Mindful of these fears, proponents of degrees, whether out of a desire merely to disperse opposition or out of real conviction, adopted a stance of reassurance. Far from making women like men, women's colleges stressed decorum and femininity; far from unfitting women for roles as wives and mothers, education, the colleges maintained, enhanced their abilities to carry them out. Barbara Miller Solomon's observation about early American women educators was equally true of their British counterparts: "Knowing well that men feared that a woman of learning would get out of hand, they promised that students would not be spoiled for family duties" (25). Early principals of women's colleges both insisted that their students observe the strictest chaperone rules and were themselves, though mostly *not* wives and mothers, models of traditional womanhood, at least in public. *Oxford Magazine's* obituary for Miss Shaw Lefevre (16 October 1914) is illustrative both of the fears and the reassurance:

> She was the very antipodes of the clumsy, masculine blue-stocking who was the favourite bugbear of the opponents of women's education. It would be difficult to imagine a more womanly woman; and the importance of such a figure-head to a recently formed women's college, exposed as it was to the freest criticism from friends and foes, can hardly be overestimated. After all, there is no teacher like example and the students of Somerville . . . were fortunate in having the daily presence of Miss Shaw Lefevre and her charming collaborator, Miss Clara Pater, in their midst. [To] them it is largely due that the presence of women-students in Oxford has given so few openings to the caricaturist, and so little cause of offence to the severest censor of morals and manners.

Womanly, charming, quite the opposite of clumsy and masculine, these women deflated the "bugbear." But this praise of Miss Lefevre suggests at the same time that she and Miss Pater, in their womanly perfection, kept the volatile women students under control. Without their constant and unfailing womanly presence, the article implies, these women of learning might, indeed, have gotten out of hand.

The chaperone rules and other regulations also seemed designed to regulate behavior so far that there was little possibility for any unwomanly activity. Not only did these rules greatly curtail any sort of mixing between men and women, they also dictated more general ladylike decorum. Women students, for example, were forbidden to go to a lawn-tennis party on foot, "because it was considered unseemly to be seen carrying a racket through the streets" (Hone, 12). The Somerville College Logbook records in 1914 a college meeting on the topic of smoking at which it was urged "that smoking as a prevalent practice attached a stigma to college and was highly prejudicial to its reputation." By 1918, the women felt strongly that, especially in view of the responsible part they and their sisters had played in the war, the chaperone rules were insultingly outdated. They even went to the unprecedented length of sending a deputation to Miss Emily Penrose asking for a revision of the rules. Although Miss Penrose seemed sympathetic and "listened, as she always listened, with the closest attention," she, "with the sense of greater events stirring" replied, characteristically: "Wait: this is not the time: wait" (Farnell, 44).

The "sense of greater events stirring" refers, of course, to the imminence of degrees for women. Miss Penrose knew better than to relax vigilance over the women's behavior, indeed to give any grounds whatever for male complaints. Here, too, one perceives the conscious but necessary repression: what Miss Penrose seemed to be saying was, let's keep it in just a little longer, just until we get what we want. Miss Penrose's ability to be ladylike while simultaneously forcing the issue of degrees, for which she had worked since her assumption of leadership thirteen years previously, is evident in male Oxford's sense that neither she nor her students had made a single unladylike demand. On the contrary, *Oxford Magazine* complimented their apparent passivity: "Our congratulations are . . . due to those who have organized women's education in Oxford with such signal tact and success. The staffs of the women's colleges can claim that the proposal of 'full privileges' (or something very like it) comes unsolicited, in response to no deputation or agitation of theirs or their pupils" (quoted in Log, Nov. 1920). Efforts such as Miss Penrose's, however tactful and subtle they may have been, required what Vera Farnell describes as "statesmanlike vision and . . . masterly powers of direction" (34). It is significant that unlike the "womanly" Miss Shaw Lefevre, Emily Penrose was sometimes characterized "as a masculine type" or as Farnell softens the accusation, as a combination of characteristics "that narrower natures of one or the other sex discard as exclusively masculine or specifically feminine" (34). There comes a point, that is, at which exclusively ladylike behavior cannot accomplish much and, though Miss Penrose tried so hard to keep that behavior the norm at Somerville, her own strength and ambition were inevitably perceived, on occasion at least, as masculine.

What this perception illustrates is that the sense or the fear that these educated women might get out of hand, though seemingly ridiculous in view of the remarkable record of good behavior which the women so carefully, so calculatedly, maintained, was in some ways entirely justified. That women students had, in the face of all manner of opposition, quietly installed themselves at Oxford, had then gradually committed themselves to a course of study more and more like that of the men, had sat, one by one, for examinations ostensibly reserved for male students, had somehow gotten themselves in the position of being fully qualified for degrees must have struck Oxford as particularly insidious, portentous, and inauspicious. There seemed to be something going on within these female walls of which men had no knowledge and to which they had no access. American educators in the early days of higher education for women, had the same sense, as Helen Lefkowitz Horowitz so interestingly points out in *Alma Mater*. She, too, sees that the fear and suspicion were not baseless. "The most carefully guarded secret of the women's colleges [was] that in a college composed only of women, students did not remain feminine. Through college organizations they discovered how to wield power and to act collectively; through aggressive sport, to play as a team member and to win; through dramatics, to take male roles" (163). In other words, despite assurances to the contrary, there was a real sense in which higher education for women *did* unfit them for marriage and motherhood; the experience of power both as individuals and as a group, the experience of winning, the experience of assuming a dominant role, changed them irrevocably. With a man's education, or as close to one as was possible given the relative lack of comforts and service in the women's colleges, these women took on male characteristics and accouterments, including such varied heretofore male prerogatives as an interest in politics, a liking for comfortable clothes, self-assertion, teamwork mentality, a tendency to dismiss the opposite sex; these women even assigned as great a value to work as to relationships and to same-sex friendship as to heterosexual involvements. This is not, of course, to suggest that women have not had and done these things for centuries but to claim that in the women's colleges they were present in abundance, aggressively, collectively, visibly, and, worst of all, successfully. Whether or not one approved of women acting like men, the fact was that, contrary to predictions, they could. And this ability, of course, called into question every assumption about women's nature. Even to suggest, as many did, that although women can act like men, they *should* not, acknowledges that what had been commonly understood as woman's nature must then be a social construct and not anything inherent.

What the women's colleges did was to force the concession that women, indeed, *could*—whether the issue was passing examinations, enduring the degree course, dealing with one another without jealousy, speaking out, developing muscles, or winning debates. Such concessions were often offhand and unconscious. *The Fritillary*, for example, quotes *The Isis* as describing a Somervillian debator's "Balliol manner." Her speech, opposing the motion "that this House considers compulsory arbitration among members of the Hague conference practicable and desirable" was, according to *The Fritillary*, "stirred and vigorous" (Dec. 1912). Producing young women who debated on complex political issues vigorously and in the manner of the celebrated debaters of Balliol college was not at all what early advocates of women's education had envisioned, at least not publicly, and was just what its opponents feared. The young women's parents might indeed have cause for concern about her marriageability. As one of Kennedy's characters remarks of his too-well-educated sister, "What man wants a wife who talks in words of five syllables?" (*Heroes*, 96); another Kennedy male "did not care for women who got Firsts" (*Midas*, 458). Oxford men did not, for the most part, take these new women seriously as prospective wives. One *Isis* contributor so instructs himself and his fellows in the special summer issue of 1914: "Women-students do not come up here to marry us but teach our children when we are married."

The poor young man who blurted out, "They don't want us" can hardly have been reassured by the female confidence, lightheartedly pompous though it was, expressed in this "Ode" to new hockey-team members, which appeared in the March 1912 issue of *The Fritillary*.

Thee scarlet-skirted Somervillians
St. Hilda's and St. Hugh's and all the male-
Abhorring brood of Margaret
Do greet

Thereto withal
That goodly fellowship of studious maids.

That even the women of the more conservative and religious Lady
Margaret Hall should present themselves as "male-abhorring" indicates the connection between sport, solidarity, and same-sex bonding so long taken for granted among young men, heretofore so
foreign among grown women. Dramatic activity as well as sport reproduced the bonding and confidence characteristic of the male
college environment. Plays became the obvious locus of an approved and circumscribed donning of male dress and subsequent assumption of male privilege. The most assertive of the students,
women like Dorothy L. Sayers and Winifred Holtby, enjoyed the
masculine roles, assumed them in plays written by others, wrote
them for themselves into all the home-grown productions. Sayers,
in the Going-Down Play of her year, which she wrote and directed,
took the part of the Oxford man she most admired, the director of
the Bach choir (Fig.8); Holtby, her friend Margaret Waley later recalls, "often chose to take male parts" which preference Waley links
to Holtby's "sexual ambivalence" (53). Even the proper Miss Emily
Penrose enjoyed dressing as a man; she once represented, in some
sort of tableau, Sir John Collier's portrait of T. H. Huxley, "holding
a skull and wearing whiskers and her nephew's coat and trousers"
(Farnell, 35).

College plays became an arena, as they had been for centuries in
the men's colleges, for acting out self-sufficiency. The women could
be both male and female; they could, even as females, be with impunity as arrogant and confident as any man. Winifred Holtby announced that she wrote the 1920 Going-Down Play "to trample
down all nasty little giggling feminine inferiority-complexes" (Brittain, *TF*, 108). One of the songs in the 1921 play, also written by
Holtby and friends, celebrated female "noise." The chorus is

Then let us raise the song on high,
All law and order we defy
With strident voice and laughter clear
We'll keep the red rag raging here.

This interesting allusion to menstruation, in conjunction with the
acknowledgement that "law and order" censure behavior in women
that would be condoned and approved in men, openly questions the

code of ladylike conduct advocated by Oxford officials, both male and female.[8] Female noise, one of the verses of this song contends, has amazing effects: "It makes the shyest spirit bold;/It makes us warm in winter's cold." Such celebration of the female surely reinforced the fears of male Oxford of the learned women in its midst.

Not every woman, of course, looked to her peers for primary relationships. One of the other songs from Holtby's "Bolshevism in Bagdad," in fact, pokes fun at a Somerville-Balliol romance:

> On Balliol bowers are bonny
> At the closing of the day
> When she and Mr. Andy
> Discuss philosophy
> Discuss philosophy,
> Which she repeats to me,
> And if I hear much more of Andy
> I shall lay me doon and dee.

Here, too, however, is the confident, self-sufficient tone that characterizes those years' home-grown dramatists. Andy is dispensable, if not to his Somerville friend, at least to her cohorts. The relationship evokes boredom rather than envy, irony rather than admiration. The narrator indulges her friend but does not take the romance very seriously. The Going-Down Play is, of course, a farce and therefore light and sarcastic, but the sure, defiant tone is consistent and pointed.

The clearest example of this tone and the female solidarity behind it occurs in the 1920 play called *The Sleeping Beauty*. It summarizes well what its authors perceive themselves to have gotten from their Somerville education and exudes an exhilarating optimism about the future of the educated woman.

> At. S.D.S. [Somerville Debating Society] who could express
>   Her views with acclamation
> Will show her bent in Parliament
>   Or bully Convocation.
> The captain who has coached her crew
>   On Cherwell or on Isis
> Will one day steer with foresight clear
>   The Cabinet through a crisis.

We mean to run this show, we are not shy
We'll make the whole world go, my friends and I.
We mean to run this show, we are not shy;
We'll make the whole world go, my friends, good-bye.
Who in the *Frit.* once did her bit
    Will write the next best-seller
She who at worst would get a First,
    Will be an All Souls Feller.
The butterfly may, ere she die,
    A tray at Buol's carry
Or on the stage will be the rage
    And some may even marry.[9]

Several things should be noted here, without, of course, taking
these lines too seriously. First, Holtby and friends have a vision of a
world run—completely—by women. Second, the lines makes explicit the connection between various talents particularly nourished
by their women's college experience and the skills needed to run
this world. Third, in this new world marriage is rather an after-
thought, something for the women who have no particular talent,
an interesting reversal of the accepted relationship between marriage and spinsterhood. In other words, the distressed undergraduate
had grounds for his complaint that "They don't want us," although
the women themselves would probably have been surprised and dismayed by such an inference.

The world of the college drama in which women could assume
male roles is, Holtby implies in these lyrics, like other college societies and activities, preparatory to analogous roles off stage. The
head of a Boston girls' school, F. A. Andrews, attacked Mt. Holyoke on the grounds that "female governance . . . might develop
new, unconventional expectations in its students to act 'the *manly*
part' upon the theatre of life" (Horowitz, 58). He was right.
College women, both British and American, learned male roles because there were no males to perform them, on stage or off. Horowitz notes that the "experience of dominance and subordination
remained at the heart of the college experience for women" but that
unlike their uneducated sisters college women, subordinate as
Freshers, gradually "acquired the prerogatives of the masculine role
with its dominant postures" (167). These women, then, took *both*

parts. They learned the roles of both women and men and learned, furthermore, to play them competently. This new-found talent makes credible and at least half serious the bravado of "We mean to run this show" and "All law and order we defy." Women who could play both roles did not have to be satisfied with subordinate ones. They could turn things around, stand tradition on its head, refuse the plot of inevitable marriage and their subordination in it, refuse to become the stock characters of that plot—the love-sick maiden, the all-sacrificing wife, the useless spinster, the devouring mother. They could, that is, act the manly part, so much freer and more powerful than their traditional one.

College women thus acted out, on stage and off, the fears of male Oxford in particular, and of detractors of women's education in general. Though their physical presence intruded little on the male university, Christopher Hobhouse's bicyclists notwithstanding, it was the self-sufficient society that most concretely embodied these fears. One manifestation of this self-sufficiency, one that was obvious and easy to attack, was the tendency of the women to develop romantic friendships. This tendency threatened not only to disrupt the law and order of society but to proclaim more loudly than anything else the superfluity of men.

Feminist scholars have written a great deal recently on romantic friendships both in and out of schools. Martha Vicinus, for example, in "Distance and Desire: English Boarding-School Friendships" discusses the prevalence of the phenomenon known on both sides of the Atlantic as "raves," "pashes," "smashes," and "crushes," and the official rhetoric that surrounded it at the turn of the century. She also explains its context:

> Middle- and upper-class young women . . . were placed in single-sex communities with a strong reforming ethos. Women leaders were pioneering new roles for their students and were under great external pressure to demonstrate the viability of their institutions. At the same time the students were eager to prove themselves worthy of the new institutions. A rave simultaneously satisfied the desire for intimacy and individuality, independence and loyalty (604).

An American educator defined the smash as "an extraordinary habit which they [students at incipient women's colleges] have of

falling in love with each other and suffering all the pangs of unre-
quited attachment, desperate jealousy, etc., etc., with as much energy as if one of them were a man" (Horowitz, 65). The women fell
in love with their peers and just as frequently with a teacher (especially in boarding high schools) or an older student. In the latter
case, when the feeling was returned, the older student often acted
the manly role in the relationship, but, of course, when the younger
woman became older, she would take on the male part in a rave of
her own. Again, the women experienced not only intense friendship, which many never duplicated in later life, but, to a certain
extent at least, the power and privilege constitutive of the masculine position in male-female relationships.

Although these romantically and erotically charged relationships
by no means originated in schools, they certainly flourished there.
College novels almost inevitably referred to them, if they did not
make them a central theme. Same-sex relationships in boys' schools
and men's colleges also flourished, of course, but, while deplored
sometimes on moral grounds, they seriously threatened no one. In
women's colleges, however, they added substance to the fear that
"they do not want us." The cause of such "unnatural" turning to
their own sex for affection (genital sexual activity was probably
minimal, if fictional accounts can be believed) was attributed, of
course, to the lack of "normal" environments and to the difficulty
of heterosexual mingling. A 1920 *Isis* correspondent, for example,
deplored "those admirable Somervillian precepts which effectively
prevent all useful social intercourse between men and women students. Erect amid the storm of 'Clubs of Both Sexes' and 'Sex Dis-
qualification Bills,' they at any rate ensure that woman shall clasp
woman at Terpsichore's shrine, when the gramophone plays Chopin"
(28 Jan. 1920). The unconsciously sexual discourse here clearly suggests worry about something more than same-sex dancing, then
common at all the women's colleges.

While women educators often used such attachments to their
own advantage—to strengthen college solidarity, for example, or,
like Sarah Burton in Winifred Holtby's *South Riding*, to exact loyalty to themselves as examples of what women could be and do—
other critics indulged in vague and veiled polemics against not only
the attachments but the institutions in which they flourished. An
opponent of Vassar and Mt. Holyoke wrote, "The system is unnatural. It is not necessary to go into particulars, but every observing

physician or physiologist knows what we mean when we say that such a system is fearfully unsafe" (Horowitz, 75). Horowitz suggests that the "great harm" which critics really feared was "the creation of a separate women's culture with its dangerous emotional attachments, its visionary schemes, and its strong-minded stance to the world" (75). That is, although the detractor refers specifically if circuitously to possible sexual relationships between young women, he actually includes all the implications of such relationships for female self-sufficiency. Martha Vicinus in "One Life to Stand Beside Me" suggests that because these friendships "symbolize[d] the single woman's sexual autonomy and economic freedom," they became increasingly suspect as women's power became more palpable (605).

Barbara Solomon notes that we cannot find out how persistent these attachments were because after the twenties, when female homosexuality had been delineated and warned against by the sexologists and their popularizers, "the women who had had primary relationships with other women usually destroyed personal evidence such as letters and diaries," but she suggests that undergraduate women "continued to accept and respect love between women" (100). A young feminist without an education argued in 1907 that "through an education girls learned to earn a livelihood and are not so liable to throw themselves away in marriage on some worthless man" (Solomon, 69). Given alternatives, she implied, many women might choose not to marry. While earning a livelihood became an alternative to economic dependence, fervent female friendship became an alternative to the emotional rewards of marriage. At the turn of the century, statistics suggested that "less than fifty percent of college women married (Solomon, 119). An early Somervillian, Miss Florence Rich, argued that men do not hate learned women, by pointing to the *one-third* of the students in her time who had eventually married (quoted in Farnell, 19). Whether the reason for this startlingly low marriage rate was, indeed, men's dislike of educated women or women's own intellectual, economic, and emotional alternatives, the fact remained threatening to a family-based society and its male-centered ideology. Women's new confidence in their ability to "run this show," their demonstrated ability to be, at least on the small scale of women's colleges, self-sufficient, and their acquisition of tools for continued self-sufficiency made male Oxford uneasy.

The giving of degrees to women, which seemed to the women

themselves and to their advocates mere justice, became for their opponents a sign of profound changes in the microcosm of the University and in the larger world. But to deny degrees to women who were fully qualified began to seem mere churlishness. No rational arguments could continue to stand up to the women's undemanding demands. Without outside influence, however, Oxford might well have continued, even without rational grounds, to deny women degrees. What finally forced the decision on 11 May 1920 to allow women almost equal access to institutional Oxford ("almost" because theological degrees were withheld from women until 1935) was the patriotic and competent activity during World War I of all British women, the same behavior which dissipated much of the opposition to women's suffrage. An amazed Mr. Asquith, for example, previously an opponent of giving women the vote, said in 1915, "There are thousands of such women [as Edith Cavell] but a year ago we did not know it" (Strachey, 348). In her history of the women's movement in Great Britain Ray Strachey adds that besides the conversion of public opinion, "the change in the outlook of women themselves" was an important prelude to suffrage. "They saw what the world was like for men; and neither Act of Parliament nor season of reaction, nor any other thing could thereafter take that knowledge from them" (349). Strachey's account was written in the twenties; its scriptural diction here indicates the intensity of the feelings of this generation of women not only for the cause of suffrage but of equal education as well.

Women at Oxford had, I have suggested, already seen what the world, at least the world of higher education, was like for men. The war, however, intensified that vision. Many students and some dons left Oxford to do war work. Vera Brittain became an army nurse after her first year at Somerville, 1914, and did not return until the end of the war. Winifred Holtby after her first year, 1917, joined the WAACs for the last year of the war. Miss Lorrimer, a Somerville Classics tutor, spent six months with a Scottish Women's Hospital Unit in Salonika, and Miss Pope, Somerville Tutor in Modern Languages since 1894, worked behind the lines in France with the Friends' Relief Women. The decision to go or to stay was not an easy one. Brittain describes the women as "victims of competing injunctions; national posters urged them to serve their 'King and Country' while the university authorities . . . anxiously insisted that it was their duty to remain, and prepare for future demands" (*WO*, 138). Holtby's decision to leave, Brittain writes in *Testament of Youth*, "inspired a Sunday-night address from the Principal on the duty of remaining at college" (154). The Going-Down Play of 1917, written in large measure by Dorothy L. Sayers, satirized the debate. The scene takes place in a nunnery and one Father Ernest urges the women to stay.

> So if the University made one mistake in letting you come up here, she's not going to make another by letting you go where you can do any harm. . . . It seems to me therefore—and this is what I just wanted to explain—that the best thing for you poor foolish women to do is to remain in the shelter of the nunnery. Much as I shudder to see the monstrous regiment of women camped in venerable Oriel.

The Father Ernest scene suggests again the ambivalent feelings of the University about its women students and the equally ambivalent feelings of the women about their role both at Oxford and in the larger world. Most of the Oxford women did remain there during the war, but almost all were involved in war work of some sort. *The Fritillary* of December 1917 mentions the students' devoting time to digging potatoes; on a loftier level, Miss Penrose organized the National Registration in Oxford and managed the Belgian Visitors' Committee (Brittain, *WO*, 140).

Thus, whether women participated directly in the war or remained at Oxford, they experienced themselves not only as able to perform work heretofore reserved for men, an experience they had had already as Oxford students, but as an integral part of the functioning of the country and of the University in a time of crisis. Somerville students, transferred to St. Mary's Hall at Oriel when their college was requisitioned as an addition to the adjacent Radcliffe infirmary, had the further experience of being at the center of Oxford University life, truncated and grim as that life was during the years of the war.[10] The austerity there, claims Brittain, was unrelieved by "gaity and stimulus" (*WO*, 116). Women heard daily reports of the deaths of friends, brothers, and fiancés. The already inadequate food was subject to rationing and, as Holtby wrote to a school friend, "in the new rations we are chronicled under the heading of 'Sedentary Occupations'!" (Brittain *TF*, 62). One practical advantage college life held for its women had nearly disap-

peared—the privacy of their rooms, a privacy some of them had
there known for the first time. Brittain says that "a shortage of coal
compelled work to be done in public rooms and over small shared
fires" (*WO*, 138). But the depressing conditions could not negate
the women's sense of being at the center of Oxford life. Byrne and
Mansfield write that "It was not in human nature, student nature
anyway, not to feel some response to this move into the heart of
Oxford, with St. Mary's chiming unusually loud across the way, the
High curving outside, and meals in a . . . hall . . . whose presincts
Sir Thomas More had haunted as an undergraduate" (41). To be at
Oriel was to have another opportunity of seeing what the world was
like for men, a world rooted in and enriched by a long history. Nor
could the depressing conditions dampen the sense of solidarity, per-
haps enhanced by working in public rooms, expressed in the 1917
Going-Down Play:

> Never fear, they're welcome one and all,
> We like all sorts in S. Mary Hall
> We've freaks and frumps and brains and butterflies and bits of
>   fluff and all
> You'll always find a kindred mind in old St. Mary Hall.

The song, while recognizing the inevitability of the labels and
prejudice to which the women continue to be subject, celebrates
their diversity, tolerance, and affection for one another. Father Ernest's "monstrous regiment of women" is an epithet of pride as well
as an acknowledgment of Oxford's continued hostility to their presence. They recognized that, like their brothers on the front, they
worked together against a common enemy. They were strong, they
were at the center of activity both academic and military. They had,
besides, comported themselves admirably, thanks to Miss Penrose's
tight rein, at Oriel, in Oxford's midst. "The general expectation
that the college in its new quarters might do something unsuitable—no one quite knew what—was not justified; and its preoc-
cupation with its own affairs, both in work and play, prevented any
misuse of its position" (Byrne and Mansfield, 43). Again, the "general expectation" was that women at Oxford's center, women, that
is, integrated into University life, on male territory, would explode,
would get out of hand, would do unspeakable things—no one quite
knew what. Indeed, the relief that nothing untoward had occurred

during the Somervillians' stay at Oriel both softened opposition and gave the women more leverage.

Also thanks to Miss Penrose, the women had furthermore taken all the right exams. In short, their position was unassailable; they deserved degrees. The first installment of women's suffrage—votes for women over thirty—in February 8, 1918, was added inducement to University authorities, especially since, by that act, Oxford women over thirty were entitled, "ironically enough" comments Brittain, "to vote for the Parliamentary representative of a university in which they were still outsiders" (*WO*, 146). "So anomalous was this position," writes Vera Farnell, "that even the most ancient and conservative of the universities could not but recognize it" (46).

A final impetus for the decision to grant women degrees was the changed character of Oxford. When "Great Tom," the bell of Christ Church College, announced the end of the war, when, the Somerville Log Book describes, the women students joined the undergraduates and the townspeople "in devoting their energies to penny whistles, gongs, flags, and all manner of vocal exercises," the worldwide influenza epidemic, which had spread quickly through the four women's colleges, was at its height. The ranks of Oxford men depleted, the ranks of Oxford women ill and exhausted, it was, according to Brittain, a "grim and dreary" (*WO*, 147) University which welcomed back the men and women returning after war service, and it welcomed them back with great anxiety. Worried that the returning students would be wild, presumptuous, grown-up, the authorities tried to pretend that there had been no war at all. Miss Emily Penrose's only concession to Vera Brittain's four years of war service was, "You are living in King Edward Street this term, I think?" (*TY*, 476). Brittain's reaction was as emotional as Miss Penrose's was contained. She wrote in her diary: "I'm nothing but a piece of wartime wreckage, living on ingloriously in a world that doesn't want me" (*TY*, 490). This world, however, was as confused about what it wanted as was Brittain herself.

On June 19, 1919, the men of Oriel made it clear that one thing they wanted was to have their hall back. The Log describes their "prolonged bombardment on the intervening wall [until] a breach was effected through which several undergraduates jumped into the quad." The young men who had invaded the women's wing cheered Somerville, "implying the mixture of their feelings with regard to our colleges," concludes the Log account. Though a mixture of feelings had persisted throughout the forty-year residence of the women's colleges, this particular mixture seems to have had a higher proportion of good humor and tolerance, indicative of the change about to come in the status of the women students. Although Oxford on the surface was again functioning normally, the ambience had indeed altered with the returnees, whose war experience made them less confident for the future than the younger members of the university, less confident, for example, in the League of Nation's ability to preserve peace. Oxford freshmen mingled with war veterans; after years of associating more or less freely during their war service, men and women found it natural to mingle more at Oxford. There was dancing. The lectures were crowded. Enrollment increased greatly—especially at the women's colleges. Women and the war had changed Oxford.

2   "The Girlies Play at Ball":

Degrees and the Somerville Novelists

It was in this changed climate that, shortly after the return of Somervillians to their college, the Statute admitting women to degrees and full membership was passed on 11 May 1920. Brittain describes the historic occasion of the first degree-giving ceremony to include women in *Women at Oxford*:

> Inside the Sheldonian Theatre, its atmosphere tense with the consciousness of a dream fulfilled, younger and older spectators looked down, moved and entranced, upon the complicated ceremony in the arena below. When the great south doors opened the five women principals, arrayed for the first time in caps and gowns, entered with Mrs. Johnson [Principal of the Home Students], supported by her ebony stick but proudly erect, in her due place at their head.
>
> After a second's silence the theatre rang with unrehearsed applause, and the Vice-Chancellor rose to receive the first women Masters of Arts ever to appear in that historic place. They walked slowly towards him, bowed, and took their seats.
>
> When the men received their degrees, cheers burst out again as the first fully qualified [women] graduates stood before the Vice-Chancellor.

At the end of her account she adds the ironic twist. What seemed to go unnoticed was "the establishment of a precedent, destined to continue for several years, by which all the men were admitted to degrees, however minor, before all the women, however impressive" (156). Despite cheers and applause and obvious excitement, however, it could not have gone unnoticed that the status of women at Oxford continued to appear subordinate. Besides the fact that the men preceded the women, the women's academic dress was, as we shall see, slightly inferior to that of the men.

Not everyone, furthermore, accepted the granting of degrees to women gracefully. A *Times* editorial suggested that the women students were seeking advantages without corresponding responsibilities; they must observe a stricter discipline. Vera Brittain wrote a characteristically impassioned response, which she quotes in *Testament of Youth:*

> It is generally assumed outside the precincts of this university that whereas [male] undergraduates are induced by the vigilance of authority to enter their college gates at a reasonable hour of the night, the women students are free to wander whithersoever they will from darkness to dawn? Are we pictured as Maenads dancing before the Martyr's memorial, or as Bacchantes revelling in the open spaces of Carfax? (505)

Nothing could, of course, have been more inaccurate than these putative visions. The women's colleges, as we have seen, had standards of scholarship as high as if not higher than the men's; the women's colleges observed discipline more strictly—but no objective records of scholarship discipline, war work, patience, or competence could entirely reconcile the opponents of degrees for women. As we have also seen, however, Brittain's bitter presentation of the ways these opponents viewed the women students is not so exaggerated as she intended. Maenads and Baccantes are precisely what opponents both envisioned and feared, Maenads and Bacchantes whose anger, savagery, and unbridled eroticism lay just under the surface, waiting.

With the granting of degrees and full membership in the University, the women were entitled to wear academic dress: Cartoons from the 1880s portray women in fancy clothes with mortarboards on their heads, an incongruous satiric costume (Fig. 4). But the mortarboard, so symbolic of the centuries-old Oxbridge tradition, was, finally, denied to the women students. In the matter of dress, as in every other, the university authorities felt compelled to make distinctions. The women wanted and assumed that they would wear both gown and mortarboard, which the Principals unanimously recommended, even arranging "a mannequin parade" for the voting delegates, but "the Proctors would have none of it" (Farnell, 114). Although they allowed the gowns, they required the women to wear a soft square black cap, which Farnell describes as clerical and which Brittain claims had an "unfortunate habit of slipping over one eye" (*WO*, 153). The quip at the time was that the cap was "a judicious compromise between Portia and Nerissa." Farnell further notes that this decision was indicative and prophetic of male Oxford's tendency "which was almost immediately perceptible, to assert authority instead of inviting cooperation" (114). Just as suggestive as this authoritarian stance is the fact that again the question of what women wear assumed importance, here to assure the preservation of some measure of femininity and difference. Significantly, it was the men who insisted on the soft cap and the women who wanted symbols of academic status identical to the men's to indicate the equality promised by degrees but never, of course, really attained.

The caps, to judge from photographs and from occasional complaints, were unattractive as well as impractical. Photographs of Miss Penrose on the day of the historic ceremony show her bareheaded next to Gilbert Murray under his mortarboard (Fig. 5). In the photograph of her during Queen Mary's visit to Somerville of 1921 she is also bareheaded, her cap in hand (Fig. 6). A decade later, when some new buildings were dedicated, Miss Penrose appears in academic gown but with a hat of her own choosing, rather larger and stiffer than the caps and not unlike the mortarboard, symbolic perhaps of her continued objection to sartorial inequality (Fig. 7). The women made more vociferous objections when the university authorities prescribed "a white blouse, dark coat and skirt, black shoes and stockings, and a black tie" for wear under the gown—and prescribed this costume for both faculty and students. Mrs. Johnson, Principal of the Home Students, "declared that she had never worn a white blouse and would take her degree in a high-necked black dress" (*WO*, 153). Subsequent photographs show little uniformity in "subfusc" (the Oxbridge term for under-gown attire), an indication that the women, ignored and idiosyncratic for so many years, would not now simply conform. The prescription itself parallels the rhetoric of keeping women within bounds and under control; the prospect of prints and polka dots under academic gowns carried the threat of women's visibility and unpredictibility that so plagued male Oxford. The attempt to regulate what was worn under the gown expressed the hope that no explosions would occur, that the conferring of degrees would not lead to the fulfillment of forty years of fears, that the inner lives of these women were as controlled, as passionless, as pliable as the outer.

The women's quiet revolt in this seemingly small matter of dress aptly epitomizes the ambiguous lives these women led. On the one hand, they had an enormous amount of freedom and autonomy in comparison to other women; on the other they were, as Martha Vicinus observes, "hedged in on all sides by social and economic constraints." They bought such freedom, she suggests, "at the price of political timidity, a frequent fear of change and a dislike of innovation" (*Independent Women*, 135). Over assertive demands, they chose unobtrusive insistence, which required constant constraint, much of it self-imposed. Women students were encouraged both to be like men and to be different from them, to aspire to male power and to renounce it. They wrote their essays and drank their cocoa surrounded by fears on the part of their own female dons that they would do something to jeopardize the tenuous place at Oxford they had acquired so patiently, and fears on the part of male Oxford that they would overrun, overtake, and destroy an ancient learning environment so dependent in many ways on the subservience of women.

Academic garb indicated success in a male world; it also cut the new members of the University off from other women and from their families. Women had been outsiders at Oxford; they were now, women with Oxbridge degrees, outsiders everywhere else. They were equal to men, said their gowns, but not quite, said their caps. They wanted to be like men, said their desire for academic dress, but not quite, said their refusal of the prescribed white shirt and ties, the subfusc customarily worn by men. In her first year at Somerville, Brittain wrote to her fiancé (who was later killed in battle), "It is a delightful change to me to be in surroundings where work is expected of you, instead of where you are thought a fool for wanting to do it" (*TY*, 110). But after three years, the women "went

down" into a world which no longer expected intellectual work
from them, a world much less tolerant of eccentric behavior, much
more certain than Oxford was about what a woman should be. As
Barbara Solomon remarks, "Whatever the educated woman absorbed as an undergraduate, in adulthood she dealt with a central
dilemma posed by the demands of society: how to live up to the
promise of her education and at the same time fulfill her female
role" (xix).

It is hardly surprising, then, that when these women write fiction, their fictional worlds are riddled with bewildering demands,
that when they create female characters who are intelligent, educated women like themselves, those characters behave in contradictory and sometimes outrageous ways. Nor is it surprising that
even when these texts attempt openly either to expand or to limit
women's role, the language and actions of the characters often undercut the attempts, and reinforce the plot of the traditional heterosexual romance. Before we look at these texts, however, it is
important to note that women's experience of themselves as Oxford
students was by no means uniform or consistent. And the women
were by no means constantly occupied with the tension they created at Oxford, with the subject of degrees, or with the general debate about higher education for women. They carried on their lives,
studying, doing war work, participating in every Somerville ritual,
writing for *The Fritillary*, debating both within the college and with
the men's colleges. Though some of their debates concerned women's
suffrage and degrees, most notably the first debate with Balliol, the
majority of the topics had little to do with women's issues; they
ranged from Sayers' opposition to the motion "that Impartiality is
neither possible nor profitable" (*Frit.*, March 1913) to Winifred
Holtby's defense of a Federal Devolution Bill (Log, 1918) to the "delightful" debate in 1919 on the motion that "Dilettantism should be
the aim of all education" (Log). (Although the women debated the
desirability of "compulsory arbitration among members of the Hague
conference" in 1912 [*Frit.*, Dec.], by 1914 there was a self-imposed
ban on controversial political matters for the duration of the war.
Interest in debates flagged accordingly during those years.)

The widely different responses of the women to Somerville itself
is clear from, for example, the intensity of Viscontess Rhondda's
dislike, so great that she left shortly after she came. The six women
whose novels I discuss all stayed for their three years at Somerville,

but their reactions to it varied significantly, as do the reactions of the characters in their fiction. In Vera Brittain's *Dark Tide*, Oxford tutor Patricial O'Neill asks an ex-student, Daphne, if she would send her daughter to Drayton, the Oxford women's college at which part of the novel is set. Daphne is not sure. Her own experience there was not altogether a good one, nor have its consequences been happy. Patricia tries to explain what might have gone wrong:

> You know you were at Drayton at a very difficult time. . . . For two years after the war Oxford was full of people who were either suffering from reaction, which made them despise work, or from the aftermath of sorrow, which made them despise play. The majority of both men and women were upset by passions and emotions which aren't at all conspicuous at a university in ordinary times (216).

Brittain herself came to Oxford in 1915 during Sayers' and Jaeger's time there, and briefly experienced Somerville, this first year, at its "normal" best. During the four years she served as a war nurse, however, both she and Somerville had changed. She later describes postwar Oxford as "abnormally normal" (*WO*, 26) and at the time expresses some of the bitterness of another *Dark Tide* character, also a war returnee, Virginia Dennison. The 1920 *Oxford Poetry* volume has one of Brittain's early efforts, "The Lament of the Demobilized," in which she complains that the ones who stayed behind "Got on the better since we were away/ And we came home and found/ They had achieved, and men revered their names,/ But never mentioned ours." The poem concludes with "the others" thinking the war returnees fools for having thrown away four years. "And we're beginning to agree with them."

The bitterness that was so much a part of Brittain's Somerville experience kept her from full participation in the life of the college. Of the group which "became popularly known in the nineteen thirties as 'the Somerville School of Novelists'" (Brittain, *LW*, 88), the two most involved in that life were Dorothy L. Sayers and Winifred Holtby. Sayers came up to Somerville in the fall of 1912; by spring of the next year she had become a frequent speaker at the Oxford Students Debating Society's debates. *The Fritillary*, usually extremely critical of debaters' styles, admitted that "Miss Sayers has an arresting manner of speaking, and was fully convinced of the rightness of her cause," which on this occasion was "that impartiality by no means necessitates lack of interest; rather, it is a necessary accompaniment to any real sense of justice" (*Frit.*, March 1913). Sayers wrote as well as spoke; she published in *The Fritillary* and in *Oxford Magazine*; she composed pieces for a select group of students called the Mutual Admiration Society, who read and criticized one another's work.[1] She also sang. The most often-repeated story of Sayers' Somerville years is of what her biographers and contemporaries describe as her "crush" on Dr. Hugh Allen, director of the Bach Choir, of which Sayers, Brittain, Holtby, and Margaret Kennedy were members. On at least two occasions, Sayers actually dressed up as Dr. Allen, once for a costume party, once in the Going-Down Play *Pied Pipings* in a part she wrote for herself. Her contemporaries and all her biographers say she was loud, flamboyant, ebulient, exuberant, eccentric, brilliant, unorthodox, bold, and dramatic. She smoked cigars, said outrageous things, tyrannized, only half in jest, her fellow students, and dressed to be noticed. Vera Farnell recalls the occasion on which

> D.L.S., as she was known to her fellow students, appeared at breakfast one morning, previous to an early lecture at the Taylorian, wearing a three-inch wide scarlet riband round her head and in her ears a really remarkable pair of ear-rings; a scarlet and green parrot in a gilt cage pendant almost to each shoulder and visible right across the hall (12–13).

Miss Penrose, always so concerned for the proper behavior of her students, nevertheless respected their rights and did not interfere directly. Rather she asked Miss Farnell to effect "the removal of the offending bedizenment by gentle persuasion" (13).

Sayers' eccentricities seem to have been both tolerated and enjoyed. Vera Brittain remembers that she "took an immediate liking to Dorothy Sayers, who was affable to freshers and belonged to the 'examine-every-atom-of-you' type. A bouncing, exuberant young female . . . she could be seen at almost any hour of the day or night scuttling about the top floor of the new Maitland building with a kettle in her hand and a little checked apron fastened over her skirt" (*TY*, 106). Although Brittain later amends this to "a red-and-white checked teacloth as an apron" (Berry, 322), both descriptions make Sayers appear rather more domestic and tame than does an anonymous marginal comment on the manuscript copy of the Going-Down play next to a song Sayers wrote about her term as "Bicycle Secretary": "In the old days the Bicycle Secretary led a dog's life and no one paid any attention to her. Miss Sayers, in her term of office, completely turned the tables and by inaugurating the simple system of impounding bicycles, was enabled to tyrannize over all college."

Contrary to Janet Hitchman's claim in *Such a Strange Lady* that "the place does not seem to have entered her soul, and her relationship with her college was always a bit off-hand" (32), Sayers seems to have felt very much at home at and a part of Somerville and Oxford in general. Brabazon asserts that, for Sayers, "To go from school to university was to go from purgatory to paradise" (42). Whether or not "paradise" is precisely the term for Sayer's perception of life at Somerville, she missed being there when she was away. In the summer of 1914, for example, she wrote to her friend Catherine Godfrey, "Oh! Tony—I got an awful wave of wanting Oxford yesterday" (Letters), and after Sayers finished at Somerville she wrote a poem which she dedicated to Muriel Jaeger and published in her first book, *Opus I*:

> Now that we have gone down—have all gone down,
>   I would not hold too closely to the past,
> Till it become my staff, or even at last
> My crutch, and I be made a helpless clown
>
> · · · · · · · · · · · · · · · · ·
>
> Therefore,God love thee, thou enchanted town,
> God love thee, leave me, clutch me not so fast.

This resolution not to be crippled by her attachment to Oxford and Somerville indicates her awareness of their hold on her. In response to news that Tony would be going to Somerville, Sayers asks her in a letter dated Sept. 22, 1915, to "Please give my love to every stick and stone you meet on your way—also to the Bursar." Though she claims in an earlier letter that she is "home-sick for Oxford—not for college" (undated), her loyalty to Somerville takes the form of snobbery toward the other women's colleges. She tells Tony in a letter of July 28, 1914, a "howler" about a young women, who, asked in an exam who the Paraclete was, replied "Peter's wife's mother." Sayers remarks laconically, "She was not a Somerville student." In a 1915 letter she notes "with much joy that L.M.H. has got two Fourths—Beast, ain't I?"

Sayers was the only one of these Somerville novelists to get a First, but like her fictional heroine Harriet Vane she did not choose to stay on at Oxford to teach. It was, however, Oxford and Somerville which inspired her most ambitious and most unorthodox detective novel, *Gaudy Night*. Somerville was not particularly pleased with its portrait but, as we will see, Sayers there invests the place with enormous power to change the lives of women; *Gaudy Night* testifies that Somerville had indeed clutched her fast.

Sayers' friend and contemporary Muriel Jaeger was a member of the Mutual Admiration Society and, like Sayers, a scholarship student. Jaeger, too, acted in plays and belonged to various clubs, but by comparison with Sayers is mentioned rarely in *The Fritillary* or the Log and is mentioned by Brittain in *Women at Oxford* merely as "a prospective novelist" (122) and in *Testament of Youth* as "subsequently the writer of several intelligent novels" (106). In a 1929 *Good Housekeeping* article called "The Somerville School of Novelists" Brittain recollects Jaeger only "vaguely" as an important third-year student "upon whom an obscure and childish 'fresher' was expected to gaze respectfully from afar off" (Berry, 322). Jaeger seems not to have been "clutched" the way Sayers was, and she wrote little about Somerville and Oxford, in spite of continued friendship with Sayers, who dedicated to her her first detective novel, *Whose Body?* in 1923: "Dear Jim: This book is your fault. If it had not been for your brutal insistence, Lord Peter would never have staggered through to the end of this enquiry. Pray consider that he thanks you with his accustomed suavity."[2] The Oxford days of the educated heroine of Jaeger's *The Man with Six Senses* are mentioned only in passing, and the novel's parable-like tone and fanciful plot would discourage even the most biographically oriented critic from identifying Hilda with her creator.

Brittain perceived Margaret Kennedy, too, as an aloof figure, in spite of the fact that the two young women, along with Winifred Holtby, read the same subject, modern history. Kennedy was, however, in her last term at Somerville when Brittain returned from the war. "I never spoke to her," Brittain says in *Testament of Youth*, "but I carried way a definite impression of a green scarf, and dark felt hat negligently shading a narrow, brooding face with arrogant nose and stormily reserved blue eyes" (*TY*, 478). Kennedy's daughter Julia Birley, herself a novelist, says, however, that Kennedy debated with Brittain on at least one occasion, and Brittain's suggestion of Kennedy's forbidding reserve is belied by Kennedy's active participation in college, including the writing of two Going-Down plays, singing in the Bach Choir ("She argued boldly with its conductor, Sir Hugh Allen, when . . . he called Mozart 'superficial'" [Birley]), as well as debating. Brittain says that Margeret Kennedy was rumoured to have announced to her fellow undergraduates that, "after leaving Somerville, she intended to live in the country and write a great novel" (Berry, 322), an announcement, Brittain assures her readers, that Somervillians would have greeted with "amused though tolerant scorn." But, "after acquiring a Second in History she disappeared from mind as well as from sight—to take the world by storm five years afterwards" (Berry, 323). The "storm" was occasioned by Kennedy's bestseller, *The Constant Nymph*, which Brittain asserts in *On Becoming a Writer* that she was "almost the last person in England to read . . . so weary was I of the enthusiasm of relatives and the black-lettered advertisement-posters decorating the escalators on the Underground" (154). When she did finally read her fellow Somervillian's novel, however, she felt foolish that she had been so obstinate.

   The Constant Nymph does give credence to Brittain's sense of Kennedy as aloof and critical. In this early novel, the educated woman destroys the "constant" love between an artist and his young, devoted, bohemian, feminine, female friend. The two 1919 Kennedy letters in the Somerville archives—both to a friend, Flora Forster—strike a distanced, scornful, and critical pose. Kennedy criticizes Sayers for being, in her book of poems, *Catholic Tales*, "so afraid of committing herself," despises fellow students Nita and Vera, proclaims the term "the very dullest . . . that ever was," and declares that she is going to start a rival magazine to the *Frit* called "The Fools' Paradise" which is "to serve as an organ for public grievances." One of her contributions to the *Frit* is a parody of a tutoring session, in which the tutor manages to confuse thoroughly his not very bright students, Miss Smith and Miss Brown. The mindless notetaking conforms to the Somerville stereotype that appears in other, male, Oxford publications. In her autobiographical *Where Stands a Wingèd Sentry*, Kennedy says little about her Somerville years except to describe the announcement of the peace in

November 1918, and even the biographical "study" of Kennedy, *The Constant Novelist* by Violet Powell, says almost nothing about Kennedy's Somerville experience except to mention her Second in history and her friendship with Eluned Lloyd. Neither Jaeger nor Kennedy, the two women seemingly most detached, even as students, from their Somerville years, directly incorporated this experience into their writing, nor did either deal directly, either in essay or fiction, with the topic of education for women. The educated woman herself, however, is an important figure, as we shall see, in the novels of both. Especially interesting is that after the second world war, by which point, as I claim in the Kennedy chapter, she had a much more sympathetic and sophisticated vision of the educated woman than is evidenced in her early fiction, she became a Dining Fellow at Somerville and dined there frequently.

Brittain does not include Doreen Wallace in her *Good Housekeeping* piece on the Somerville novelists, since Wallace had not in 1929 yet published her first novel, but Wallace became one of the most prolific of the group. Like Brittain, Wallace came to Somerville as an "exhibitioner." She worked on the staff of *The Fritillary* and did some speaking but seems to have given most of her extra time to writing poetry, which she published regularly and which won several prizes. In her second year at Somerville, Blackwell published a book of poems, *Esques*, which she wrote with Eleanora Geach. A reviewer for *Oxford Magazine*, who assumes that the volume was written by *Misters* Geach and Wallace, praises it highly, especially Wallace's "memorable poems": "People whose palates are fresh enough to enjoy words like sardonyx, chrysolite, and nenuphar, however and wherever they occur, as a child enjoys plums, should buy and read *Esques* (25 Oct. 1918). The poems are critical of Oxford, but later Wallace admitted that her Oxford days afforded her "the quick thrust-and-parry of good talk, the joyful recognition of a point of agreement, the keen hunt along the track of a new line of thought" (*In a Green Shade*, 136), which she had not, thirty years later, otherwise experienced. The noticeably masculine images she uses here contrast sharply with the feminine choices she made for her life—marrying a farmer and, she adds, a farm, having several children, and writing only "when work in house, garden, and fruit fields permits" (*Green Shade* jacket)—choices for which Sayers pities and blames her, if we are to credit Janet Hitchman's identification of Wallace with Catherine Benedict in *Gaudy Night*.

Wallace met Sayers, who had returned to Oxford to work for Blackwell's after two years' teaching, when Wallace herself was a second year student at Somerville. Hitchman describes Sayers' new friend as "also tall and slim, with a rapier-like mind [and] . . . an easy command of language" (42). She says that the two argued a great deal, "Dorothy the Christian, back in the fold after her flirtation with agnosticism, and Doreen the unbeliever, neither moving one inch from her stance" (43). (In fact, the two women argued fiercely in later life over a religious issue, the tithe, which Wallace opposed passionately even in her fiction and Sayers, the church-woman and parson's daughter, supported. This issue, Wallace maintains in a *Times* obituary, "to my lasting regret" caused the demise of their relationship.) The young Wallace, however, was part of Sayers' rhyming club and "coffee party" set which included the Sitwells, Brittain, and Holtby (Hone, 32).[3] Wallace's first novel, *A Little Learning*, embodies all the ambivalence about higher education for women that is the concern of this study. Of the Somerville novelists' texts, hers make the harshest comments about the all-female world of the women's college yet evince the most bitterness toward the heterosexual world inhabited by women after college and portray most dramatically the demands and privations of that world. When she admitted in her gardening book, *In a Green Shade*, that she had not experienced "this exhilarating mental release since I came down from Oxford," she longed for another quality of Somerville conversations—"one talker helping the other" (136). Thus, though the "good talk" has the masculine qualities of thrust-and-parry and the keen hunt, it sounds, in retrospect at least, more supportive than competitive, more, if we credit current assessments of differences between male and female conversing habits, feminine than masculine. So critical, then, of an all-female academic world, Wallace remembered, nevertheless, its advantages and admitted its attraction even after thirty years. Her fictional creations, too, long for such intellectual stimulation, illustrating thereby the power of the recollected college experience.

Unlike her fellow student Doreen Wallace, Winifred Holtby did not write an Oxford novel, but she does discuss, in her journalism and in *Women and a Changing Civilization*, issues of women's education. She notes, for example, that "the burden not only of domestic responsibility but of masculine discouragement lies heavily on the woman student . . . the conflicting claims of family and professional duties rend her" (WCC, 58). One of the sub-chapters of *Women and a Changing Civilization* is titled "The Inferiority Complex," a phenomenon which, we have seen, she was determined to eradicate even in her Somerville years. The piece delineates the cultural reasons for this complex in women and suggests that even the most educated, intelligent, and successful women suffer from it.

Holtby's direct involvement in feminist causes parallels her thorough involvement in life at Somerville. Even in the depressed Somerville of the war years, she found Oxford life full and fun, perhaps because, as she once claimed, "I was born with a love of committee work in my blood" (Waley, 39). She described her first days at Somerville to a friend: "I spend my time . . . tearing about Oxford on a very rusty cycle, flying from lectures, tea parties, concerts, lacrosse matches, and all the thousand and one other things that insist on taking place at the farthest possible point from my headquarters" (Brittain, *TF*, 62). When she returned to Somerville after her year of war service, she resumed her frantic pace. Besides singing with the Bach choir and acting in and/or writing nearly every play produced at Somerville during those years, she was president of two debating societies and a member of many committees and all three political parties. "But how can I know which I like best till I've tried them all?" (Brittain, *TF*, 87–88).

Holtby's sense of fun and freedom at Somerville extended even to her examinations, the source of such anxiety and terror to most students. At her *viva* (the oral exam at the end of the degree course), she wrote to Jean McWilliam, "I enjoyed myself and laughed, and made the examiners laugh . . . but I never gave them a single piece of useful information, though they gave me chance after chance to do so, and I knew most of the things really. So I shan't get a First; but I had a good run for my money" (*Letters*, 53). Brittain claims in *Women at Oxford* that Holtby explained afterwards "that she lost her First by a facetious reference to the private life of Henry VIII" (144). Holtby's sense of fun made her popular and approachable as well as active. Her room became a gathering place for friends and younger students who wanted advice, tea, or sometimes just a warm room for a party. Brittain claims that but for "Winifred's watchful and persistent care," Hilda Reid (later a writer of historical fiction) "would probably have perished of starvation or insomnia" (*TF*, 90). Holtby wrote in a notebook from her first year back after the war that "People have been pouring their emotional crises all over me till I can't breathe" (Brittain, *TF*, 90). Holtby's most lavish care was expended on the friend of her final year at Somerville, with whom she lived on and off for the rest of her short life, whom she loved with all her passionate energy, Vera Brittain. Indicative of their relationship and of Holtby's generosity are these lines from a letter to Brittain during one of their early periods of separation: "I don't care twopence whereabout in the scale of your loves I come, provided that you love me enough to let me love you and that you are happy, whatever else befalls" (Waley, 55).

In *Testament of Friendship* Brittain makes clear that Holtby's experience at Somerville was not all positive. She and Holtby both complained, she writes, "that the eager, immature, bewildered students at the women's colleges did not receive sympathetic guidance from female dons who appeared to place themselves on pedestals and to regard the perplexities of adolescence as beneath their dignity" (85). She also quotes an unpublished letter to Jean McWilliams in which Holtby writes that at Somerville "there was not a soul to whom one could go to ask for advice about knotty points, or even who held up any sort of suggestion about behavior—only about brains" (86). These reservations, however, seem to have resulted from irritations of the moment. Brittain admits that "In the end, Winifred was to remember her years at Somerville with gratitude" (87). In fact, in her will Holtby made Somerville the beneficiary of the proceeds from her posthumously published works. The successful, prize-winning *South Riding* continues to provide funds for scholarships.

In none of these six women is Somerville's power to "clutch" so obvious as it is in Vera Brittain herself, whose time at Oxford, especially the two years she spent there after the war, was painful and alienating, yet who writes about it constantly in both her novels and her non-fiction as a place of energy and hope. During her first term back at Somerville after the war, she was enormously bitter about the place; she resented Holtby's youth and energy (she and Holtby shared a history tutorial and disliked each other heartily their first year together); she felt that "I'm nothing but a piece of wartime wreckage, living on ingloriously in a world that doesn't want me" (*TY*, 490). During the next two terms she had a near nervous breakdown, symptoms of which included a conviction that she was growing a beard and turning into a witch. Gradually, however, she began to recover, thanks, she claims in *Testament of Youth*,

to *Oxford Poetry 1920* (a Blackwell publication which she edited
and contributed to), the triumphant struggle for degrees, and Winifred Holtby (500). By this time the two women's "foolish rivalry"
had turned into "something really blest," as Brittain acknowledged
in a letter to Holtby (*Letters*, 17).

With her recovery, Brittain's bitterness abated. Her memories
of Somerville in *Testament of Youth, Testament of Friendship, The
Women at Oxford,* and *Lady into Woman,* while not without pain,
are tempered and are distanced from, if indulgent toward, the an-
grier, younger self. She praises Somerville unstintingly in her *Good
Housekeeping* article of 1929. In an attempt there to explain why so
many novelists came from this small college, Brittain stresses its un-
orthodoxy and diversity: "it never promised to turn out 'perfect
ladies,' . . . . Religion . . . matters not at all; . . . nationality is
unimportant; . . . class is also a matter of indifference; . . . Age
presents no difficulties."[4] She concludes that "In such a community, with its large choice of companions and its wide range of ideas,
the inquiring, unconventional mind of the creative writer finds
ample opportunity for unrestricted development along its own lines"
(Berry, 321). In *On Becoming a Writer* Brittain admits an even more
practical advantage of Somerville: "The scales of opportunity still
tend to be weighted against women, and any extra educational asset
that a woman can acquire helps to redress the balance." She cites
the success of the Somerville novelists as well as Storm Jameson and
Phyllis Bentley to support her suggestion that "for women writers a
college background has permanent value" (29).

She acknowledges, too, the inspiration of "the Somerville celeb-
rity," successful author Rose Macaulay, whose "youthful eccentricities . . . had already become a legend" (Berry, 321). Macaulay's
witty, satirical, and polished fiction was itself peopled with Somerville students, like the feminist Stanley Garden, whose resentment
over the joking treatment of women in Parliament, of which she
was a member, leads to the narrator's comment: "Women may and
often do regard all humanity as a joke, good or bad, but they can
seldom see that they themselves are more of a joke than men, or
that the fact of their wanting rights as citizens is more amusing than
men wanting similar rights" (*Told by an Idiot,* 223). Somervillians,
too, are Pamela and Frances, a happy pair in *Dangerous Ages* who,
without narrative censure, "had mothered one another at Somerville eighteen years ago, and ever since" (75). Jane Potter, fictional

editor of *The Fritillary,* has a wayward mother who, after spending eight weeks at Oxford, wants, over her daughter's vehement protests that there are already too many, "to write an Oxford novel. Because, after all, though there might be many already, none of them were quite like the one she would write" (*Potterism,* 4).

Though these portraits are amusing and satiric, they are also sympathetic. Macaulay's women are forceful, sexual, productive, intelligent, and fun, and Macaulay herself was an independent woman who remarked in 1926 "that she could not understand why anyone should chose to live with someone else rather than alone" (Smith, 105). One imagines a Sayers "coffee" in 1920 with the six prospective novelists (though Kennedy would not have been included), discussing the recently published *Potterism* and exulting in Mrs. Potter's rationale for writing the Oxford novel, a rationale of which Wallace, Brittain, and Sayers doubtless availed themselves. Brittain admits that Somerville students exchanged Macaulay legends, culled from a college servant, such as her lying in bed for days at a time "attended by two or three devoted friends, interminably scribbling on loose sheets of paper, which she would leave lying about the floor or push into her dressing-table until the drawers refused to close." Brittain admits, too, that such discussions led to a temporary outbreak of similar behavior "in the mistaken but persistent belief, common to the young, that by imitating the eccentricities of the great, one somehow acquires their genius as well" (Berry, 321).

More important than Macaulay's eccentricities, however, and her own lavish use of the figure of the educated woman, was her success. She left Somerville in 1903, published her first novel in 1906, and published steadily thereafter. Not only did these young Somervillians all have their work appear in Oxford publications, they had the early and constant publication of one of their predecessors concretely before them. "To Winifred and myself," Brittain writes in *Testament of Youth,* "she was a portent, a symbol, and encouraging witness to the fact that a university education could produce writers of a non-academic yet first-rate calibre" (510). By 1929 when Brittain wrote the *Good Housekeeping* piece, all but Doreen Wallace (whose *A Little Learning* appeared two years later) had published at least one novel. Macaulay's success was, of course, only one of many experiences of success for these women. They had helped win a war; they had wrested degrees from an ungiving Oxford; they had written, directed, and acted in plays; they had taken on the roles of both men and women; they had run committees and won debates; they had been nursed and nurtured by one another, women on their own. It did not, then, seem odd to Brittain and Holtby to set off alone on a six-week holiday in Italy, which Brittain says was "the most perfect holiday of my experience" (*TF*, 111) and after which Holtby wrote, "And we will go again. There are heaps of lovely places to see and things to do. Never doubt that I want to see and do them and that I ask no better travelling companion than you" (*TF*, 112). It did not seem odd for the two friends to rent a cheap flat together in London where they could launch their writing careers.[5]

The easy optimism of the Going-Down Play verse which Holtby wrote—"We'll make the whole world go/My friends and I"—continued into their early post college lives, but easy optimism was a very small ingredient in the lives of these novelists' educated-women characters, who reflected all the contradictions and ambiguities of the women's college experience, who emerge triumphant, defeated, hero, villain, savior, and even *monstrum horrendum informe*, a male don's judgment in 1921 of a woman in cap and gown (*TY*, 508).

3 *Unnatural by Degrees:*

Dorothy L. Sayers'

Overachieving Murderess

In an unpublished tribute to her former tutor, Mildred Pope, Dorothy L. Sayers professed that Miss Pope typified "some of the noblest
things for which the University stands. The integrity of judgment
that gain cannot corrupt, the humility in face of the facts that self-
esteem cannot blind; the generosity of a great mind that is eager to
give praise to others; the singleness of purpose that pursues knowledge as some men pursue glory and that will not be content with the
secondhand or the second best" ("Toast" ms). Sayers' novel *Gaudy
Night* portrays a college world in which these noble things exist, not
perfectly by any means, but palpably. Dean Martin, Miss Lydgate,
Miss de Vine, while they have their quirks and limitations, at least
approximate Miss Pope's virtues—the virtues most closely associated for Sayers with a university education. And it was the women's
colleges, "mapped out on freer democratic lines" than the frequently "autocratic, old-fashioned" men's colleges, that could most
easily instill these virtues into their members (*UO*, 129).

Sayers was not, however, interested in these virtues only in the
context of a college community. Her heroine Harriet Vane, writer
of detective fiction, and, in fact, most of the other educated women
in the Sayers canon, exercise these virtues in their own, non-
academic, spheres. Miss Meteyard in *Murder Must Advertise*, for

example, though she writes the "vulgarest limericks" (13) ever re-
cited within the walls of Pym's advertising agency, earns Wimsey's
respect for her intelligent judgments and thoughtfulness, and it is
she who, with her singleness of purpose, first penetrates Wimsey's
disguise. Sayers says explicitly in her "Toast" that in her own experience a university education was an asset to the advertising firm,
that Oxbridge graduates had "the scholar's habit of orderly thinking
that makes for efficiency, whether you are dealing with metaphysics
or with margarine. They knew how to handle words—and that is as
useful in writing a slogan as in writing a sonnet. And they had the
scholar's habit of looking upon knowledge of any sort as a thing to
be freely shared without jealousy and that made for good will between them [and] other people in the office" (MS.). The most
generous-spirited moments at Pym's are occasioned by the Oxford-
educated Death Bredon and Miss Meteyard.

Not all Sayers' independent and competent women are explicitly
linked to a college but they are, nonetheless, an educated lot, well-
read and pursuing careers. Eiluned Price in *Strong Poison* and Ann
Doland in *The Unpleasantness at the Bellona Club*, untrusting and
crusty young women, both display sense and sensitivity in tracking
down murderers. Marjorie Phelps, Peter Wimsey's artist friend, puts
aside her romantic feelings for him to aid him in freeing her rival
from a murder charge. The notable exception to this pattern of
large-spirited, generous, honest, self-respecting "new women" is,
however, Sayers' most vicious, frightening, and violent villain, Mary
Whittaker in *Unnatural Death*. This inexplicably cold-blooded murderer bears significant resemblance to the uncontrolled and uncontrollable hidden woman that Oxford feared to be under the surface
of the studious and disciplined woman students. The text is a bewildering one: Mary's motives, at first clear and comprehensible,
quickly become quite the opposite; the attempt to sort out "natural" and "unnatural," "normal" and "abnormal," and their relation
to those motives adds verbal to psychological confusion. Seven
years later, Sayers' only other text with a female villain offers a new
version of this vicious creature, a version which in its re-sorting of
"natural" and "unnatural" exploits Oxford's fears of the educated
woman in order to question the widespread assumption that the romantic plot is the good and true story of a woman's life.

When Mary Whittaker's parents are killed in an accident, Miss
Agatha Dawson, lifelong companion of Mary's late great-aunt Clara

and heir to her considerable estate, asks Mary, a nurse and a distant relative, to live with her. Miss Dawson makes clear that she intends Mary to have the Whittaker money after her own death. But Mary Whittaker cannot wait and uses her sophisticated medical knowledge to secure for herself her great-aunt's legacy. At first she seems to the reader (who does not, of course, know that she is the murderer) much like Sayers' other educated women. Even when one suspects, as one does early in the novel, that Miss Whittaker might have killed Miss Dawson, one rather admires the clever woman and notes the extenuating circumstances: Miss Dawson was old and dying anyway; the money promised to Mary might, as a result of a new piece of legislation, go elsewhere if Miss Dawson lived too long; Miss Dawson was becoming increasingly unreasonable. Mary Whittaker's hastening of the inevitable natural death seems, though not excusable, at least understandable.

As the plot unfolds, however, as two more women are murdered and three other people (including Peter Wimsey) viciously attacked, Mary Whittaker becomes unquestionably sinister and horrible. While we certainly must allow Sayers her female villains, we can, nonetheless, ask why a woman, and an educated woman at that, should murder more and in colder blood, than any other Sayers killer. A second and related question is why this villainous murderer is a lesbian. While woman-as-murderer is entirely in keeping with Sayers' brand of feminism and while the destructive lesbian relationship in the novel is balanced by a lesbian relationship that is less suspect and more respectable, the problem of the excess of physical violence in the novel remains, and it is that excess that points to the fear of the eruption of violence—reputedly lurking in educated women—rampant in the degrees-for-women debate.

Women exerting emotional violence—on men but perhaps especially on other women—are commonplace in literature. We think of the early suffering of poor Pip at the hands of Miss Havisham and Mrs. Joe, Jane Eyre at the hand of Mrs. Reed, and Cinderella at the hands of her wicked stepmother and jealous stepsisters. The detective novel, permeated as it traditionally is with violence, not only allows the use of physical violence to explore and carry out the emotional violence more characteristic of women in both literature and life, but almost demands it. Subtle violence seldom holds the detective-novel audience. Readers have complained, for example, that *Gaudy Night* does not properly conform to the genre because

there is no corpse. It is, then, almost a necessity that any exploration of violence among women in a detective novel be, if it is to
compete with male violence, physical and fatal.

In addition to the requirements of detective fiction, Sayers'
views about equality between the sexes also demand a female villain as violent and cruel as her male villains. Sayers' most explicit
writings on women, "Are Women Human?" and "The Human-
not-quite-Human," both maintain that women and men are human
beings before they are gendered beings. She rejects any notion of
limitation on individual women's abilities and rejects equally any
suggestion that women are in any way superior to men or that "all
women are well-fitted for all men's jobs" (*UO*, 136). Further, "It is
stupid to insist that there are as many female musicians and math-
ematicians as male—the facts are otherwise, and the most we can
ask is that if a Dame Ethel Smith or a Mary Somerville turns up,
she shall be allowed to do her work without having aspersions cast
on either her sex or her ability" (*UO*, 136–137). Analogously, she
would agree that more men commit murder than women (the question why in the case of musician, mathematician, or murderer is
not a topic she addresses), and she would defend vigorously the
right of individual murderesses to be as bloodthirsty as their brothers in crime.

Indeed, in an unpublished manuscript, "The Profession of Murder," she argues playfully that "there is no profession so freely open
to men and women . . . as that of murder." Murder is not, she continues, "by any means incompatible with being an excellent wife
and mother" (PM). She does suggest that men's greater physical
strength make "bashing, throat-cutting, strangling, and the more
energetic forms of stabbing" more appropriate to them, and "poisoning, on the other hand . . . a very pretty feminine accomplishment." Again, however, if men can be good poisoners, they have a
right to this method and if women have the strength for strangling,
they are equally entitled to its benefits. The detective who ignores
these possibilities does so at his or her peril. In *Strong Poison*, for
example, Harriet Vane is the most likely suspect and, being a
woman, is assumed to be particularly suited to the poisoning of her
lover. In fact, the murderer is the victim's male cousin. In both
mysteries with female villains, the women attempt strangulation, a
method more suited to the brawny male; neither of the female villains uses poison. Mary Whittaker's successful method can perhaps

be described as one of the less energetic forms of stabbing; she uses a weapon well suited to her profession as nurse (murder is, presumably, as compatible with being an excellent nurse as with being an excellent wife and mother)—a hypodermic needle.

Sayers, then, by creating a female murderer, only carries out her own conviction, both serious and tongue-in-cheek, that we must allow women to pursue freely their chosen professions. There are, of course, numerous female murderers in crime fiction, most frequently in crime fiction written by women, for perhaps the simple reason that women writers tend to create strong female characters (they also more often create female detectives) and see nothing unnatural in the fact that women, too, have murderous impulses, some of which, at least, must be played out in order to make an exciting detective novel.

The existence of a female murderer is, therefore, hardly surprising. What elicits more concern and comment is that Mary Whittaker is a lesbian. Virginia Morris suggests that Whittaker's "confused" sexual identity, her motive—financial gain—and her attempts at a male method of murder—strangulation—are closely related and meant to draw attention to her masculine qualities (488–489, 493), but nearly all Sayers' women have "masculine" qualities and in her essays Sayers is adamant that such qualities are human and that women have a right to them as well as to other masculine prerogatives like knowledge about Aristotle and the wearing of trousers (*UO*, 131–132).

Kathleen Maio sees *Unnatural Death* as a "testament . . . of [Sayers'] paranoia about lesbianism" (9). Miss Climpson, the spinster detective introduced in this novel, seems the spokesperson for this paranoia. She refers to the attachment between Mary Whittaker and Vera Findlater as "unhealthy" (78), and "thoroughly undesirable" (154), and she assures Vera "that it is more natural—more proper, in a sense—for a man and woman to be all in all to one another than for two persons of the same sex. Er—after all, it is a—a *fruitful* affection" (158). Miss Climpson here invokes a kind of "natural law" argument, common in the Catholic and Anglo-catholic circles in which Miss Climpson moves, against homosexuality. Yet the real focus of Miss Climpson's concern seems to be that Vera is being "preyed upon" (154) by Miss Whittaker and that the attachment is immature: it is a "pash" (78); Vera is "*schwärmerisch*" (154). Not once does Miss Climpson make a derogatory remark about the Clara Whittaker–Mary Dawson relationship though those two women were, much more than Vera and Mary Whittaker, "all in all to one another." In fact, Miss Climpson argues against Mary Whittaker's father's conviction that Clara Whittaker ought to have left the money in the family (that is, to him) rather than to Agatha Dawson: "he inherited the *bad, old-fashioned* idea that women *ought not* to be their own mistresses, or make money for themselves, or do what they liked with their own!" (79)

Miss Climpson, furthermore, cannot be taken as spokesperson for Sayers' "paranoia." Though she is a woman of good sense and unusual ability, as a result of her lack of education she lacks the power to discriminate, as is illustrated by the constant underlining in her reports to Lord Peter. She should have been a lawyer, she says; she "should have liked a good education, but my dear father didn't believe in it for women" (35). Another indication that Miss Climpson's judgments are not always sound is the narrative information that "For Miss Climpson, men were intended to be masterful, even though wicked or foolish. She was . . . a perfectly womanly woman" (154). Although the epithet does not carry in this text the unequivocal condemnation which it acquires in *Gaudy Night*, it is not a term, even here, of approbation.

Sayers created Mary Whittaker just after her marriage—just after, that is, she had renounced the single life and with it a certain amount of independence and the possibility of casting her lot with another woman. Lesbianism might, under these circumstances, pose a certain threat and/or cause regret, but Miss Climpson's acceptance of the Whittaker-Dawson relationship and numerous hints to the reader that Miss Climpson's judgments are not always trustworthy, as well as the portrayal of other lesbians of a much less threatening cast, both in her other novels, and, more importantly, in *Unnatural Death* itself, argue against the accusations by critics of any "paranoia."[1] It seems important to elaborate this argument because the question of same-sex relationships is, in the context of women's educational communities, inextricable from the question of higher education for women itself, as we have seen.

Among Sayers' cast of lesbians are the cynical but loyal Eiluned Price of *Strong Poison* and the charming couple in *Five Red Herrings*, Miss Selby and Miss Cochran, who occupy "adjacent cottages," and are continually "taking tea in each other's living rooms or bathing together in the sands at the Down" (66). They are both talented artists and "Wimsey liked them . . . because they had no nonsense about them" (66). The most explicit, however, aside from Mary Whittaker and her companion Vera Findlater, are Clara Whittaker and *her* companion, Agatha Dawson, Mary's first victim. These two are portrayed not only as a lesbian couple but as a stereotypical one. Miss Clara supported them with her excellent business sense and was the aggressive, more active partner. "There was a many gentleman as would have been glad to hitch up with her, but she was never broke to harness . . . wouldn't look at 'em, except it might be grooms or stablehands in a matter of 'osses. And in the way of business, of course" (121). Miss Dawson, on the other hand, "was the 'domestic' partner, and looked after the house and servants" (179). She was, further, "more timidlike. She'd go by the gates, and we often used to say she'd never be riding at all but for bein' that fond of Miss Whittaker and not wanting to let her out of her sight" (117). The villagers respect these women and accept them as different but not at all unnatural. As Mr. Coking, musing about both his animals and the two women, says, "Well, there is some creatures like that. . . . The Lord makes a few of 'em that way to suit 'Is own purposes, I suppose" (121). Even Miss Climpson, so adamant, as we have seen, in her harsh judgment of the Whittaker-Findlater relationship says not a word against that of the older women. This, in spite of the fact that the two relationships are carefully paralleled by the women's rhetoric. Mrs. Coking, former maid to the Dawson family, reports that Miss Agatha often said to her, "I mean to be an old maid and so does Miss Clara, and we're going to live together and be ever so happy, without any stupid tiresome gentlemen" (125). Vera echoes this sentiment closely when she says later in the novel to Miss Climpson, "Well, I mean to be an old maid, anyhow. . . . Mary and I have quite decided that we're interested in things, not in men" (156).

The Dawson-Whittaker relationship is not only accepted and respected but is central to the plot of the novel. The motive for murder hinges on the fact that "when Clara Whittaker died she left *all her money* to Agatha, passing over her own family!" (79)—a legacy which clearly expresses that these women were "all-in-all to one another" and which, furthermore, does not, even among the conservative villagers and the Catholic Miss Climpson elicit any disapproval. It is important to establish at some length the general goodness of Sayers' educated women in general and lesbian women in particular, to eliminate simple prejudice or "paranoia" as explanations for her creation of this independent woman/lesbian villain. The issue here is more complex, centered not on the fact of Mary Whittaker's new womanhood or lesbianism, but on their conjunction with the excess and nature of the violence she perpetrates and the terror and disgust she elicits.

A Sayers detective text usually limits itself to one corpse. In *Gaudy Night* there is no corpse at all; *The Nine Tailors* and *The Unpleasantness at the Bellona Club* both have a corpse but no real murderer. In *Unnatural Death*, however, there are three corpses and three aborted attempts at murder. As suggested above, the first murder, that of Miss Agatha Dawson, is not a surprising one. The victim was old and ailing; she refused to make a will, even when it seemed that the person she wished to inherit her money might not, in fact, under an imminent law, automatically do so; even the charitable Nurse Philliter describes the old woman as "obstinate, you know, and what they call a character, at the best of times" (42); she was constantly in pain from cancer. If her desired heir should relieve that pain and hasten her death just a little, the reader might almost forgive her, as he or she is invited to forgive Ferguson in *The Five Red Herrings* and Tallboy in *Murder Must Advertise* (though in both those cases the victims were impossible to sympathize with, as is not the case in *Unnatural Death*). Instead, however, of limiting herself to what might almost be judged a mercy killing, Miss Whittaker begins to attack everyone who might slightly suspect her complicity in her aunt's death. And the attacks are not spontaneous strikings-out, but cold-blooded and elaborately planned. The three aborted attacks and possibly one or two of the murders are done in disguise; the so-called Mrs. Forrest has a London flat, a car of her own, and a bank account—all indications of a well thought out plot.

Inspector Parker attempts to account for this excess of violence: "When a woman is wicked and unscrupulous . . . she is the most ruthless criminal in the world—fifty times worse than a man, because she is always so much more single-minded about it." Lord Peter Wimsey concurs, "They're not troubled with sentimentality, that's why, . . . and we poor mutts of men stuff ourselves up with the idea that they're romantic and emotional" (204). But, like other generalizations about women made by men in Sayers' novels, this one is undercut by both the subtle disapproval of the narrator (Parker says this "sententiously") and inherent lack of logic (why should lack of sentimentality, traditionally associated with men, suddenly make a female murderer fifty times worse than a male one?). The text, then, like Sayers' essays, makes its point that statements about women in general apply to no one; one can only say that this woman, Mary Whittaker, is a more ruthless criminal than Parker and Wimsey are used to and that Miss Whittaker should be as free to compete in the world of nasty murders as Mary Somerville should have been free to compete in the world of mathematics and Dame Ethel Smyth in the world of music. This individualistic feminism should perhaps deter the critic from attempting to unearth any cause for Mary Whittaker's violence other than her right to this "masculine" vice.

Again, however, it is the puzzling excess that keeps the question alive. Though we as readers do not accept Charles Parker's pronouncement, we sympathize with the desire for an explanation. We too sense that this murderer exceeds the conventions of the genre, oversteps the boundaries. Significantly, Mary Whittaker offends, oversteps, and destroys in precisely those areas in which the opponents of degrees for women predicted that the educated woman would offend, overstep, and destroy.

Mary Whittaker, a "well-educated, capable girl . . . self-reliant, cool . . . the modern type" (18), stops at nothing to gain financial independence. She commits her first murder for precisely this reason—to insure that Agatha Dawson will die before the new law that will threaten her right to inherit comes into effect. In killing Agatha Dawson, Mary does away with the last representative of an older, more genteel and aristocratic world and replaces it with her own hard, businesslike approach to life, indicated, even before she is revealed as murderer, by her refusal to continue the £100-a-year allowance Miss Dawson had made to a distant relative, Hallelujah Dawson. Miss Dawson, we know, had no head for business; her educated heir has head for little else. This illustrates one of the first fears of Oxford men and their supporters—not only does the world seem headed in a bad direction anyway, but aggressive, hard, educated women will contribute to a world without the traditionally feminine virtues.

Mary Whittaker, true to all dire predictions about granting women educational equality, from one point of view, is unsexed. One of the strangest and interpretively unresolvable incidents in the novel is the attempt by Mrs. Forrest (Miss Whittaker in disguise) to murder

Lord Peter. She tries to drug him sufficiently to allow her to use the empty hypodermic syringe with which she injected air into Miss Dawson's artery and tries frantically to keep him at her flat while the drug has time to take effect. There follows a kind of seduction scene, in which Wimsey, desperate to find out what she is up to, feigns growing passion for the "epicene" woman, whom he had previously experienced as "something essentially sexless" (152). He puts his arm around her and feels "her body stiffen," then kisses her. "He knew then. No one who has ever encountered it can ever again mistake that awful shrinking, that uncontrollable revulsion of flesh against a caress that is nauseous" (153). The simple sequence of action in this scene consists of Whittaker's desire to detain a man whom she correctly perceives as a danger to her newly won independence; her indication to him that she expects him to seduce her; his complicity, for his own ends, in her plan; her distaste for his admittedly "exaggerated passion" (153). But the charged language here makes the scene much more sinister: "awful shrinking," "uncontrollable revulsion," "no one who has ever encountered it can ever again mistake." With the apparent complicity of the narrator, Wimsey evinces the same reaction to unyielding women as the detractors of the women's colleges do. Whittaker is perceived as unsexed because she is not heterosexual; as awful and uncontrollable because not responsive to a man's violent and feigned embrace. We have suggested the fears that underlie those worries about unsexed women; the text's portrayal of the unsexed woman as murderer gives concrete shape to these fears. At the same time, we must note that the shrinking, the revulsion, the nausea are Mary Whittaker's; while this murderer is consistently seen from the outside, while she has heretofore been rational, passionless, and faultlessly competent, in this scene she reveals something important about herself, some vulnerability which allows the reader a fleeting sympathetic response to her, qualitatively different from any other in the novel. That this brief revelation concerns Whittaker's sexuality suggests again a textual ambivalence about her that is not easily resolved.

Whittaker's second victim is Bertha Gotobed, a former maid of Miss Dawson, who had overheard Whittaker's argument with Miss Dawson over the will and had been subsequently dismissed by Mary Whittaker on a flimsy pretext. Bertha is a *good* girl: "There wouldn't have been any carryings-on with her young man—nothing of that" (96). Though pure and virginal, Bertha is engaged to be married to a respectable young man—she will, that is, as her name implies, go to bed, and she is not, therefore, unsexed, as is her murderer. Bertha's sister Evelyn, another potential victim, remains alive, Wimsey speculates, only because she has married and followed her husband to a Canadian farm. Mary, then, the text implies, threatens not only the aristocratic world of her aunts but also the world of the virtuous working-class woman who, though she may have to support herself for a time as a maid or waitress, looks forward, unlike the man-hating Mary, to a "natural" life of husband and children. This threat to Bertha also embodies those fears that the educated woman will overturn the values of a stable society.

The third corpse is the woman who has been portrayed throughout the novel as, in one way or another, Mary Whittaker's victim—Vera Findlater. Miss Climpson cannot at first see why Mary has chosen such a "very gushing and really *silly* young woman" (78) as a constant companion, but decides later that "she likes to have someone to admire her and run her errands. And she prefers it to be a stupid person, who will not compete with her" (154). Miss Climpson becomes, in the course of the novel, genuinely fond of Vera and tries, as we have seen, to urge her to a more "natural," that is, heterosexual relationship. Vera, however, has learned well the lesson her friend taught her: "They [men] haven't got any ideas. And they always look on women as sorts of pets or playthings. As if a woman like Mary wasn't worth fifty of them!" (155)

Before she finds out that Vera has been found dead in mysterious circumstances, Miss Climpson reconstructs what she imagines goes on between the two women: "Humiliating, degrading, exhausting, beastly scenes. . . . Damnable selfishness wearying of its victim. Silly *Schwärmerei* swamping all decent self-respect. Barren quarrels ending in shame and hatred" (216). Like Peter Wimsey's fierce condemnation of Whittaker's sexlessness, Miss Climpson's language here betrays a ferocity of response so far unwarranted by the situation. The reality, later revealed, that Mary Whittaker is the murderer not only of Miss Dawson and Miss Gotobed but of her friend appears to justify both Wimsey's and Climpson's reactions and to embody their fears. In killing Vera Findlater, who, as her name implies, finds the truth, not just later but too late, Whittaker again plays out masculinist anxieties about the new woman. First, she is not content to be herself a spinster but must recruit innocent young women to this "unnatural" state. With her superior education and new-woman self-confidence and competence she seduces Vera, who in her gushing innocence is a perfect candidate for marriage and motherhood. Even more threatening, however, is Mary's obvious assumption of the male role. She becomes, for Vera, both teacher and provider. We recognize *her* rhetoric in Vera's words; it is Mary's money, inherited from her first victim, that is setting them up on their chicken farm, Mary's worldliness that allows the inexperienced Vera to leave home, to spend time in London, to contemplate an alternative future. Whittaker has assumed a male prerogative in her very choice of a mate. Miss Climpson's speculation about Whittaker's psychology amusingly parallels the stereotypical man's view of marriage: he wishes a wife to admire him and run his errands, prefers someone less intelligent than himself who will not compete with him. In response to Vera's panegyric on friendship, Miss Climpson even uses the Whittaker-Findlater relationship to expose a basic fallacy of male-female relationships. She quotes "a most *splendid* priest" who "said that Milton's remark about Eve—you know, 'he for God only, she for God in him'—was not congruous with Catholic doctrine . . . it was *out of proportion* to see everything through the eyes of another fellow-creature" (158). Thus, she implies that the "natural" heterosexual relationship she prescribes for Vera may well be as "unnatural" (out of proportion) as this homosexual one, which is "unnatural" in turn either because it is not fruitful or because in it Mary Whittaker plays the part of a man and finally brutally kills her "wife"—while wearing a pair of men's boots.

In "Are Woman Human?" Sayers regrets the "tendency on the part of the women's colleges to 'copy the men' on the side of their failings and absurdities" and the women students' "foolish trick of imitating and outdoing the absurdities of male undergraduates" (*UO*, 132). Mary Whittaker, the "well-educated . . . capable . . . modern type" concretely and drastically embodies Sayers' fear that educated women might end up replicating men's failings. She embodies, too, the fear voiced by detractors of women's education that educated women might in any way act the manly part. In an amusing paragraph indicating a passage of time in the solving of this grisly case, the narrator makes a list of headline world events, seemingly significant but actually silly: "Chamberlain and Levine flew the Atlantic, Segrave bade farewell to Brooklands . . . , England's supremacy was challenged at Wimbledon." Among the events is

"Oxford decided that women were dangerous" (183). In its context this event partakes of the silliness of the others, yet in Leahampton is a woman dangerous indeed. "Oxford," then, is both hopelessly silly and absolutely correct. Women are dangerous, especially when, educated and competent, they become like men. Furthermore, they are most dangerous to traditional victims—other women. All the corpses in the novel are female. The attempts to kill Peter Wimsey and Mr. Trigg are aborted before any harm is done, but Miss Whittaker's attack on Miss Climpson results in serious injury. The fear underlying this world of female victims seems two-pronged: on one hand, the fear expressed by male Oxford that the educated woman will disturb the "natural order" by assuming the male role of victimizer of women, and the fear expressed by women like Sayers that educated women will repeat, will replicate, this order and that the sufferers will be not men but other women. As usurpers of the traditional roles of men, including seduction and murder, women could create a world in which they are both oppressed and oppressors. In either scenario men nearly drop out of the scheme entirely as they have nearly dropped out of this text.

Before we examine further the almost single-sex world of *Unnatural Death* in which victims, villain, and detective are all women, and its relationship to that other single-sex world Sayers created in *Gaudy Night*, it is important to reflect briefly on the significance of the book's title. It refers directly to the fact that the deaths of both Miss Dawson and Bertha Gotobed are officially declared "natural" deaths, but are actually murders, that is, the most unnatural of deaths. Doctors and coroners first judge the deaths natural because they find no signs of violence, struggle, or poison. The beauty of Miss Whittaker's method is that she kills with a natural substance—air—injected into an inappropriate place. Yet no matter how simple and natural-seeming the method, the fact remains that she kills. And this malevolent human agency becomes the distinction here between natural and unnatural.

Similarly, in a discussion between Peter Wimsey and Charles Parker about "normal" and "abnormal" crime, the distinction hinges on human agency—abnormal crimes are "the failures. The crimes that have been found out" (83). This discussion, however, undercuts the original distinction. Does Miss Dawson's death become unnatural because Mary Whittaker killed her or because the crime was discovered? Another possibility, however, is that the title refers primarily to Vera Findlater's death, which Whittaker makes no attempt to hide as natural but, on the contrary, makes seem the result of an elaborate plot that includes a black male attacker, drugs, kidnapping, and theft. And it is here that Whittaker begins to make the obvious mistakes that lead to her capture. Like Chaucer's Nicholaus in "The Miller's Tale," Mary overelaborates. She creates a plot less and less "natural," which eventually exposes her. The text's plot, too, as it becomes more elaborate, as it adds on corpses, disguises, and plots within plots, exposes its own artifice, and thus subverts any correspondence between death in fiction, always artificial, and death, natural or unnatural, in the world. Finally, the title includes Whittaker's suicide—she strangles herself with a bed sheet after she is caught—a death unnatural because it is self-imposed, because it uses a man's method, and because it uses as its instrument something associated with the natural functions of sex and death.

The seemingly simple opposition, then, between "natural" and "unnatural" is complicated by the ubiquitousness of its application and by the discussion about those related words, "normal" and "abnormal." And the distinction becomes even more complicated when the words are applied in a different context. We have seen that Miss Climpson uses "natural" to characterize the relation between a woman and a man, which, unlike one between two women, can be "fruitful." The Whittaker-Findlater relationship not only results in an unnatural death but is in itself an unnatural relationship, according to Miss Climpson. As in the case of "unnatural" applied to death, however, other considerations confuse this commonly used line of reasoning. First, as we have seen, Miss Climpson makes no such judgment on the Clara Whittaker-Mary Dawson relationship, which was, according to Miss Climpson's criterion of "fruitfulness", just as unnatural as the Mary Whittaker-Vera Findlater one. Furthermore, as we have also seen, Miss Climpson objects to the latter because it partakes so strongly of the commonly accepted and assumed "natural" male-female relationship—that is, Vera Findlater wants to live her life through her friend. Miss Climpson repeats with approval the judgment that such a relationship, the exemplar of which is that most natural pair, Milton's Adam and Eve, is "out of proportion" (158), that is, unnatural.

Dawson Gaillard notes that the characterization of Miss Climpson as a "womanly woman" indicates that she "belongs in the natural order but has been frustrated by society" (40). Yet the term "womanly woman" comes to carry a certain opprobrium for Sayers. She says, for example, in the introduction to *Unpopular Opinions* that the second section of the book (where we find her feminist essays) "will offend all those . . . who use and enjoy slatternly forms of speech, all manly men, womanly women, and people who prefer wealth to work." In such despicable company, a womanly woman can hardly be the object of much sympathy. And we recall the context of this remark about Miss Climpson: she believes that "men were intended to be masterful, even though wicked and foolish" (154). Furthermore, the juxtaposition in *Unpopular Opinions* of "those who use slatternly forms of speech" and "womanly women" reminds us of Miss Climpson's own slatternly speech. Shrewd and observant as she is, she rambles, she gets the emphases wrong because she emphasizes too many things. We recall that Miss Climpson could have been a good lawyer but did not have the education. The implication here is that Miss Climpson is a womanly woman because, educationless, deprived for so long of meaningful work, she does not know any better. Again, human agency marks the distinction—the womanly or natural woman needs education to correct her slatternly forms of both speech and judgment.

The text of *Unnatural Death* does not attempt to sort out centuries of controversy over "natural" and "unnatural"; it does, however, recognize the confusion and complication of this distinction whether applied to death, sex, or gender roles, and recognizes further its relevance to the issue of education, because education is, as Rousseau reminds us, a sort of interference with the natural. Women need education just as men do, but in educating women we run the risk of their acquiring, in the freedom and worldliness that education confers, the less desirable qualities of their brothers. The detractors of degrees for women are correct: educated women are dangerous. Given freedom they are just as capable as men of murder for financial gain, of murder cold and calculating, of murder ugly and violent. That this text emphasizes the risk and emphasizes it so dramatically and excessively indicates conflict and division in the text itself, a conflict to which the title calls and recalls our attention, between fear that educated women will become dangerous and conviction that education is nevertheless necessary to them.

Sayers' own experiences of education for women was, of course, at a single-sex institution. As we have seen, life at a women's college for a British woman in the first half of the century was very much woman-centered. Feminist critics especially have discussed the significance of this issue in *Gaudy Night*, which takes place at a women's college patterned on Somerville. But critics have over-looked the existence of the woman-centered world in *Unnatural Death*, a world less organized than Shrewsbury College, to be sure, but woman-centered nonetheless. We have noted already that in this novel victims, villain, and detective are all female; further-more, the victims, villain, and detective are all part of distinct and distinctive networks of women. None of the networks is idealized like Shrewsbury College; the predominant sense in the text is that a single-sex environment, while sometimes necessary and acceptable, is severely limited and perhaps "unnatural."

Unnatural Death features Lord Peter Wimsey and Inspector Parker, but the main detecting is done by Miss Alexandra Katherine (who becomes in later novels Miss Katherine Alexandra) Climpson, whose job is a philanthropic invention of Lord Peter's to employ "superfluous women" (37). Miss Climpson only hints in *Unnatural Death* at the establishment of what in later novels is known as The Cattery, a kind of detective agency, "my eyes and tongue . . . and especially my nose," as Wimsey says of Miss Climpson herself (37), made up entirely of "old maids, simply bursting with useful energy, forced by our stupid social system into hydros and hotels and . . . posts as companions, where their magnificent gossip-powers and units of inquisitiveness are allowed to dissipate themselves" (36). The Cattery turns the stereotypical feminine vice of gossip-monger-ing into the masculine virtue of seeking truth and justice. Though Miss Climpson in this novel is still picking out the future members of the firm, its structure and function are clear. The agency's em-ployer and director is Wimsey himself, though in later novels the agency functions more autonomously. When the novel begins, Miss Climpson has been interviewing and collecting information about hundreds of women whom the firm might suitably employ. From this female environment Miss Climpson moves into the female Leahampton world; she boards with Mrs. Budge and cultivates the acquaintance of the village women, all eager to give their opinions about the death of Miss Dawson and the respectability of their neighbors.

"You know, Wimsey, I think you've found the mare's nest," Par-ker remarks after Miss Climson reports on her initial contacts. The "mare's nest" refers to Peter's assumption that someone murdered Miss Dawson; Parker suspects that she died a natural death. But besides denoting an illusion, the phrase creates an image entirely appropriate for the Agatha Dawson-Clara Whittaker milieu with its combination of domesticity and horsiness. The image works even more precisely for Miss Climpson's new milieu—the Leahampton world of females, gossip, confusion, and finally illusion—in which the mares and "mères," Mrs. Peasgood, Miss Murgatroyd, Mrs. Tredgold, Miss Findlater, Miss Whittaker, and Miss Climpson, discuss one another and discuss as well Nurses Philliter and Forbes, the late Miss Dawson, and the absent Mrs. Budge. So thoroughly female is this world that the presiding deities are "the avenging Errinyes" (51) and the invoked author Sheila Kaye-Smith (53). Not only does Miss Climpson move from the potential Cattery to the Leahampton mare's nest, but she refers to her own history as a "woman-ridden existence" (78), and the narrative voice mentions Miss Climpson's "woman-ridden life" (216). It is this history and her reading of another woman novelist, Clemence Dane, who wrote "a *very clever* book on the subject" (78), which alerts her to the "unhealthy" (78), "*schwärmerisch*" (154) relationship between Vera Findlater and Mary Whittaker.[2]

The detecting Miss Climpson's female worlds overlap in many ways with the female worlds of the villain and her victims. We have already seen the great-aunts' relationship, a relationship which commenced in a girls' school (124) and from which the formidable Clara Whittaker dispelled all men. Even the more timid and domestic Miss Dawson "was never one for flirting" (125). Clara was a rich woman but her money was not inherited from her father; rather she "had built up her fortune *entirely* by her own exertions" (79). Nor did she leave the money to the "son"—her clergyman nephew Charles Whittaker—but to her life companion, Miss Dawson, who in turn leaves the fortune, not to another family clergyman, Halleluja Dawson, but to Mary Whittaker. Matriarchy or mare's nest, the world is decidedly female.

Even the world of the least central victim, the engaged Bertha Gotobed, consists primarily of her sister Evelyn and her loyal landlady, Mrs. Gulliver; these are the only of her associates to appear in the novel. The male companion whom the police suppose to have shared the fatal picnic lunch turns out to be illusory, as do the male kidnappers that seem to have murdered Vera Findlater and carried off Mary Whittaker. That the police so eagerly pursue these male red herrings testifies to the tenacity of the assumption of villain as

male and to the threatening exclusivity and autonomy of these female realms. Miss Climpson is quick to point out to the police the
jealousy, hatred, and selfishness that can permeate a woman-ridden
world, Parker quick to proclaim women murderers fifty times worse
than their male counterparts, Oxford quick to decide that women
are dangerous. Whether the atmosphere of *Unnatural Death* owes
its sinisterness, it violence, its unnaturalness to its femaleness, as
Miss Climpson, Parker, and Oxford imply, is impossible to decide,
in part because of the slipperiness of "natural" and "unnatural,"
their tendency to overlap, ther tendency so easily to take on and so
promptly to shed, each in turn, moral and social opprobrium. We
must look, finally, at this atmosphere in conjunction with Sayers'
other women's world, which both partakes of and overcomes these
qualities, Shrewsbury College in *Gaudy Night.* There "natural" and
"unnatural" do not simply slip and overlap but eventually sort
themselves out by reversing themselves entirely.

4   Of Catteries,

Colleges, and Whimsical Weddings

Archibald: Besides . . . if there were no men, how would
    there be any civilization? For all the ladies would be oc-
    cupied with bringing up their children and would have no
    time . . . for inventing machines and navigating the ocean
    and delving in ruins and doing the hundred-and-one other
    things needful for our well-being and security.
Nurse: How is this matter arranged, pray, among the bees of
    whom you think so highly? The workers there are all fe-
    males, who, by a suitable provision of nature, have been
    relieved from household cares and have both leisure and
    strength to perform all the tasks for which this civilization
    calls (22).

This dialogue between the nurse and her young male charge comes
from Sayers' enigmatic book, *Even the Parrot: Exemplary Conversations for Enlightened Children*, written seventeen years after *Unnatural Death* and nine after *Gaudy Night*. We will discuss the end of this
particular "conversation" later; the scrap above serves as a reflection on the women's world of *Gaudy Night* and gives it, by way of
analogy with a beehive, a foundation in the natural order of things.[1]
In *Unnatural Death* a women-ridden existence is presented and very

nearly dismissed as in one way or another unnatural; *Gaudy Night* confronts the issue openly and asserts the naturalness of a highly un-natural—that is educated, civilized, cultivated, and women-ridden world. The tool for the exploration of this paradox and the delinea-tion of its terms is Harriet Vane, the detective-novel-writing hero-ine who makes her first appearance in *Strong Poison*, published in 1930, three years after *Unnatural Death*. In *Strong Poison* Vane has been arrested for the murder of her former lover. Like Mary Whit-taker, Harriet is a well-educated, competent, strong woman. Also like Mary, "quite the modern type," as is evidenced by her uncon-ventional relationship with Philip Boyes and her independent spirit. Unlike Miss Whittaker, Vane, though guilty of a sexual rela-tionship outside of marriage, is not guilty of murder. In the course of the novel she is tried for both.

Like Miss Climpson, Harriet is a detective of sorts, shrewd and observant, but with a kind heart. Unlike Miss Climpson, Harriet is an Oxford M.A., too young to be thought a spinster, morally and artistically tolerant, and confident of her abilities. In *Strong Poison,* Harriet takes on Miss Whittaker's role as potential villain but she reverses the role and becomes the heroine; in *Gaudy Night* Harriet takes on Miss Climpson's role as detective and reverses it, too. Miss Climpson, under orders from Peter Wimsey, insinuates herself into a women's community to which she does not belong, as a spy; Har-riet Vane, working on her own at the request of Shrewsbury Col-lege, openly considers the problem of a women's community to which she *does* belong: "They can't take this away, at any rate. Whatever I may have done since, this remains. Scholar, Master of Arts; Domina; Senior Member of this University . . . ; a place achieved, unalienable, worthy of reverence" (13).

In creating Harriet, then, Sayers creates a woman who fulfills not male Oxford's fears but female Oxford's ideals. And because Harriet partakes of both the outside world and the women's intellectual community, she can bridge the wide water between them; because she belongs to both only marginally she can probe, question, and criticize them. Several critics have discussed the Shrewsbury schol-arly community at length. Nina Auerbach suggests that the initial vision of it as "an oasis of detachment governed by wise and faithful women" breaks down as the outside world necessarily contaminates it "and these strong women recede rather shamefacedly out of the action" (165); Meredith Cary notes that in this novel (interestingly, she omits to observe this about *Unnatural Death*) "Sayers assigns all the basic detective fiction roles to women. Women are the victims, the criminal, the witnesses, the investigator. At first glance such a cast of characters suggests that Sayers has set up a separate world where women can escape from male violence and power" (264). Like Auerbach, Cary claims that such a "first hopeful vision" (264) breaks down in the course of the novel.

On the other hand, Carolyn Heilbrun testifies in an *American Scholar* review to the importance of Sayers' "portrayal of a female community and a moral universe" (553), to Heilbrun's own sense of the possibilities open to women. That such a community is not a utopia perhaps allows it to inspire the intelligent young woman "for whom the female destiny of flirtation, wedding, and motherhood is insufficient or even unattractive" (553). Harriet Vane, then, might be seen not only as connecting the outside world of the novel with the inner female intellectual world but also as connecting the world of the reader with that of the novel. Sue Ellen Campbell suggests this possibility when she asserts that the creation of a heroine, "a figure for whom there is no established formula [in detective fiction] . . . consequently forces both characters and plots out of their usual molds" (498).

Besides Harriet's ability to bridge these worlds, or to extend and/or blur their boundaries, she has the power both to bridge and to blur traditional distinctions among fictive roles. We have seen that in *Strong Poison* Harriet is alleged villain, victim (in that she is almost sent to the gallows, in that she is judged guilty of being an immoral woman), and detective (by extension of her profession as a writer of detective fiction). A suggestive passage in *Have His Carcase* (1932) shows Harriet humorously conflating the detective and the villain:

> Harriet pleased herself over the coffee with sketching out the career of an American detective-novelist who contracted a fresh marriage for each new book. For a book about poisons, she would marry an analytical chemist; for a book about some-body's will, a solicitor; for a book about strangling, a hangman, of course. There might be something in it. . . . And the vil-lainess might do away with each husband by the method de-scribed in the book she was working on at the time (37).

Harriet's mind plays with possibilities, overlappings, and breaks with tradition (the wayward writer is an American, that ubiquitous British symbol of the unexpected). In *Gaudy Night* Harriet more explicitly and self-consciously moves from writer of detective fiction to detective. And she forces this character, too, out of its mold: she fails to solve the case, ironically enough because there is one character—the single woman—whose mold she cannot break into or out of.

Gaudy Night begins with Harriet's return to Shrewsbury. Unlike most of her fellow students, she had not visited between the taking of her degree many years before and this Gaudy in 1935, "at first because she had loved the place too well, and a clean break seemed better than a slow wrenching-away" and then because her unconventional life seemed not what "Shrewsbury expected of its old students" (8). These reasons together with the nostalgic depiction of the college buildings and gardens, invest the community not only with the power of enormous influence but with a kind of moral purity which renders it utopian. Harriet returns to her college not with romantic longing for the spires of Oxford but with hesitation and anxiety. As a sexually experienced woman and a woman accused of murder she has, she thinks, become as much outsider as member. When Harriet meets the Shrewsbury women, however, she perceives the college as less judgmental, less potent, and more subject to human foibles. The Dean, for example, assures Harriet right away that no one bothers about her past at all (14). That this is not altogether true only points to the real and human differences among the scholars. Harriet's encounters with women of her year remind her that three years at university do not guarantee a lifetime of intelligent work, and her short discussions with Miss Barton and Miss Hillyard establish clearly that prejudice and jealous meanness do not disappear amid lofty towers, peaceful lawns, and well-stocked libraries.

This initial vision is, nevertheless, one which—expanded, contracted, and modified though it is in the course of the book—persists. The vision of Shrewsbury as Auerbach's "oasis of detachment" or Cary's "separate world," changes as much because Harriet has reestablished herself as part of it and has made it a part of herself as because of internal jealousies and external pressures. Harriet's nostalgia for Shrewsbury is, as nostalgia tends to be, based on an idealization. "If only one could come back," she thinks, "to this quiet place, where only intellectual achievement counted, if one could work here steadily and obscurely . . . undistracted and uncorrupted" (20). At dinner that night the noise of "two hundred female tongues" (24) reminds Harriet that the place is not always quiet, yet quiet times and places throughout the novel become sources of stability and creativity for her. In her room one night, for instance,

> In that melodious silence, something came back to her that had lain dumb and dead ever since the old, innocent under-graduate days. The singing voice, stifled long ago by the pressure of the struggle for existence and throttled into dumbness by that queer, unhappy contact with physical passion, began to stammer a few uncertain notes. Great golden phrases . . . swam up out of her dreaming mind (188).

Though the "high, clamorous" voices at table drive her almost mad, Harriet recovers her own voice, her own lyric, not of innocence but of experience, in the Shrewsbury silence, precisely because this silence is constitutive of a place in which women, even women with a past, have a voice.

Though it becomes clear from Miss Hillyard's misanthropy, Miss Cattermole and Miss Flaxman's silly romantic rivalry, Miss Shaw's exaggerated idea of her influence on her students that Shrewsbury is not a place where *only* intellectual achievement counts, it is nonetheless a place where intellectual achievement does count. As the mysterious villain makes more bizarre and sordid threats, it becomes clear that "undistracted" and "uncorrupted" apply with serious qualification to this women's world, but it becomes equally clear that they *do* apply. In spite of the great temptation, occasionally succumbed to, to turn on one another, engendered by the atmosphere of suspicion and threat, the women, like Miss Pope in Sayers' tribute, remain generous, humble, and loyal. Peter Wimsey reminds them at the end of the novel "that the one thing which frustrated the whole attack from first to last was the remarkable solidarity and public spirit displayed by your college" (36).

Harriet decides, in the end, not to stay at Shrewsbury. She decides, too, to accept, finally, Peter Wimsey's marriage proposal, but she makes these decisions on the basis of personal vocation, not out of any conviction that marriage is superior to membership in the Senior Common Room. Harriet's philosophy that "one should do one's job, however trivial, and not persuade one's self into doing something else, however noble" (44) allows her to reject for herself a life she finds congenial, worthwhile, and admirable, to reject it because it cannot make use of her own talent. That Shrewsbury has no real niche for a writer of popular fiction in no way implies that the life there is not a valid and "noble" one. Life with Wimsey, on the other hand, might have such a niche, though conventional marriage does not if the writer happens to be a woman.

Phoebe Tucker, one of Harriet's friends from college, serves as an illustration that marriage need not necessarily dull the mind nor corrupt the judgment, but she is the only such example in this book. Catherine Freemantle, a friend who married a farmer, is worn-out and frustrated. Harriet feels "she would rather be tried for life over again than walk the daily treadmill of Catherine's life" (42). Mary Stokes seems "cut off from them by sickness, by marriage" (13). Even Peter Wimsey, who tries throughout the novel to get Harriet to agree to marry him, admits that "of all the devils let loose in the world, there [is] no devil like devoted love" (332). We will see that in this novel traditional marriage, in fact, wreaks havoc on the intellectual life of women in very dramatic ways. Harriet, when she rejects the female community for herself, asserts a kind of hope that she and Peter and any offspring they might have could create an environment as supportive of her talents as Shrewsbury is of another sort of talent.[2]

Harriet thus acknowledges the viability of the Shrewsbury community by rejecting it—that is, she considers it seriously as a way of life with its own validity and its own very real attractions. Mrs. Goodwin, the college secretary, theorizes that the "disorders" plaguing Shrewsbury "tend to occur in celibate . . . communities. It is a kind of compensation . . . for the lack of other excitements" (68). Even at the height of her suspicion that the theory is true, Harriet vacillates: "Once again, she felt Wimsey as a dangerous alien and herself on the side of the women, who, with so strange a generosity, were welcoming the inquisitor among them" (279). This vacillation between the world of women and the wider world serves as a bridge between them, acknowledging the validity of the separate existence of the former and affirming their interdependence. The overt dramatization of her role here does not occur until *Busman's Honeymoon*, Sayers' next novel, in which Harriet and Peter finally marry—"from a women's College, of all places," (12) as a guest writes. Harriet substitutes Shrewsbury for church and home (she has no living relatives to complicate the issue), the Senior Common Room for friends and family: "The bride came attended by the most incredible assortment of bridesmaids—all female dons!—and an odd dark woman to give her away, who was supposed to be the Head of the College" (12). Wimsey's shocked sister relates the details of this strange wedding between Harriet and her brother, between a college and "the world," between an institution by its nature female and an institution by its nature double-sexed. In giving Harriet away, the Head of Shrewsbury replaces the expected father and Harriet becomes the daughter not of a traditional heterosexual union but of a community of women. Like Clara Whittaker, who breaks the paternal chain of inheritance by willing her money to Agatha Dawson, Harriet breaks, in an even more radical move, the paternal ritual by which women, like property and as property, are passed from man to man, from father to husband.[3]

Virginia Morris asserts that "Harriet's decision at the end of [*Gaudy Night*] to marry Peter Wimsey demonstrates Sayers' conviction that an assertive, independent woman can be a good wife and is probably her most radical, most feminist idea" (493). This idea was, as we have seen, a persistent tenet of the advocates of degrees for women but an idea that Sayers herself would have scorned. The implication of Harriet's decision is much more radical: the educated woman, reborn in her college, re-formed through the agency of other educated women, can reform the role of wife by always pushing at its boundaries, always rebelling at and refusing its traditional demands. Harriet in *Busman's Honeymoon* does this explicitly with the word "husband," which she notes is "A repressive word . . . when you came to think of it, compounded of a grumble and a thump. The man in possession. The man with rights—including the right not to be made a fool of by his belongings" (36). What finally convinces Harriet, after five years of April Fool's day proposals, to consider marrying Wimsey is his recognition of her right to risk her life for her work, which recognition she takes as "an admission of equality." "If he conceived marriage along those lines, then the whole problem would have to be reviewed in that new light; but that seemed scarcely possible. To take such a line and stick to it, he would have to be, not a man but a miracle" (GN, 184).

Wimsey is, of course, not a man but a character in a novel written by a woman. Harriet's marrying him is a creative act, not a real or a social one, and the object of that creativity is marriage itself. Harriet, reborn of a world of women, marries Peter, whim of a woman, to make concrete a vision, not of things as they are, but of things as they might be. An assertive, independent, educated woman cannot make a good wife by the very definition of the word wife, as Harriet knows well throughout *Gaudy Night*. Even Phoebe Tucker, the archaeologist, the only married woman in the novel who has not compromised her mind, has had to fly in the face of accepted behavior. She "casually" dumps her "trio of youngsters . . . upon delighted grandparents before hastening back to the bones and stones" (17). "Casually" is important here: Phoebe's work comes first and she, without guilt or anguish, makes the arrangements necessary to do it. What Harriet as an educated woman must do is recreate the institution of marriage to accommodate the lesson of Shrewsbury—that one's work is the important thing. One cannot do someone else's job nor can one *be* someone else's job, because those imply, as Miss de Vine points out, either "devouring or being devoured" (151).

This image of the devouring or devoured woman, which, as we shall see, amounts to the same thing, occurs again and again in the novel and serves to summarize Oxford and the larger world's fear of the educated woman. Miss de Vine here reverses the fear and suggests that it is the traditional wife, not the educated woman, who devours or is devoured. Miss de Vine's insight alerts the reader to the true culprit in the novel, but the reader—like Harriet herself and like the community of women affected by poison pen letters, scrawled obscenities, destruction of academic work, attempted strangulation—has deep-rooted prejudices which prevent her or him from recognizing the clue. The plot that Harriet, the Shrewsbury dons, Mrs. Goodwin, and the readers are reading is similar to the plot of *Unnatural Death*. They anticipate the repressed and then excessively expressed rage of the independent woman who, like Mary Whittaker, finds her position threatened; they follow the line of popular Freudianism and look for the strong emotions seething beneath the surface in women who have chosen to forgo marriage and presumably sexual relationships for a career. The violent, threatening, distasteful acts perpetrated upon the college and its members seem to come in turn from each of the women dons, whose psychology becomes subject for speculation by Harriet, by the other dons, by students, by the staff.

The first attack upon Shrewsbury consists of drawings and paste-up notes. Harriet finds a sketch of "a naked figure of exaggeratedly feminine outlines, inflicting savage and humiliating outrage upon some person of indeterminate gender clad in a cap and gown" (36). Shortly after the Gaudy, a sort of reunion weekend for former students, she discovers a message in her gown sleeve: "You dirty murderess. Aren't you ashamed to show your face?" (51) Both sketch and note depict a violent woman; the latter suggests a male victim. As she goes through the list of suspects, the first phrases that then come to Harriet's mind are "soured virginity," "unnatural life," "semi-demented spinster," "starved appetites and suppressed impulses," "unwholesome atmosphere" (66). The narrator describes these phrases as "ready-minted for circulation," which implies Harriet's unquestioning adherence to the romantic plot which prescribes, at least in its post-Freudian version, the sad state of single women. Miss Hillyard, the history tutor, bitter and anti-male, seems to embody these phrases and becomes, therefore, Harriet's prime suspect. To Miss Hillyard and only to her, however, the events suggest "the usual masculine spite against academic women" (87), even though Harriet points out that no male had access to the sites of the disturbances. What might seem on Miss Hillyard's part—given her "prejudice" against men—also "ready-minted" sentiments may not be. Her conclusion, correct as it turns out, may stem rather from her work: to read history is to read about men and what they have done. Informed by popular psychology and romance rather than history, Harriet's unthinking sentiments, her ready-minted phrases, are echoed and embodied by the villain herself, the scout Annie, who thinks it "dreadful" "to see all these unmarried ladies living together. It isn't natural . . ." (102). For readers of *Unnatural Death*, the application of "unnatural" to women living together is a familiar one and implies again the unnatural woman—educated, assertive, independent—as villain. Here, however, the accusation does not come, as it does in the earlier novel, from the sympathetic detective but from the villain who, wife and mother, perpetrates these "disorders," a term like Miss Climpson's "out-of-proportion," similar in both structure and meaning to "unnatural."

The gist of the fifteen messages collected by the college for Harriet's detecting is that women should leave men alone. At first the text mentions no specifics of language or imagery except that the notes and the scribblings on walls and mirrors are vulgar, coarse, and unpleasant; we learn later that one directed at Miss Hillyard reads, "No man is safe from women like you" (359). While the theme that women are a threat to men is vague and imageless, Padgett, the porter, articulates a more vivid and specific threat. In a conversation structured and placed as a spot of Shakespearean comic relief, Padgett and a fellow employee decide that the country needs a Hitler to "keep the girls at 'ome" (101). The man suggests that for someone with that attitude, Padgett's job as porter at a women's college is an odd one, and he inquires about Padgett's previous employment. Padgett informs him that he took care of camels at the zoo. The man asks, "Wot made you chuck it?"

"Blood-poison. I was bit in the arm," says Padgett. "By a female" (101). Here the motif of the devouring female occurs in a comic conversation, but that conversation is echoed only two pages later by a serious one between Harriet and Annie the scout, in which Annie uses diction similar to Padgett's. "But it seems a great shame to keep up this big place," she says, "just for women to study books in . . . Books won't teach them to be good wives." Harriet replies, "What dreadful opinions! . . . Whatever made you take a job in a women's college . . . ?" (103) Instead of answering, Annie accuses educated women of having no heart and offers "the Bible" in support: "much learning hath made thee mad" (103). That Annie should use to condemn educated women a Roman accusation against the apostle Paul calls attention to her disorderly mind and calls into question her hints that Miss de Vine is behind all the "funny things" going on at Shrewsbury. Though there is no explicit devouring imagery here, the similarity of this to the Padgett scene and Annie's ferocious dislike of educated women imply that fear. A subsequent prank makes the fear more explicit. The villain, not yet revealed to be Annie, hangs a dummy clothed in academic robes in the chapel. The paper "pinned to its middle by the bread knife" (129) contains a Latin quotation from Virgil: "No more dreadful monster. Birds with the face of a maiden, foul discharge from their bellies, hooked hands and always pale with hunger" (my translation).

Miss Hillyard sees a man behind this choice of quotation; it expresses the most dramatic misogyny, including disgust of menstrual blood and fear of the lurking monster. In *The Aeneid* the lines describe the Harpies, who have just eaten food out of the mouths of men—precisely what Annie accuses the women academics of doing—but even this has not assuaged their hunger. Miss Hillyard, the woman who most obviously fits the stereotype and, on that account, chief suspect, has guessed correctly. It was Annie's husband

who quoted these lines, in his suicide note. The diction is especially appropriate to the situation: "*tristius monstrum*" echoes precisely Annie's feeling that the lives of these "unmarried ladies" is
"dreadful" and not "natural"; "*virgineus,*" though a broader term
than the modern "virgin," underscores the fear of thwarted, unfulfilled sexuality that afflicts even the "virgins" themselves. And,
of course, the "*fame*"—hunger—carries out the devouring woman
motif, which becomes most explicit when the mysterious culprit attacks Wimsey's nephew, Lord Saint-George. The black figure grabs
him, not to harm but to warn: "Go away. We murder beautiful boys
like you and eat their hearts out" (174). The many references in the
novel to food and meals bring out the irony that underlies Annie's
warning: if anything, it is the men at Oxford who eat the food out
of women's mouths. We have seen the contrast between the prod-
ucts of the Christ Church oven, for example, and Shrewsbury fare.
We have learned that the women's college has had to make do by
"cheeseparing," a word that emphasizes the homely ascetic of these
women's lives, so different from Annie's vision of their devouring
propensities.

Annie is, by Miss de Vine's definition, a devoured woman. She
has, quite consciously, made someone else her job. No matter what
he did, Annie claims, she would have stood by her husband; she
made him the focus of her life. And that, she says *is* a woman's job
(372). Now that he is dead, she lives for her children. Annie fears
and hates educated women because they will not be devoured. Because traditional male/female relationships allow, Annie assumes,
only for a devoured and a devouring partner, by her logic those who
refuse to be devoured, become devourers—of men. She sees concrete evidence for this in Miss de Vine's behavior toward her
husband. When Miss de Vine discovered that he had repressed evidence in order to save his own research, and when she realized that
he knew perfectly well what he had done, she reported him. Because he lost his job and his degree and eventually committed suicide, Annie believes that Miss de Vine killed her husband and ate
his heart out.

Annie, however, becomes the real devourer, and the distinction
between the devoured and the devouring blurs. Like Miss Cattermole, who Miss de Vine says is in danger of being devoured by her
parents (151), Annie's two children are in danger of being devoured
by her. When her eight-year-old daughter tells her and Harriet that

she wants to ride a motorcycle when she grows up, Annie rebukes her. She is bringing them up to be, not motorcyclists, but "good wives and mothers" (191), she tells Harriet firmly. Reflecting later on this conversation, Harriet finds "curious . . . this desire to possess children and dictate their tastes, as though they were escaping fragments of one's self" (351). Peter Wimsey says that he will not marry a woman who "adores being protected" because "she would always be deceiving me in the kindest manner, for my own good" (270). That this deception, itself a kind of devouring, becomes a favored strategy among dependent, devoured women is a commonplace in feminist rhetoric. The survival of the devoured depends on such strategies.

Virginia Morris asserts that "By turning her rage outward, Annie . . . becomes . . . a liberated woman" (492) because she initiates and carries out violence, but the text suggests that she does so out of a passion and hatred that devour rather than liberate her. To divert suspicion from herself after an attack on Harriet, Annie pretends she has been forcibly locked in the coal cellar. She is found "in such a state, what with coal-dust and hammering her fists on the door . . . pounding and shouting" (353–354). The image here is a significant one: the devouring, enraged woman, here devoured by the darkness of the coal cellar, shouts unheard for hours, while above her the academic life of Shrewsbury College goes on. Confined to the cellar, Annie loses her power—her days and weeks of violence against educated women are over except for her vituperative outburst as she admits her guilt. Morris asserts that on creating this working-class villain, "Sayers falls back on [a] tired elitist formula" (494), but the text seems to suggest something much less simple—something which this portrait of Annie in the coal cellar presents quite concretely: failure to train the intellect, to put it in control of the powerful but destructive urges of "devoted love"—that "overmastering brute," as Wimsey calls it (332)—creates figures like Annie. Repressed passion may twist and warp a personality, but it is love, making another person one's job, that is truly dangerous, as Miss de Vine opines early in the novel (151). An educated woman, then, is less likely to be guilty of villainy of this devouring sort, "unnatural" though she may be.

In both *Gaudy Night* and *Unnatural Death* the unnatural woman, implying, as she must, a threat to societal order in general and to men in particular, looms large. But while *Unnatural Death* in its attempt to explore simultaneously "unnatural" sexuality, murder (that is, unnatural death), and unnatural states (for example, spinsterhood) produces only confusion, *Gaudy Night's* claim is quite clear: the "unnatural woman" turns out to be the civilized human being and the hope for a saner society; the natural woman, the womanly woman, not the educated woman, is the real danger.

Significantly, there are no lesbians in *Gaudy Night*. The epithet "unnatural" never refers here to sexual orientation or activity as it did in *Unnatural Death*. Rather, the text applies it specifically and approvingly to women who acknowledge claims other than personal ones, who put, for example, "professional honour" above "personal loyalties" (336). Annie is the natural woman, the woman who fights for her man no matter what he does, whose violence is unchecked by a trained intellect. *Gaudy Night*, like *Unnatural Death*, uses the related phrase "womanly woman" but here with no ambiguity. The womanly is linked explicitly in the novel to Naziism: Miss Barton's book, a copy of which Annie burns, "attacks the Nazi doctrine that women's place in the State should be confined to the 'womanly' occupation of *Kinder, Kirche, Kuche*" (360); we have seen the comic exchange in which the porter and the foreman long for a Hitler to keep British women at home. Peter Wimsey notes that the word "womanly" is almost more offensive than its opposite (291), and assures Harriet that she at first escaped Annie's venomous attacks because in sneaking a young man into the college chapel she gave Annie the idea that, unlike the members of the Senior Common Room, she was a womanly woman (366). But later Harriet destroys this illusion when she informs Wimsey in Annie's presence "that personal attachments must come second to public duties" (368).

What Harriet learns in the course of the novel is that one of her instinctive, "ready-minted" responses to the vulgar violence at Shrewsbury—that the members of the Senior Common Room lead an "unnatural life" (66)—is, in fact, correct, but she learns as well that this unnatural life, far from being the source of violence, is an antidote to it. It is Annie, the villain, who articulates the sentiment that "all these unmarried ladies living together . . . isn't natural" (102). Though such rhetoric is not in vogue among the "unmarried ladies" themselves, Miss Hillyard points out that they secretly fear its truth: "The fact is, though you will never admit it, that everybody in this place has an inferiority complex about

married women and children. For all your talk about careers and
independence, you all believe in your hearts that we ought to abase
ourselves before any woman who has fulfilled her animal functions"
(194). The dons protest the accusation but, having themselves
fallen prey to popular Freudian suspicion of spinsterhood, they continue to fear that the culprit is one of themselves.

Harriet fears this, too, as we have seen, until Wimsey sets her
straight. At one point in the investigation, she is "suddenly afraid
of all these women . . . she knew the ancient dread of Artemis,
moon-goddess, virgin-huntress, whose arrows are plagues and
death" (220). This reversion to the mythical reinforces the depth,
the cultural pervasiveness, of the fear of the unnatural woman. Not
simply a fear born of Oxford's nervousness over the women in their
midst, the dread of the independent, assertive woman is "ancient,"
rooted in the myths of the civilization that Oxford exists to per-
petuate. The fear is liable to express itself even in the lives of
women dedicated to their right to independence, even in their fiction, which is likewise rooted in these myths. To her credit, Harriet, though this ancient dread clouds her judgment, does not allow
it to undermine her own convictions about the preeminence of objectivity, truth, and the life of the mind.

It is only, however, the men in the novel who, not themselves
under suspicion either of being the culprit or of living an unnatural
life—though one of them is a bachelor in his forties—have the distance born of privilege to poke fun at the natural or womanly
woman. When Harriet tells Lord Saint-George that "uncle Peter"
was quite right to go to Paris on a diplomatic mission, the nephew
jokingly exclaims, "What an unnatural woman you are! He ought
to be here, weeping into the sheets and letting the international
situation blow itself to blazes" (356). In fact, he is delighted with
Harriet's stance. Lord Saint-George is not, though, immune to the
charms of the womanly woman. He does not, for example, "encourage women students," because they are "too grubby"for his tastes
(173). Uncle Peter, whose legacy of generations of ownership is
firmly controlled by an educated mind, wants, not a womanly
woman whom he can own, but Harriet with her "devastating talent
for keeping to the point and speaking the truth," (280), a talent
honed or perhaps brought into being by her Shrewsbury education.

We have seen Wimsey's casual scorn of the womanly woman; the
justification for this attitude comes in the denouement—the reve-

lation of the womanly woman as villain and of the ultimate stability
and goodness of the female intellectual community, willing to see
its own faults and to correct them. Miss de Vine, the original object
of Annie's attack, accepts partial responsibility for the consequence
of her years'-old reporting of Arthur Robinson, Annie's husband.
Miss de Vine recognizes that intellectual integrity required her to
do it but blames herself "not for my original action . . . but for the
sequel . . . Miss Lydgate would have done what I did in the first
place; but she would have made it her business to see what became
of that unhappy man and his wife" (375).[4] It is here that the dis-
tinctiveness of a community of educated women becomes apparent.
Even Peter Wimsey, that most compassionate and sensitive miracle,
objects that Miss de Vine cannot require of herself Miss Lydgate's
noble spirit. The women, however, know better. When Annie
screams that Miss de Vine "wouldn't have cared" (371) even if she
could have foreseen the consequences of her action, the reader
knows that she is wrong. During the course of the novel, we like
Harriet have "marvelled . . . at the untiring conscientiousness" of
the Shrewsbury dons and their community in which "Nobody's interests ever seemed to be overlooked or forgotten" (40). They continue this solicitude with their conscientious treatment of Annie
herself, against whom they evince surprisingly little bitterness and
whom they want not incarcerated but "medically dealt with" (378)
in keeping with Miss Lydgate's habitual charity. Thus although the
idealized academic haven of *Gaudy Night's* opening is continually
attacked and modified by the novel's subsequent events, the community emerges sound and whole as one place in which stern adherence to intellectual integrity and insistence on the importance
of one's work does not imply neglect of human needs and lack of
compassion.

Though Auerbach has perhaps some justification for her complaint that the "vision of self-governing Shrewsbury fades away"
(165), replaced by "the self-congratulatory, cloying idyll of Lord
Peter's marriage to Harriet Vane" (in *Busman's Honeymoon,* Sayers'
last novel), she underestimates the significance of the female intellectual community which allows Harriet, through her immersion in
its world, to return and to revise the entrenched institution called
marriage. That she does not return and revise so thoroughly as
we might like (that she insists, for example, on retaining in the
ceremony the promise to obey) does not obviate the principle

established here: that the very existence of such a community, an agency for re-forming the "natural" woman, encourages the re-formed, educated woman to carry its values into the wider world, an act that makes possible an alteration and ultimate undermining of patriarchal institutions. Harriet, though she embraces domesticity to a limited extent in *Busman's Honeymoon*, does not therefore accept that traditional union of male and female which privileges the male and represses the female. In *Busman's Honeymoon*, for example, she resents the male scorn for the foolish, pathetic Miss Twitterton. "Harriet was angry . . . men; when they got together they were all alike—even Peter. For a moment he and Kirk stood together on the far side of a chasm, and she hated them both" (138). The identification of male bondedness with callousness, implicit here and in *Gaudy Night*, becomes explicit in *Even the Parrot* in which, as we have seen, the beehive becomes an analogue in nature of the all-female community. Matilda, Archibald's sister, reflects that if women are "relieved from household cares" and can thus "perform all the tasks" of civilization men must lead "anxious and desperate" lives, must therefore persuade themselves and women that they have not "outlived their usefulness" (23). Archibald suggests that they will always be needed—at least to fight the wars. Nurse protests,

> Why, Master Archibald, if there were no men to make the war, I think the women and children would manage very well, since they would only need to be protected from one another. Therefore, it is very much to the interest of men to invent the occasions and instruments of war, so as to create an occupation for themselves wherein their services may be supposed indispensable (24).

Far from fading away, then, the Shrewsbury/Somerville vision gains in this text, seven years later than *Busman's Honeymoon*, a "natural" base and an explicit utopianism. Whether *Even the Parrot* advocates any sort of political/social enactment is not the question here. What it does do is keep alive the tension between Somerville and the world. The continued existence of a community of women calls into question not only, as in *Gaudy Night*, the adequacy of accepted institutions of both marriage and the male academic community, but in *Even the Parrot* the place of men in society as well. In a humorous passage in "The Human-not-quite-Human," Sayers comments on "how strange [a man's] life would appear to himself if it were unrelentingly assessed in terms of his maleness" (*UO*, 143), if he were constantly barraged with articles on the "Position of the Male" and claims that "we do need a more definite conception of the nature and scope of man's life" (144). This, she implies, would seem to men the questioning of the supposedly unquestionable, yet it is just what a functioning community of women does, by its very existence, question: if women can live productive, honest, and compassionate lives on their own, what is the "nature and scope of a man's life?" It is at this moment that the issue of lesbianism seems to come to the fore, but it is precisely at this moment that we can see why it need not, and why lesbianism is absent from *Gaudy Night.*

Lesbian relationships can be seen as "problematic" only relative to a world in which male/female relationships are the norm and in which marriage and family are seen as central to the functioning of society. The world of *Unnatural Death,* in spite of its pervasive femaleness, is such a world. Eve Kosofsky Sedgwick notes the "relatively continuous relation of female homosocial and homosexual bonds" in our culture (5), and the world of *Gaudy Night,* unlike that of *Unnatural Death,* implies that relation: with the possibility of a female community that is not centered in marriage and family, female/female relationships, whatever their physical content, lose their "unnaturalness" and their marginality. Further, this text seems to intuit that, in Peter Brooks's words, "deviance" and "detour" are "the characteristics of the narratable" (104) and that therefore, in the world of *Gaudy Night,* lesbianism loses its narratability, because in this context relations between women are no longer deviant. This is not to suggest that Sayers herself was comfortable with the idea or reality of lesbianism, but only to observe that *Gaudy Night,* set in a single-sex institution, gave her easy opportunity, which she passed by, to portray a lesbian relationship as aberrant, sinister, or immature—an opportunity that other writers of this period did not neglect.[5]

The fact remains, of course, that Harriet Vane, that most sympathetic heroine, chooses marriage over female community or a single life, but this choice is, as we have seen, an attempt to find scope for her gifts as well as lifelong companionship. And marriage with the rich, sensitive, egalitarian Wimsey is far different from traditional

marriage and quite explicitly a fiction in which Harriet can continue to create fictions. When Harriet gets stuck on the plot of her
new detective novel, Wimsey suggests that she depart from the conventions of popular detective fiction and make a rounded character
out of Wilfrid, the wrongly suspected villain. "But if I give Wilfrid
all those violent and lifelike feelings," Harriet objects, "he'll throw
the whole book out of balance." Peter replies that she would "have
to abandon the jig-saw kind of story and write a book about human
beings for a change" (256). Harriet knows that such an abandonment would "hurt like hell" but she admits her desire to write such a
book and amazement that Wimsey takes her work so seriously, more
seriously, perhaps, than she herself has been wont to take it. Her
previous lover, Philip, had taken only his own writing seriously, in
spite of the fact that the two of them lived on what Harriet's writing
earned.

Harriet's writing of popular fiction thus takes on several functions
here—all of them addressing the relationship between gender and
genre, a relationship foregrounded by her choice to marry Peter.
First, her writing becomes, by their responses to it, a touchstone for
the soundness and generosity of the other characters in the Harriet
novels—a touchstone that divides the characters along gender
lines. Miss de Vine, stern scholar that she is, likes and admires Harriet's books. All the members of the Senior Common Room eventually respect her craft. On the other hand Philip Boyes and his
friends in *Strong Poison* call her work trash. Ryland Vaughan, one of
the Boyes set, is convinced that Harriet killed Philip "just because
she couldn't write anything but tripe herself. Harriet Vane's got the
bug all these damned women have got—fancy they can do things.
They hate a man and they hate his work. You'd think it would have
been enough for her to help and look after a genius like Phil" (67).
The snobbery, misogyny, and fear of the educated woman expressed
by Phil and his friends contrast markedly with the attitude of Harriet's female friends. Eiluned Price opines that Philip "couldn't forgive Harriet that she took her work seriously and sold books" (74).
Peter Wimsey is the exception to this gendered response: he urges
her to take her work even more seriously.

The "male" response becomes a clue that Harriet's unconventional liaison with Boyes simply reproduced traditional marriage—
yet she refused to marry him. The proposed marriage to Wimsey,
seemingly traditional, is a much more unconventional relationship

in content, having more in common with the college female/female friendships—it is based on mutual respect for one another's work, it has endured without sex for five years—than with male/female romantic attachments. It might thus be more accurate to say that Harriet chooses marriage not *over* the female community but *out* of it. It is there she has learned what her priorities must be, and she brings them to this marriage, thus subverting the institution while preserving many of its elements.

The second function of Harriet's work is to provide another model for this subversion: while preserving elements of detective fiction, her novel begins, with the re-creation of Wilfrid, to subvert the genre, and this subversion, too, has its roots in the female community of academic women where one must pursue excellence even at the cost of personal pain. Making over Wilfred will hurt like hell but "What would that matter, if it made a good book?" (256)

Finally, Harriet's work elucidates and asserts the experimental status of *Gaudy Night* itself and the importance of such experiments. This novel, like Harriet's, while preserving the traditional elements of detective fiction refuses to content itself with the "jigsaw kind of story" and rounds out at great length its characters, especially the Harriet and Peter of the earlier novels. Sayers acknowledges this deliberate move in her essay on *Gaudy Night*: "I could not marry Peter off to the young woman he (in the conventional Perseus manner) rescued from death and infamy, because I could find no form of words in which she could accept him without loss of self-respect" (Roberts, 79). Harriet's work, then, explains why *Gaudy Night* is such an anomaly in detective fiction and reminds the reader that the text has claims beyond the unravelling of plot.[6] Similarly, in stretching the detective novel to its limits by probing Wilfrid's psychology deeply and widely, Harriet serves again as the tester of boundaries, the breaker of molds, which have become so limiting as to be unacceptable. This testing and breaking reminds us constantly that although the text conforms in major ways to traditional narrative, we must look beyond its conventions, whether of detective fiction or of romance narrative.

What we see when we do is that *Gaudy Night* centers not on couple-based romance but on some alternatives to it. Peter and Harriet work out their relationship in the course of the novel but do so in the context of a female community which asserts both by its very existence and by its explicit rhetoric that personal relation-

ships are secondary to intellectual integrity, work, and the functioning of the community. Because Harriet has absorbed these
values, she must refuse one alternative, the academic community
itself, because she cannot do her work there—work to which, as we
have seen, significance has accrued both in and among these texts.
But the female academic community serves its educative function
well by offering an alternative in addition to itself to traditional romance. Far from turning in on itself, it undertakes the re-formation
of that most deeply rooted pattern of both narrative and ideology,
the traditional relationship between woman and man. And it does
this not only by posing itself as an alternative which, in any case,
could serve only the few whose temperaments and abilities suit
them to the scholarly life, but by sending from its enclave young
women who have lived the alternative, if only briefly, if perhaps not
very consciously, and in that way have absorbed its standards and
values. Harriet's return to Shrewsbury has reaffirmed the validity
and importance of her chosen work and of work itself, has redeemed
the single life for women which had so confused and frightened her
at the beginning of the novel, and has, in offering a serious and
valid alternative to "couple-based romance," given that relationship the status of a choice, not a destiny. It has thus shaken and
disputed the fiction of the inevitability of heterosexual union and
made that union, therefore, a possible path for the educated woman,
who can re-form it now that it is no longer fixed in "nature" and
assumed to be the only "natural" way of life. Such a union, can,
that is, now complement her vocation rather than become it.

Several critics, including Sayers herself, have noted and discussed the changes that Peter Wimsey undergoes in *Gaudy Night,*
changes which make possible Harriet's acceptance of their marriage. M. Hannay, for example, points out that "Wimsey's weak-
nesses did not exist before this novel, but they have been skillfully
projected back into the past" (48). During the years between *Strong
Poison* and *Gaudy Night,* Harriet moves from accused villain to heroine, and Wimsey from detective hero to flawed human being. As
Sayers, in this godlike manner, fashions for her heroine a fit helpmate and for her hero a suitable female counterpart, Stanley Wetherall, one of her nastiest villains—aping the role of creator and thus
exposing the danger inherent in the creative process—fashions
himself a wife, and by doing so comments forcefully on the differ-

ence between marriage according to Harriet and Peter and the conventional heterosexual romance.

We have seen that much of the rhetoric used to justify women's
education focused on the suitability of an educated woman as companion to an educated man. In an article on Wilkie Collins and
Sayers, E. R. Gregory notes that Sayers was drawn to Collins because, unlike Meredith, who seemed to her all along to want, along
with Tennyson, "women freed and educated so as to be better companions for men, . . . Wilkie is hardly interested in woman as a
complement to man. He sees her as a creature of independent personality and intelligence" (55).[7] The figure of Stanley Wetherall in
"The Incredible Elopement of Lord Peter Wimsey" exposes the fallacy and the danger of the former attitude, an attitude which is, as
we have seen, a clear component of an updated romance plot. An
intelligent and ambitious young doctor with a speciality in thyroid
problems, Wetherall treats a child, Alice, a cretinous imbecile.
With daily doses of thyroid extract, he turns her into a functioning
human being. She emerges from his treatment "tall, beautiful, with
gold hair and blue eyes like the Madonna" (304), and when she is
seventeen, the "over forty" (306) Pygmalion—Wetherall—marries
the golden girl he has sculpted from the thick, ugly cretin and has
educated at his expense.

Not content with Alice as sculpture, Wetherall reinforces her
status as art object by having Sargent paint her portrait. Formed by,
educated by, owned by, not a nurturing female community but a
self-centered man, Alice is at his mercy. When the Basque scholar
Langley openly admires her, the irrationally jealous Wetherall, who
can, in fact, weather nothing, takes her off to an isolated Basque
area, in the hope that Langley will eventually find his way there,
and begins systematically to undo his handiwork. Wetherall, in
spite of Alice's pleas and attempts to escape his fiendish cruelty, deprives Alice of her thyroid treatments and delights in watching her
revert to the unformed state in which he found her. The analogoue
to her "thick and slouching body," her drooling mouth, and her
"half-bald scalp" (310), that is, her reversion to the unformed material of art, is her de-education. Wetherall sees "her eyes grow vacant, her speech die away into mere animal noises, her brain go to
mush" (327).

The narrative actually begins with Langley's discovery that his
old friend Stanley Wetherall is living outside the village Langley is

studying. He writes Wetherall a note and is invited to their house. The reader's introduction to Alice is the noise she makes in place of speech, "a kind of low animal muttering . . . a suckling, slobbering sound, [which] ended in a series of little grunts or squeals, and then there was silence" (308). This noise and subsequent silence contrasts interestingly with the opening paragraphs of the story in which the inhabitants of the village chatter "freely . . . in that strange Basque language which has no fellow in the world, and is said by some to be the very speech of our first fathers in Paradise" (302). Before Alice has had time to acquire, as her husband eventually does, as Langley has done, the fathers' tongue, she is made dumb by the same father/artist/god who gave her speech. The villagers agree that when she first came "she was beautiful. She laughed and talked in her own speech" (306). The last sound the villagers have heard from her lips is a shriek at the sight of her husband.

The villagers' sense is that some jealous god has worked a spell. Stanley Wetherall is, indeed, a jealous god. When Langley goes to the Wetherall's house, Stanley explains that his wife suffers from "premature senility" (310) and that he decided to settle in this isolated spot away from everyone who knew the wonderful, beautiful, educated Alice. "I can bear it better here, in this wild place where everything seems possible and nothing unnatural" (311). There is, then, a sense in which the Alice to whom we have just been introduced is "natural." With her deficient thyroid, Alice is physically formless and stupid. We see here another foray into the complicated natural/unnatural opposition. Sophisticated medical intervention and expensive schooling have saved Alice from her natural fate but have allowed her to live the life of a natural woman—the possession, like the Sargent portrait, of her husband. Totally dependent on him for her powers, including the power of speech, she represents in extreme form the plight of every woman, especially every natural, womanly woman. Educated by and for a man, she is subject, at his whim, to de-education.

Stanley, however, educated in his own right, suffers little from the primitive conditions and isolation of the village. "I get the latest medical journals . . . I'm writing a book, you know, on my own subject, so I don't vegetate. I can experiment, too." The subject of his experimentation, that which keeps him from vegetating, is, of course, the vegetation of his wife. To accompany his vigorous intellectual life are the trappings of his class and sex: after dinner he brings out for Langley "brandy and a box of cigars" (312), symbols of that civilization which exists side by side with the total degradation of his wife, a coexistence inherently possible in an institutionalized relationship of dependence such as marriage.

Langley, upset by his evening with the Wetheralls, accidentally encounters Lord Peter Wimsey and tells him as much as he knows of the story. Disguised as a powerful wizard, Wimsey appears in the village in Wetherall's absence and sets about undoing the spell. The magical talents of the stranger who has come to rescue the speechless Alice are largely verbal and closely allied to that education which Alice has been given and of which she has been then deprived. Wimsey speaks "the language of the Apostles" (315), pronounces "sacred . . . words . . . in the right order" (317), uses "the language of the faith" (308), converses with angels (315). In reality, the magical incantations are "the remnants of classical education" (328). He intones Greek (320) and Latin (321), sometimes in the same sentence, and produces "an atmosphere of gloom and mystery" (328) with recordings of classical music. All this he accompanies with daily doses of thyroid extract smuggled into the Wetherall house. Thus, the sophisticated medical technology and the educational tools, especially the tool of classical language, begin to undo the de-education of Alice. One day "the wizard had spoken many things in a strange tongue, and the lady had spoken likewise. Yes—she who for so long had only grunted like a beast, had talked with the wizard and answered him" (323). This return of speech is the most obvious sign of hope for Alice's recovery. Wimsey contrives to help her escape from Stanley Wetherall and the oppressive marriage that has made the horror possible. Ironically Wimsey practically delivers her, still "bewildered" and "like a child" (324), into presumably another marriage. This predictable happy ending is surprisingly uninspired and off-hand after the high drama of the "elopement." She'll be "right as ninepence," Wimsey assures Langley, and she can probably get a divorce. "After that— it's up to you" (328). Again, then, Alice must depend for her re-education on a man, this time the kind-hearted Langley, of course, who will presumably love her more adequately than Wetherall, but she will remain a child without the possibility of belonging only to and being educated only for herself—without, that is, the female educational community of *Gaudy Night.*

What *has* been gained here, however, results from Wimsey's

intervention. Its simultaneously rational and supernatural character indicates something important about the protean Wimsey and his function in the fiction we have been discussing. We noted that in *Gaudy Night* Harriet reflects that for Peter to regard her truly as an equal makes him "not a man but a miracle" (184). In "The Incredible Elopement" more than any other work, he appears miraculous, even though he has an explanation for every bit of miracle he performs. More than the miracles themselves, however, three suggestive elements in the story establish Wimsey as an exception to mankind. First, the thyroid extract he gives Martha to give Alice is in the form of "enchanted wafers" (322) in a "casket of shining metal" (321), which suggests, of course, communion wafers magically transformed to the body of Christ. Second, when Alice comes to the cottage and, to Martha's surprise, actually speaks to the wizard, Wimsey draws "strange signs upon the floor around the lady and himself," an allusion to Jesus' drawing on the ground when faced with the woman caught in adultery. As Jesus saves the suspected woman from stoning, Wimsey frees the suspected Alice from a similar fate. Finally, his role here as rescuer of Alice from the Evil One parallels the Christian notion of Christ as rescuer of humankind from Satan's rule. These parallels and allusions in "The Incredible Elopement" associate Wimsey with the Christ figure, an association not surprising, since Wimsey in his careful and balanced treatment of women in general and of Harriet in particular corresponds closely to Sayers's construction in "The Human-not-quite-Human" of Jesus' own behavior. Sayers speculates, "Perhaps it is no wonder that the women were first at the Cradle and last at the Cross. They had never known a man like this Man—there never has been such another" (148). Never, that is, until her own creation of Lord Peter Wimsey, who manages to inspire affection even in the man-hating Miss Hillyard; whose behavior corresponds to that

> prophet and teacher who never nagged at them, never flat-
> tered or coaxed or patronized. Who never made arch jokes
> about them . . . who rebuked them without querulousness and
> praised without condescension; who took their questions and
> arguments seriously; who never mapped out their sphere for
> them, never urged them to be feminine or jeered at them for
> being female; who took them as he found them (148).

Sayers even added a few improvements: Wimsey is a scholar, a gentleman, and incredibly rich. As Carolyn Heilbrun wryly remarks of him in "Sayers, Lord Peter and God," "he was to show from the beginning what God could have done if only He'd had the money" (462).

Although Hannay is surely correct in her analysis of the changes Wimsey had to undergo in order to be a fit helpmate for the educated woman, it is important to recognize that those faults and foibles which make him human enough to marry do not affect his relationships with women. In that sphere at least he remains and perhaps improves, becoming, in Sayers' understanding, Christlike and more miracle than man. "There never has been such another," she proclaims in 1938, which reminds us again that Peter is not "such another," but a fiction, as is the Vane-Wimsey marriage—both creations of a woman writer. And, as we have observed in the discussion of *Busman's Honeymoon,* even this miracle man, because he, though fictional, belongs to the male sex, cannot wholly overcome Harriet's resistance.

The unsatisfactory ending of "The Incredible Elopement," unsatisfactory in that it replicates on some level the original marriage of Wetherall and Alice, though satisfactory in its adherence to the romance, reminds us that the happy, romantic ending of *Gaudy Night* is also ambiguous. Harriet's resistance to Wimsey as male in *Busman's Honeymoon* is only a logical extension of the scene in which Harriet finally accepts Wimsey's proposal. After telling her that if she marries him it will give him very great happiness, he inquires "Placetne, magistra?" Although asking in the language of the Oxford degree-giving ceremony if the proposal pleases her and addressing her with an academic title are signs that he respects both her intelligence and her accomplishments, they are also reminders of other uses of Latin which mark misreading, misogyny, and exclusion. Peter uses Latin phrases in "The Incredible Elopement" purely for their magical, impressive effects. The phrases cannot be read because they mean nothing. Similarly the Latin note affixed to the dummy in *Gaudy Night* does not, in fact, connote what it seems to. The phrases themselves are, as only the anti-male Miss Hillyard can see, not the expression of a classically educated, frustrated female don, but of an uneducated, vindictive embodiment of the perfect wife echoing her misogynist scholar-husband quoting Virgil. As Miriam Brody observes, "surely some misgiving must haunt Harriet

as she hears the Latin words Wimsey has chosen . . . some memory
that all Latin signifiers do not lead ultimately to signifieds that their
writers are scholarly or that they are work-finders, breach-healers,
and can make severed halves whole" (114–115). The Latin in the
proposal calls to mind the note and calls to mind, too, the misogyny of the classics and the use of Latin as the language of a priest-
hood which excludes women altogether.

Insofar, then, as Peter is a fiction, more miracle than man, Harriet can accept him; insofar as he is "real," she must resist him, because the "real" man is more like Stanley Wetherall, perhaps not
with his intentional cruelty but at least with his desire to have the
educated woman under his control and to punish her if she shows
signs of independence. Women are right to be suspicious, the Harriet texts suggest. Not only do men themselves often despise women
but they teach women to do likewise. Like Annie in *Gaudy Night,*
like the dons themselves on occasion, Harriet in *Have His Carcase*
lumps women with children and assumes that they "would be useless in an emergency" (16); she realizes only later that her assumption that "a man would display superior energy and resourcefulness"
is, after all, a "foolish relic of Victorianism" (24). Her suspicion of
other women, especially of the independent, educated woman, is
finally laid to rest in *Gaudy Night* where the female community in
its combination of intellectual integrity and compassion assuages
the fears played out in *Unnatural Death* and illustrates vividly the
difference to women between education received in this context
and that received at the hands of men, the latter so chillingly accomplished and reversed in "The Incredible Elopement." Wimsey's
role in both story and novel allies him with the female educational
community, while warning the reader that such male allies are citizens not of the real world, but of female utopias.

In spite of its numerous foibles and problems, the women's-college
world of *Gaudy Night* is a kind of female utopia—in a tradition that
includes Mary Astell's *A Serious Proposal to the Ladies,* Christine
de Pizan's *Book of the City of Ladies,* and Sarah Scott's *Millennium
Hall*—but a utopia invaded by a mystery, which is in turn invaded
by elements of more mainstream fiction. The resultant hybrid is, I
think, one of the most successful strategies used by these Somerville
writers to accommodate the educated woman. Unlike the traditional novel, a detective fiction does not have to repeat in its broad
outlines (though of course it does in its details and assumptions) the

romance plot. Sayers found it, for that reason, a congenial genre. Yet with women as murderers and detectives as well as victims— with women as main characters—the romantic plot, cultural baggage carried by all women, inserts itself and demands that the text contain a love interest. Agatha Christie and Patricia Wentworth circumvent this demand by making their detectives elderly women who, according to the romance narrative, are no longer interested in sex and love; Sayers, however, obliges by making the romantic plot itself of central concern and the detecting, the clue-finding, the readings and misreadings apply not only to the college's poison-pen case but to the romantic plot which is embedded in the villain's life-story and which plagues the developing relationship between Harriet and Peter. *Gaudy Night* thus exploits the detective genre by turning the lens onto the romance, the romance-run-amok.

Here the educated woman becomes the detective—reader, interrogator, clue-finder—a job to which her education has eminently suited her. Harriet applies her research skills as well to assist Miss Lydgate in *her* detecting, a project which Brody disparagingly labels "a model of the work the Great Detective must do—as it is also a model of logocentrism, a search for the center" (101). But Miss Lydgate herself, a neat revision of the corruptible researcher and her male namesake in *Middlemarch*, recognizes that achieving such mastery and capturing the complete truth is impossible; hence the delays, the last-minute additions, the pain of parting with the manuscript. The educated woman, reminded by Annie's wanton destruction, knows that the research project is not what it seems, as she knows that the detecting project is not what it seems. Harriet can no more "solve" the mystery than Miss Lydgate can complete the text, because there are too many things which intrude, which demand attention, which complicate. Annie's husband circumvents the intrusions of complicating evidence by destroying the evidence of these intrusions. *His* text rather than Miss Lydgate's, becomes the "model of logocentrism," of phallocentrism, of mythic mastery—a model which leads to death accompanied, appropriately enough, by a text of Virgil's misogyny. Annie's husband's work, not Miss Lydgate's, is the real model of what the Great Detective must do, and *Gaudy Night* with its relentless and "feminine" insistence on the importance of digressions, complications, and intrusions— who will be hurt and how? what effect does the mystery have on the communal life of the college? are single women repressed? is undestructive heterosexual love possible? is the life of the mind natural?—calls into question the genre itself and its logocentric assumptions, while it more overtly calls into question the romance plot. Peter Wimsey, male-ally-as-fiction, deus ex machina, solves the case, but even the man-as-woman's-whim cannot solve it whole. Annie's fate and the fate of her children will haunt Shrewsbury just as uncertain loyalties will haunt Harriet's marriage to Peter. Harriet must continue to revise her fiction and her "fate"; the detecting must go on—a suitable job for an educated woman.

1. Somerville College, Oxford.
Photo courtesy of the Principal and Fellows of Somerville College, Oxford

2. (*above*) Somerville College converted to an infirmary during World War I.
Photo courtesy of the Principal and Fellows of Somerville College, Oxford

3. (*above right*) A 1920 prediction of the horrors of a Junior Common Room invaded by women pursuing degrees.
Photo courtesy of the Bodleian Library, Oxford (*Per G. A. Oxon 4to145*, page 8)

4. (*right*) A cartoon from the 1880s which suggests women's "real" reason for seeking Oxford degrees and which portrays the Somervillians with the mortarboards they were never allowed to wear.
Photo courtesy of the Bodleian Library, Oxford (*G. A. Oxon 4to415*, folio 699

1940 A.D.   THE OLD J.C.R.

A STUDENT OF SOMERVILLE HALL GAINS A FELLOWSHIP

5. (*above*)   Emily Penrose and Gilbert Murray on the day women received degrees for the first time. Miss Penrose is not wearing her cap. Photo courtesy of the Principal and Fellows of Somerville College, Oxford

6. (*above right*)   Visit of Queen Mary to Somerville College in 1921. Again Miss Penrose (back to camera, right front) is bareheaded. Photo courtesy of the Principal and Fellows of Somerville College, Oxford

7. (*right*)   Three women wear the women's caps, but Miss Penrose (second from left) chooses her own hat—rather like a mortarboard. Photo courtesy of the Principal and Fellows of Somerville College, Oxford

8. (*above left*)   Margaret Kennedy.
Photo courtesy of Julia Birley
9.   (*left*)   Dorothy L. Sayers impersonating Dr. Allen, 1915.
Photo courtesy of the Bodleian Library, Oxford (MS. Eng. misc. c. 698, folio 36r)

10.   (*above*)   Doreen Wallace gathering strawberries on, the book jacket insists, "her husband's" farm, 1949.
Photo courtesy of Doreen Wallace

11. Winifred Holtby at Brigne,
1921.
Photo courtesy of the William
Ready Division of Archives and
Research Collections, McMaster
University Library, Hamilton,
Canada

12. (*right*) Vera Brittain in her
VAD uniform, 1916.
Photo courtesy of the William
Ready Division of Archives and
Research Collections, McMaster
University Library, Hamilton,
Canada

5 Muriel Jaeger's
Educated Woman and the
New Nativity Narrative

Muriel Jaeger, the "Jim" of Sayers' early letters and member of the Mutual Admiration Society, is the least known and the least prolific of these Somerville novelists. Though she wrote a play and three short novels, most of her work is nonfiction and little of it directly addresses the topic of the educated woman or women's role in the world. Like Sayers, however, she takes for granted a woman's right to whatever life she chooses. In her chapter on George Sand in *Experimental Lives*, a collection of biographical pieces, she praises the courage and conviction of the woman who chooses to break new ground. "People—especially women—have certainly been freer because one immensely courageous and highly vocal woman explored the uncleared country for them" (215). A book of essays published late in Jaeger's life, *Shepherd's Trade*, complains good-humoredly about the hazards of being such a "vocal woman." She and her writing friends have suffered, she says, from the story of Jane Austen writing "her books with easy placidity in the common sitting-room, putting them aside at every domestic and social demand and calmly resuming them when the interruption was over." Jaeger suggests that the story is not truth but fiction, used to chide women writers who express the "difficulties of authorship in our harassed existences" (50).

Her fiction, with the exception of *The Man with Six Senses*, addresses these issues only obliquely. In the earliest novel, an ironic utopian fiction called *The Question Mark*, the protagonists are all male, and her portrait of the twenty-second century is unremittingly man-centered. She does, in good utopian fashion, describe the relationship between the men and women in her future society: in the "normal" class, the future looks worse for women than the present. Ena, a "normal" woman, tells Guy, the twentieth-century man transplanted into the twenty-second century, "You're not like the rest. You don't think girls are for nothing but to tease and make love to" (230). More alarming than this implied limitation of women's role, there has developed in this new society a fashion for harems. Yet in the "intellectual" class, women are theoretically equal; this suggests that education not only determines class but levels sex. But like the division of future humans in *The Time Machine* this division into "normal" and "intellectual" has robbed each class of important human qualities. Sylvia, the "intellectual" woman in the novel, has an exciting and independent life, but both she and her fiancé are rather detached, cold sorts, having, apparently, sacrificed heart for head.

Sylvia plays a minor role in *The Question Mark*, but in Jaeger's next novel, *The Man with Six Senses*, the figure of the educated woman, though she is neither the eponymous subject nor the narrator of this quirky book, is the center of all energy and activity. An Oxbridge graduate, a confident, independent, career-minded woman, Hilda takes on the "man with six senses," Michael Bristowe, and with him the future of humankind. However, before we examine this portrayal of the educated woman and her unusual adventure, we must look at the portrayal of the narrator through whose eyes we see her, lest, unwary readers, we be seduced by his sophistication and disarming common sense into reading only *his* version of the story.

An intelligent, patronizing, and pedantic man, the narrator, Ralph, mirrors closely those Oxford males who, quite supportive of degrees for women, saw the educated woman primarily as a complement to the educated man. Himself a "highly educated man" (30), an intellectual, a writer of essays, Ralph wants to marry the beautiful Hilda. Both their families have plotted the union, but both sets of parents are dead by the time Hilda finishes her university degree. Ralph, several years older than she, has watched her grow up and has become convinced that she is exactly suited to him. His mother, while she was still alive, wanted him to propose to the eighteen-year-old Hilda, but Ralph decided to wait because, unlike his mother, he quite approves of his future wife's educational aspirations. His mother, he says, "did not understand nor accept our later maturing, due to the increasingly complicated demands of civilized and cultured life, which make a longer period of growth essential if a completely adequate personality is to emerge" (11).

Ralph congratulates himself on his liberal attitude—"I have never been against the higher education of women, as, openly or covertly, are many of my contemporaries"—but immediately follows this declaration with a shift of focus that reveals what is to him the chief benefit of this higher education: "I think an educated man all the better for having an educated wife, who is able to be an intellectual companion to him, to be interested in his work, and to follow the movements of his mind" (14). Though few of his contemporaries would have approved so enthusiastically of a university education, not just for women in general, but for their intended wives, Ralph's diction nevertheless constantly betrays his failure to see Hilda as a human being. He imagines her, for example, "as the young heroine of an old Teutonic epic or of an Icelandic saga" (11). Later, when she is staying at Marling, Ralph's home, he sees her "as the Princess of Thule, . . . bestowing gifts in her father's high hall" (197). Thus while he casts her as a heroine, almost a goddess, equally he relishes having her under his roof and rule. That his home becomes "her father's high hall" indicates the paternal attitude which he assumes is constitutive of marriage and in which he frequently indulges. While on the one hand he idealizes Hilda as more-than-human, on the other he frequently characterizes her as less than himself and dependent upon him: "Young and innocent," "unawakened" (5), attractively shy and immature (15), "a lonely and pathetic figure in need of my help and protection," "a child still—the precious child whom I loved and had to save, at all costs, from herself" (226).

When Hilda does not live up or down to his expectations, he is disappointed. When she comes back from college, for example, a "self-possessed girl who welcomed me so graciously in the pleasantly austere sitting-room," who had "just that additional confidence, that social aplomb, which I had counted on her gaining," he "missed the old shyness" (15). Not only does she disconcert him with her newly acquired social confidence, but she also destroys his vision of himself as "welcome rescuer" (16) and admired mentor. Instead of the enthusiastic praise for his book and a pupil's interest in its subject matter, she discusses his theses as an equal. "I suppose," he comments, "that one is liable to forget as one grows older the possibilities of rapid mental development in the early twenties" (18). Even, then, when she demonstrates her ability to be an intellectual companion, he notes condescendingly, as one would of a child, how much she has grown. And he admits that this new Hilda was "not entirely welcome to a man coming in search of solace" (18).

Ralph's need for solace is occasioned by an affair he had in Italy which, he implies, turned out rather badly. Though he allows himself the license of other relationships, even sexual ones, he is jealous and resentful of Hilda's nonsexual interest in Michael Bristowe. And though Ralph himself is absorbed in his work, he is sure that Hilda does not take hers very seriously and resents her refusal of his marriage proposal on grounds that she likes what she is doing. He does not suggest that she could continue working after marriage, because a wife should interest herself in *his* work and "follow the movements of his mind." While both his sexual experience and his devotion to work seem natural to him, he can accept neither in Hilda. Later in the novel, after her husband's death, Ralph decides not to renew his proposal of marriage, because "the idea of marrying a widow has always been distasteful to me" (269). He does not explain his distaste, but one assumes that it is rooted in the kind of possessiveness Doreen Wallace's Margery in *The Time of Wild Roses* describes so cynically: "If there is one thing which will turn a man from a rational human being into a he-ape incapable of thought, it is the notion that another male is sharing the body of his female" (145). Though the other male in this case is dead and was never anyone Hilda desired sexually, Ralph does not even attempt to explore, much less overcome, the irrational "distaste." It is there; it seems altogether natural to him. Indeed the romance plot depends on woman-as-virgin-waiting-to-be-awakened. Thus Ralph not only writes out but judges his own experience in terms of this plot.

What Ralph ultimately resents most about Hilda is her rationality. A traditional complaint of men about women is that they are irrational. Yet it is this very irrationality which gives men power over women and easy grounds for dismissing their claims. While Ralph sees rationality as highly desirable in a helpmate, while the acquisition of rationality strikes him as a good effect of the education of women, its actual presence in Hilda disconcerts and angers him because it diminishes his power and augments her claims. By being rational, Hilda deviates from both roles he has cast her in: she is neither mythical nor helpless. Besides her failure to live up to his fantasies, this rational woman argues with his work, as we have seen, and points out his specious arguments. Furthermore, as if rationality leaves no room for romantic myths, her rational approach to life seems to make her immune to falling in love. Ralph expects at least a spark of ardor from his proposal of marriage, but Hilda only answers calmly, "It's pleasant to know that you want me, Ralph," (77), as she refuses him. He expects to dissuade her from what he regards as her destructive plan for life. When she says she has tried to be as rational and practical as she can, he attacks her: "Rational! It's rationality that is the matter with you" (232). Ralph wants Hilda to be irrational so he can use that irrationality to manipulate her: "I felt sometimes that if I could only get Hilda to waver in her poise for a moment, to say something thoroughly irrational and unjust, to lose her temper, there might have been a chance to make progress" (81), progress meaning, to Ralph, the possession of Hilda.

Ralph's most significant and self-revelatory attack on Hilda's rationality is his admission that, having lost a simple argument in which he was using an irrational generalization about women to convince her to give up her work, "I went away in impotent rage against the rational woman and all her works" (81). The choice of words here, like the rhetoric of male Oxford, reveals the intense emotions conjured up by the figure of the woman with a degree. First, the use of "impotent" suggests fear that educated woman emasculates: not only is Ralph unable to find a hole in her reasoning, not only, that is, is he intellectually defeated by this young woman, but in his eyes her refusal to marry him threatens and/or effects impotence as well. While he looks to the educated woman as fit helpmate, she quickly becomes his equal and insists on such independent action as turning down his proposal of marriage, thus depriving him of those powerful symbols of potency, a wife and children.

Second, "rage" suggests that underneath his own rational veneer Ralph himself is irrational; in spite of his ostensible approval of the idea of educated women, the actuality threatens to strip him of the fruits of his own education. That civilized, cultivated life of the mind, nurtured by the university, so long a prerogative of men, rests perhaps, like male power itself, on displacing its opposite onto the other sex. When that is no longer possible, when women claim a right to such an educated life, men experience the irrationality in themselves, here as rage. Finally, the reference here to the baptismal formula in which the person to be christened is asked to denounce Satan and all his works, suggests the extreme response, so far from Ralph's conscious thought, to education for women—that it is diabolical, that it turns women from angels to devils, from willing servants to adamant rebels against the rule of the male god. It was, further, a woman's lust for the fruit of the tree of knowledge which allied her to Satan in the first place, according to Christian myth. Ralph's rhetoric implies this connection between the Eve wanting to be educated and the educated Hilda, and simultaneously asserts his own position on the side of the angels. That both men in the text have angels' names (Raphael, Michael) underscores this gendered alignment and hints, perhaps, at a covert alliance between the men. In any case, Ralph's apparent feminist sympathies work only at the level of his rhetoric and function only when they result in his own aggrandisement. He relishes the vision of himself as tolerant and forward-looking in his approval of women's education and independence but is unable and unwilling to accept the consequences of this attitude.

Besides lashing out in rage, he resorts to the most traditional cliches about women and thus suggests that the educated woman is not at all what he really wants for himself. When Hilda announces her plan to marry Michael Bristowe, an arrangement she regards as both practical and rational, Ralph cannot believe that "an adult woman should speak to me in this manner about the supreme experience of her sex" (226). Ironically, in his desire for the child bride Hilda will never be, Ralph immediately decides Hilda is not, in fact, an adult woman. What he wants is a woman who does regard marriage as the supreme experience. That he adds "of her sex" indicates that marriage is not, of course, the supreme experience for his sex, for himself. He has, after all, his work; his wife should abandon hers and take up him as her job. The irrationality of this position can be ignored only by his positing a dichotomy between adult men and adult women. Unlike the adult man, who is independent, dedicated to his work, and able to see love and marriage in practical terms, a woman who acts and thinks likewise must be immature.

As Ralph has tried unsuccessfully to get Hilda to marry him, so he tries unsuccessfully to prevent her from marrying Michael Bristowe. In the conversation which follows Ralph's expression of "incredulity" about Hilda's willingness to marry without love, Hilda expounds her agnostic, evolutionary philosophy. Ralph comments that he "had had glimpses before of this philosophy of Hilda's" (227). Again we see that Ralph, while approving of the educated woman in the abstract, has little interest in her in the concrete. He has not been interested enough to hear her expound her "philosophy," though he has repeatedly wanted to hear her accept his marriage proposal—that is, the content of her intellectual life is quite secondary to her sexual and social function as his future wife. That she is beautiful and intelligent is enough; only when she acts in a manner he finds incredible is he willing to listen to her exposition of the beliefs out of which she acts. Here, too, there is a suggestion of Ralph's irrationality. He has not heard Hilda because he has not been interested; he has not been interested because he has feared to hear, feared that Hilda is not the ideal woman he has set her up to be.

This carefully constructed contrast between Ralph's apparent approval of educated women, his tolerant, man-of-the-modern-world manner, and the fear and irrationality which underlies these attitudes, reveal him to be a partly unreliable narrator whose interpretation of Hilda and her story readers must constantly question. He admits at the outset, in fact, that his narrative is not "the account of Michael Bristowe's strange career that Hilda asked me to write" (5). Requested to tell the story of another man and his special gift, Ralph, writer and egoist, can tell only the story which touches him more personally, the story of the educated woman and all her works. A woman's story, though, even an educated woman's story, is traditionally assumed to be a romance. Ralph therefore tells the story of a woman and a man, and in doing so he tells the story of himself because he assumes that Hilda, whom he regards as his "natural mate" (217), can have no story apart from him. The text, however, though it presents the story only from Ralph's point of view, refuses to limit itself to his version. Hilda, in her attempt to alter the romantic script prescribed for her life, alters as well Ralph's narrative. Both Ralph's direct reports of conversations between him and Hilda and the ironies implicit in his self-portrait alert the reader to a subtext, a new story for the new woman—educated—whom the traditional romance plot cannot accommodate. In order to sort out the elements of this new plot from the old, we must look briefly at the story Ralph tells. I present here the outline of that story, with little narrative comment, as a context from which to extract the threads of Hilda's more hidden narrative. As we have seen, Ralph has known Hilda for many years: he regards their marriage as "a longstanding family plot" (12). When she leaves the university, she takes a job as secretary to "one of the political women who hoped to be in the next Parliament" (16) and lives alone in a small Bloomsbury flat. Meanwhile Ralph has indulged his wish to travel and to become a man of the world. When he returns after some time in Italy, he finds Hilda equally desirable but changed not altogether to his liking. For one thing, she talks to him as an equal about his work. But the main problem is that she has taken up again the company of a man he regards as thoroughly undesirable, Michael Bristowe, who, Hilda has come to realize, has a strange and special gift. It manifests itself at first as a dowsing ability—that is, he can recognize the presence of water and other substances even under ground. One day Hilda, Ralph, and Michael are out in the country; Michael, reacting violently to his sense of something horrible nearby, discovers a corpse. The journalist who subsequently tries to make use of Michael for police work writes of him as "a truly terrible young man" who "informed me . . . that the elderly gentleman of military appearance who shared our compartment . . . was wearing corsets with steel in them and that the pearls of the opulent-looking lady who had been sitting near us at luncheon were imitation. What a disturbing element Michael Bristowe would be to introduce into smart society!" (133) Smart society, however, is little inclined to take up someone who detects not only metal and corpses but hypocrisy as well.

Hilda wants to help Michael because she thinks his gift significant, and she knows that he is an unreliable sort who has little ability to make his way in the world. After Michael fails as a detective and a finder of oil, jobless, he becomes extremely unhappy with himself, carelessly contracts pneumonia, and, Ralph says, would have died but for Hilda's determination that he recover. He does recover, in part, but is weak and constantly depressed, and when Hilda takes him to Marling, Ralph's house, to convalesce, Ralph begins to believe in the sixth sense, but he perceives it as alienating and menacing. An old dowser who recognizes Michael's ability urges Hilda to look after Michael well because "There aren't many of his kind" (218).

Because the dowser's injunction corresponds to her own sense of responsibility, Hilda decides to marry Michael. Michael is, she says, helpless without her, and she is convinced that "If *he* goes under, humanity may lose a chance that may never come again. . . . And I'm the only person who can do anything" (223). She does not love him; she only senses that he is her temporary responsibility (222). She knows, too, that he will die shortly and that "we may have a child . . ." to inherit his gift: "It's the only chance" (225). Ralph is appalled at this turn of events. He is devastated by the death of his hopes of marrying his "natural mate" and incredulous that Hilda could be so unwomanly as to marry out of social responsibility rather than love. He has not been able to convince her to marry him, and nothing he says can change her mind about marrying Michael; when he accuses her of making Michael into a Messiah, she agrees, in so far as the "Michael Bristowes are the only sort of Messiahs we can expect now that we have lost our omnipotent God. Our God is one who needs our help. And it seems clear that this is my opportunity to help" (232).

Ralph goes away for some months while Hilda and Michael marry and settle in the country. As Hilda and the doctors predicted, Michael does not live long. Ralph returns after Michael's death knowing that Hilda would no longer be the girl he loved: "that girl seemed to have died the day she embarked on her inadmissable enterprise" (244). Ralph determines to stay away but Hilda writes to him urgently because she has no money and he is "the nearest thing to a brother that I possess" (245). It is then that Ralph discovers that she is, indeed, pregnant with Michael's child. She has the baby in the nursing home of a friend, Lettice Platt; it is a hard delivery— both child and mother are ill afterwards. The surprising thing, what no one anticipated, is that "this young prince [coming] into his kingdom" turns out to be a girl. Hilda seems not terribly interested in the baby, which Ralph attributes to its sex and Lettice to Hilda's weakened state. But it is clear that Hilda remains hopeful that the child will have Michael's gift. Ralph accepts a journalism assignment on an expedition; she returns to her job. Ralph believes that Hilda would marry him at this point but, as we have seen, he is not interested in marrying a widow. He concludes his narrative with what he believes and desires that Hilda has learned from this experience,

that life is, and must be, chiefly ruled by Fear—that the man who tries to practise ideals in this world is like one who composes an Ode to Peace while the enemy is setting fire to the

Thatch. The world is no longer her oyster—the oyster of her intellect. She begins to understand too, in what elementary manner one needs the help and support of one's fellow creatures, the comfort of contact (269).

But he says he will not exult in the fulfillment of his prophesies, because Hilda did, after all, make a "valiant attempt": "It would be a poor thing to triumph over one who has made an effort beyond human strength because, when the thing was accomplished, her strength failed and she fell below herself in compensation" (270).

This is Ralph's version of the story and his patronizing interpretation of its significance, an interpretation which projects his own values on the silent/silenced Hilda. In *Paradise Lost* Raphael tells Adam and Eve the story of the angels' rebellion and warns the pair that they, too, might fall. Similarly, Ralph sees in Hilda's failure to read/heed correctly the lesson of the old story—that is, to stop rebelling and to marry him—her fall, like Eve's a fall from innocence to experience, from trusting dependence to disillusioning independence. It is not surprising, then, that Ralph's antidote to this story is to insist even more adamantly on the romance plot: Hilda will either come to her senses and marry (admitting thereby her need for "the help and support of one's fellow creatures") or she will be punished by failing strength and/or death.

Clearly, Ralph's tendency to write the romance into Hilda's story, the resemblance of his rhetoric to that of male Oxford, and his oddly irrelevant and inflated rhetoric call his conclusions into question. Is Hilda now willing to marry Ralph? What has she really learned from her experience? What is its significance? And if Ralph's assessment is, indeed, accurate, what are we to make of the new, defeated Hilda? Since we have only Ralph's version of the story, which he confesses is not the story Hilda asked him to tell, we must look more closely at the story Hilda, in spite of Ralph, is trying to tell. First of all, Hilda has asked Ralph to write, not her story, but "the account of Michael Bristowe's strange career" (15). Throughout the novel, Hilda has that objectivity, that "singleness of purpose that pursues knowledge" which Sayers attributes to the educated woman. Even her relationship to the man she marries is objective and purposeful: she is not in love with him, she simply feels a duty toward humanity. She realizes, as well as Ralph does, how unlikable Michael is, but knows that he or at least his gift is her "strongest interest" (222). The story she requests is not then, in any way, a romantic or personal one; it is an "account;" an account, not of Bristowe the man, but of his "strange career," that is, of the gift she believes him to have possessed.

Secondly, the story that Ralph tells—the heterosexual, couple-based romance between himself and Hilda with its predictable obstacle, the "other man"—is the very story Hilda consistently and explicitly rejects. Ralph suggests at the start that his marriage to Hilda is "a long-standing family plot" (12). It is this plot which, as Ralph's mother senses when she hears about Hilda's "university career," Hilda will refuse, unravel, reject, and rewrite. Ralph implies throughout the novel that it is Hilda's interest in Michael which is keeping him from his "natural mate." He refuses, that is, to take seriously Hilda's own plot for her life. In the romantic narrative there are few things which can keep a man from his true love. Family opposition is one, but here there is family support. The obvious other is another man, and it is this plot element which Ralph seizes and exploits in his version of the story. The term "long-standing family plot," furthermore, suggests burial as well as wedding. In rejecting Ralph, Hilda rejects not only the families' plans but her place in the graveyard at the end of a life as dutiful daughter and wife, a life which would require her to bury her own needs and desires. All three plots—the grave, the plan, and the story-line—she recognizes as attempts to entrap her, to take away her independent existence, to make her into a Viking princess in her father's hall. In contrast to the family plot and father's hall, Hilda's residences emphasize her status as independent woman. She begins in a Bloomsbury flat and moves with Michael to a cottage of her choosing after realizing that Marling has no place for her and her chief interest. In both places she is, as Ralph notes with some chagrin, "very much upon her own ground" (16) as opposed to being in or on the family plot.

Hilda's first explicit rejection of the plots occurs with Ralph's marriage proposal, which takes place, as does much of the story, on Hilda's ground. She is neither shocked or thrilled by the proposal, but considers it with rational detachment. No, she says, "she did not want to marry at present . . . , she was keenly interested in her work, . . . she was enjoying her life of independence in London, and had no desire for the ties of domesticity" (76). Though Ralph records her answer, the most salient point he infers is that at least he has no "fears of a rival" (76). He has earlier tried to dissuade her from seeing too much of the disreputable Michael. She makes very clear not only that she will not take his advice, but that "it might be the worst sort of crime one can commit if I did not help him" (58). Since Ralph's response is to absent himself for a while and then to return to give her, as he says, another interest—himself and his renewal of the marriage proposal—he sets himself up as Michael's "rival" though Hilda assures him that Michael is not a rival and though he seems to accept that assurance. Ralph repeats the romantic story even when it is groundless.

Hilda's refusal to marry Ralph is a rational one. She does not reject marriage altogether: "she had no special feeling against it," but she rejects it only for herself, only at this time. Ralph's unwarranted, irrational inference here is that he has permission to persist in his suit. She asserts her interest in her work; this above all Ralph resents and refuses to take seriously. In fact, it is this interest, this "chief pretext for remaining unmarried" (81) that, reassured about Michael, he sees as his best target for attack. His approach is silly and predictable. "You can't like working for Mrs. Hastings . . . . Women always bully women. Everyone knows that" (81). Again, Ralph adheres to an old story, and Hilda denies it in order to tell her own: "Some do and some don't . . . just like men. Mrs. Hastings is very pleasant to work for" (81). Like the marriage and family plot, this story may be sometimes true, but not in this case, not for her. It is at this point that Ralph leaves "in impotent rage" (81): Hilda, the rational woman, insists, simply and clearly, on shaping her own story and thus ruins his. Later, when Hilda tells Ralph that she is going to marry Michael, Ralph returns bitterly to the question of her work. He thinks he has discovered a hole in Hilda's story. Work "had been a sufficient reason for refusing to consider marriage with me; it apparently had no weight against the necessity of nursing Michael Bristowe" (194). Again, Ralph believes that his story is the true one: women willingly give up their work for marriage or for nursing men. But again, it is Ralph's story which is wrong. He discovers later that Mrs. Hastings was, in fact, "keeping the post open for her" (194). Hilda has no intention of abandoning her work; she only wants to devote herself for a time to a limited project which seems to her of enormous significance.

When Ralph leaves Hilda at the end of the novel, furthermore, she has engaged a nurse for the baby and expects "to be back at

work again in a few weeks' time" (265). Little as he likes it, Ralph
cannot tell Hilda's story without her work, just as Hilda cannot tell
her own story without it. It establishes her identity at the beginning
of the tale; she returns to it in the end; it comes up in conjunction
with both Ralph's marriage proposals. Though Ralph attempts again
and again to minimize its importance, its appearance at crucial
points in the text works against his claim.

Refusal of the marriage proposals and insistence on work, whether
political or personal, are both attempts on the part of Hilda and the
text itself to deny the romantic story that Ralph keeps trying to tell.
A third attempt is Hilda's consistently unromantic attitude toward
Ralph, toward other men, and even toward the man she marries.
Ralph complains early in the novel, for example, that Hilda treats
him "as an old friend with whom a possible future business arrangement had been left temporarily in abeyance" (80). At the end of
the novel, as we have seen, she writes to him for financial help because he is "the nearest thing to a brother" (245) that she has. The
"warmest" comment she makes to him is, "It's pleasant to know
that you want me, Ralph" (77). Her regard for Ralph as an old
friend, as a brother, as a partner in the enterprise that is her chief
interest, indicates clearly that Ralph's romantic story is a fictional
account, not because Ralph is either novelist or conscious deceiver
but because he is himself entrapped in the romantic plot. Though
he tries to find hints of some more romantic interest on Hilda's part,
though he attempts to see Michael as a romantic rival, he must admit that Hilda is less "sex-conscious" (80) than any other woman
he has met. When he takes her to his club for dinner, he cannot
decide whether it is "admirable" or "pathetic" that "she was obviously utterly unconscious of the discreetly admiring glances of my
fellow-clubsmen" (31). He responds here as predictably as Doctor
Bays in *Ashley Hamel*, a novel by Somervillian Hilda Reid: "He had
been scandalized earlier that morning by the advertisement of a se-
ductive woman, but the sight of a woman who practised no seduc-
tive arts shocked him more profoundly still" (53). Doctor Bays and
Ralph, two educated men, cannot use their own intellectual tools
to overcome the prejudices so deeply embedded in the romance plot
that writes their lives.

Hilda herself says explicitly that she has a different plot in mind
for her own life. "I've never been in love . . . the way books describe it. I think, that I am probably not capable of that" (222).

The books describe something Ralph and others seem to understand but she does not. Their plots and experiences are not hers. What shocks Ralph most, however, is not that she is not "in love" with him or is impervious to the romantic feelings she inspires in others but that she is not in love with the man she intends to marry. Though as Hilda points out, Ralph has himself defended "the French *marriage de convenance*" (235), he finds similar sentiments in a woman incredible and unwomanly. Hilda's comment reveals Ralph's own irrationality and unquestioning adherence to the convention that marriage, while a pleasant and desirable addition to a man's already mildly successful and amusing life, is for a woman the "supreme experience of her sex" (226).

Hilda's most open rejection of Ralph's romance is her expression of surprise that "I should ever hear you talk like a best-seller" (235). Hilda's use of the derogatory "best-seller" rather than simply "book" implies that Ralph's story is a more thoroughgoing and less well-intentioned fiction than an ordinary novel. She here sees through Ralph's hypocrisy and his histrionic, irrational attempt to make her change her mind about marrying Michael. He speaks of the "horror" of a marriage without love, as though the tale he spins is not just romance but gothic romance, forgetting, but perhaps enacting, the gothic insight that it is most often the erotic which generates the horror. Hilda, the educated, rational woman, refuses to attend to his warning. The inflated rhetoric of the conclusion—the speculation on what Hilda has learned, Ralph's sense of Hilda as "desperately . . . clinging to the hope that her sacrifice had not been in vain" (268)—must be seen in the light of this gothic rhetoric, in light of Hilda's perception that Ralph is talking like a best-seller. What he has written down is not the story Hilda asked him to tell, but a best-seller, a gothic romance that casts Hilda as properly chastened by the disastrous results of her Faustian, Frankensteinian "inadmissible enterprise" (244). Ralph then writes himself off on a romantic expedition, having rejected the now awakened, no longer innocent woman, having, like the uninvited crone, cursed the newborn child under pretense of blessing her: "I cannot help suspecting that it may be the happiest thing for little Stella if she turns out, after all, to be completely commonplace" (256).

Unable to "share a happy and normal life" (217) with Hilda, unable, that is, to succeed in turning Hilda's story into a romance,

Ralph hopes for a romantic script for Stella. Hilda, on the other
hand, wants her daughter to have Michael's gift, to have it "in a
higher degree than Michael" (93). Again, we see the conflict between Ralph's plot and Hilda's; again we note that Hilda's breaks
new ground. Like the American who, Ralph asserts, is "capable of
seeing freshly without preconception" (163), the educated woman
has a vision. Unlike the American, who sees freshly only for his
own profit, Hilda harbors ambitions for her child that center not on
her own gratification, not even on Stella's future, but on the good
of all humanity, "a chance that may never ·come again" (223).
While, then, Ralph's plot is a romance, Hilda's is a vision; his is
personal, hers social; his is conservative, hers adventurous, "an adventure of the race" (229).

Finally, it is by the sex of child that the text significantly alters
the romantic plot, and by her response to the sex of her child that
Hilda definitively breaks into Ralph's romance. According to Ralph,
Hilda herself had never considered the possibility that the inheritor
of the gift would be female. "Master of Arts as she was, and as much
of a feminist as are most educated women nowadays, Hilda, like any
Victorian, had attached her exceptional hopes to a young prince"
(257). The text, however, has prepared the ground for the child's
sex by the reference to von Reichenbach, a nineteenth-century
German scientist, and his discovery of "a new sense in human beings" (93). Unfortunately no one paid attention to his work because
his most gifted subjects were "invalid girls." Stella, too, is an invalid girl: she is ill for weeks after birth, "small," "helpless," "pathetic" (256) and she is in-valid because she is a girl. In Hilda's
mental plot, at least as much of it as we can glean from Ralph's de-
risive summary, Hilda, the almost-virgin "Madonna" (257) will
bear a "young prince," a Messiah whose path she has made smooth
(252). To conform to its Biblical analog, the expected child should
have been a son. But unlike Ralph, who cannot change his plot to
accommodate new information, Hilda is able to turn her invalid
girl into a valid messiah and to turn the biblical narrative into a
modern story.

She names the child Stella, as "star" an indication both of the
continued connection with the Christmas narrative and of the departure from it. She rejects the plot of motherhood to return to
work, leaving Stella in the charge of "a highly trained nurse" (265).
Contrary to Ralph's allegation that Hilda has an aversion to Stella

because of her sex, Hilda seems clearly to have made the adjust-
ment in her expectations. "Do you see?" she asks Ralph "in an almost awe-stricken whisper," "she's trying to get her hands free"
(267). Miss Platt denies Ralph's explanation of Hilda's indifference
to the child when she notes that Ralph is "upset, like most men,
when they find that all women haven't the maternal instincts of a
broody hen" (259). And Hilda's reverential awe belies even the indifference. Further, the struggling hands of the child imply that,
like her father, she will use her hands to "feel," as instruments of
her sixth sense. The "trying to get her hands free" suggests also that
as a female child she, like her mother, will refuse to be trapped by
the romantic plot and will, unlike von Reichenbach's invalid girls,
use her gift in a positive, rational, and valid way. Though Stella
may inherit her father's gift of seeing beneath the surface, it is her
mother who is her real creator, who will make sure that the child
has "a better chance than poor Michael," that she does not "start
with everything against [her]" (229). In this revision of the Christmas story the mother takes the initiative to produce the new messiah, since in the post-war world "our God is one who needs our
help" (232). The death of the father and the investment of hope in
the daughter emphasize the newness of this narrative.

At the end of the novel we see, with Ralph, a Hilda exhausted by
her undertaking, alone, subdued. Unlike Ralph, however, we do
not see her ruled now by fear and need; we do not see her as a failure. Ralph is quick to make these judgments yet has no ground for
his pessimism but his own desire for feminine mediocrity for both
mother and daughter. Though he consoles himself with the "incipient fulfillment of [his] prophecies" (270), his own failure to participate when invited in what the text invites us to see as a messianic,
evolutionary experiment has itself made Hilda's project more difficult than it need have been. He could not relinquish the romantic
plot; he abandons Hilda after her marriage and is no longer interested in his "natural mate" once she has acted contrary to his
wishes, once she has married, however briefly, however practically,
another man. Theoretically supportive of women's higher education, Ralph is as frightened and horrified of its consequences as its
opponents are. His setting off, at the end of the narrative, on an
expedition, is flight as well as male adventure. He takes refuge in
the masculine prerogative of foreign travel and novel excitement
while Hilda, the real adventurer, goes quietly back to her work with

Mrs. Hastings and to her evolutionary task. Ralph continues to write his romantic tale; he renounces his love for fallen Hilda and moves into another romantic adventure, while Hilda, the rational woman, continues to rewrite the conventional tale. If, as Ralph thinks, she could now accept his proposal, it would be as companion and friend that she would marry him; she arranges rationally for child care; no story of maternal instincts prompts her to give up her work even though the child is a very special one.

Although Hilda constantly revises Ralph's romantic narrative, she does not herself write or have an interest in writing. That task she gives over, too trustingly, to Ralph, the professional, with the request that he write the account of Michael Bristowe's strange career. Ralph cannot, however, write this account because it is not his story. In fact, the text suggests that Ralph senses that an account of Michael Bristowe would be not the story of a man at all but a testament to the creativity of an educated woman. Ralph watches the development of Michael with great anxiety, in part because the gift itself frightens him, but more because of Hilda's creative role in it. "It frightened me," he admits, "to remember that Hilda had deliberately helped to develop it, so that its potentiality had become infinitely greater than they [sic] need have been" (191). It is Hilda, then, who has taken a simple enough gift of physical discernment and worked systematically to improve and expand it. To Ralph's romantic mind, the creation has taken on, like Frankenstein's experiment, a life of its own "half wizard and half monster" (213), has become "a live menacing entity" (215). Hilda is, then, a powerful if unconscious creator whose material is not words on paper but the stuff of the human race; she is not Ralph's serving goddess, but a creator god/goddess; Michael Bristowe's story is, in this very concrete way, her own. Her decision to reproduce Michael's gift and Michael's story can be seen, of course, as her acceptance of the womanly role. Even her motives, while not sexually romantic, are altruistic and self-denying in the way that the romance plot conventionally dictates the good woman's motives to be. Three things, however, work against this interpretation. One is the very feminine nature of Michael and Michael's gift. Although his sense begins as something sex-neutral, an ability to detect the presence of metals and various objects, with Hilda's encouragement and tutoring it becomes an ability to sense people, both their presence and their motives, and to communicate in some intuitive, wordless way. The sixth sense, in other words, is very like "women's intuition"; Michael himself is stereotypically feminine. Helpless, unambitious, sickly, moody, he welcomes Hilda's taking charge of his life. Thus Hilda devotes her energy not to a romantic man but to a weak and irritating one, not to a man's gift but to a woman's.

Second is Hilda's clear sense of her mission's limits. She knows that Michael will not live long. She even asks her employer to hold her job. Far from the all-encompassing and life-long commitment demanded by the romance, Hilda's commitment is circumscribed and temporary. Third is Ralph's own acknowledgment of Hilda's role in Michael's gift and life. He believes she has saved Michael's life; he believes she has created this "half wizard and half monster." Ralph can give no reason for his sinister interpretation of Michael's sixth sense; perhaps its very association with the feminine frightens him. Aside from Ralph's rhetoric, the sense appears valuable and fairly congenial. Although readers have no grounds for adopting Ralph's attitude toward the gift, his account of its development seems reliable enough: it is as much Hilda's creation as Michael's potential. Her decision to reproduce can be seen as the decision to continue, despite Ralph's warnings and objections, her own plot line. Ralph acknowledges this in an extravagant simile at the end of the tale when he asserts that someone who "tries to practice ideals in this world is like one who composes an Ode to Peace while the enemy is setting fire to the Thatch" (269). We could turn Ralph's simile on himself and see him as the idealist whose project/plot—both of marrying Hilda and of writing her romance—is set fire to by Hilda, the subverter, like Bronte's fire-wielding Bertha, of traditional values and of traditional texts.

In Ralph's text, though, the idealist is of course Hilda, the educated woman, who in the simile takes on the dimensions of a composer or poet whose work is continually subverted by "the enemy." Such subversion is easy if the enemy appears as friend, and Ralph's own role has become that of the enemy in the guise of supporter and friend, the man who, unlike "many of my contemporaries . . . [has] never been against the higher education of women" (14). Nevertheless, he subverts Hilda's efforts, in large part because he does not want Hilda to succeed in her creation, in what the text sees as her daring enterprise. What he wants is to settle down with her as princess of his hall; by setting fire to her Thatch he hopes to smoke her out of her own territory and into his—a kind of manuscript-burning, which he is too civilized and rational to do in reality, but which he effectively accomplishes by turning her story into his own romance. Only when the reader recognizes the enemy in friend's clothing does Hilda's story emerge and does the ending reflect not, as Ralph would have it, a woman punished for refusal to play her proper part, but a woman, like Jaeger's Sand, "immensely courageous and highly vocal," who makes people freer because she "explored the uncleared country for them."

Jaeger's juxtaposition of a secular, female-centered nativity narrative with a thwarted tale of romance becomes her strategy for circumventing the romantic plot. She portrays the educated woman as trapped by the text, trapped by the romantic story the narrator wants to tell. By providing another layer, however, a tale of origins and destinies, a tale, moreover, which revises and reverses that myth, both etiological and teleological, of Christianity, Jaeger allows her heroine to slip out of the more literary text and into the mythic one, in which elements of romance diffuse themselves in confrontation with the sacred. Although the sacred here is secular, the otherworldly this-worldly, the powerful father-god a weak human man, the submissive woman a powerful mother-creator, the male savior a female star, tiny, weak, but growing, the effect and significance remain the same: next to the blueprint for the future of the human race, the heterosexual romance pales. No rhetoric on the part of the narrator can inflate that plot to comparable proportions.

The Oxbridge education sets in motion this shift from plot to myth and epic because it replaces shyness with confidence, submission with initiative, fairy tale with reason—in other words, powerlessness with power. The romantic plot is, for women, the origin and embodiment of powerlessness. Trapped in it, women only repeat it. One way out, Jaeger's text suggests, is through the uncleared country of originary myth where women can start over, this time with education and power on their side.

6 From the Mistresses' Grove

to the Master's Garden:

The Doreen Wallace Plot

In her chatty, book-length meditation on gardening, *In a Green Shade*, Doreen Wallace asserts that

> It is quite possible to write good psychology without recourse to the deplorable stream-of-consciousness technique, so wordy and so formless; so disingenuous too, for with all its meanderings it is not really a stream of consciousness—if it were, one day would fill three volumes. It is only a selection of consciousness, so why not be a bit more selective and get on with the story? I turn the pages of James Joyce, Dorothy Richardson and Virginia Woolf (Philistine that I am) in the vain hope that sooner or later something will happen (51).

Unlike some of her famous contemporaries, Wallace, like the other Somerville novelists, eschews technical innovation in favor of getting on with the "story." The basis of Wallace's stories is the "couple-based romance," but in these texts the "romance" invariably sours; what we are left with is similar to what Susan J. Rosowski calls "the novel of awakening," in which the heroine comes to "an awakening of limitation" (49)—limitation of the possibilities of her life as a woman. In *Land from the Waters*, a Wallace novel set, unlike most

of her works, in an earlier century, the narrative voice comments
on the independent, undomestic, "unnatural" (45) heroine who refuses marriage because she is not "the right kind of woman": "But
without much conscious effort and simply by doing each task because it had to be done, she became that kind of woman. Life
moulded her" (138).

Wallace's interesting and consistent contribution to this "novel
of awakening" is the injection of the complications attendant upon
women's education. Some of her heroines, like Eliot's Maggie, resent the contrast between their brothers' education and their own
lack of it. Elinor Fairlie in *Elegy* describes her family: "Our two
brothers were educated at British public schools, but we girls were
educated only by Father and Mother; the household arts and the
Bible were all any woman needed" (14). But even among these late
Victorians, Wallace includes the educated exceptions, like Elinor's
sister Harriet who "needed more. She won tough battles against
Father by pointing out, from the example of men, that medical mis-
sionaries were twice as useful as spiritual ones" (14). Harriet becomes a doctor, but the struggle and "strength of mind" that the
struggle necessitated have made her "quite intolerable" (14). Later
in this novel—and later in the century—a male character deplores
another effect of women's education:

> It did not take me long to discover the sexual proclivities of
> most of the Piers set . . . a carry-over from school no doubt.
> Undergraduates are almost always at the peak of sex-develop-
> ment, and in these days [the 1920's], the women students were
> an unalluring lot who took no pains to attract men . . . men
> were not their objective (108).

Offensive personalities and deviant sexuality, so distressing to the
associates of these women, are not the complications of education
most painful to Wallace's educated women themselves, who have
constantly to deal with lives in general and men in particular who
demand less of their minds than they have been trained to give and
more of their bodies than they want to give. The Austen-like opening of Sayers' *Have His Carcase*, in comment on Harriet Vane's predicament after her acquittal of Boyes' death, asserts that "The best
remedy for a bruised heart is not, as so many people seem to think,
repose upon a manly bosom. Much more efficacious are honest

work, physical activity, and the sudden acquisition of wealth" (9). Later, marriage for Harriet becomes, not a refuge, but a rewarding addition to an already interesting life. Jaeger's Hilda, though she marries a man she does not love, does so as a sacrifice for the future of humankind, and she looks forward to an early and productive widowhood. Unlike these protagonists who choose marriage freely, Wallace's educated heroines fall into it, betrayed by the perverse circumstances of their lives or by the perverse exigencies of their own bodies. Bridget in *Land from the Waters* recognizes that "I have surrendered to womanhood. We have no choice, unless we be rich" (146), a circumstance echoed in the lives of her more contemporary sisters. Audrey in *Barnham Rectory* surrenders everything to marriage, to Alan's passion:

> For a moment the fierce virginity of the intellectual woman fought for its life, then mere human nature gave in to his superior strength. He kissed expertly, sweetly, warmly, and he called up from the depths of Audrey a tremulous response of which she was ashamed. If she were to give herself up to this sort of thing, what would become of Audrey the socialist, Audrey the idealist, Audrey the proud? Not only did she despise, she also feared the female animal concealed deeply in her which was beating its way upward to her lips and would not be denied (266).

Marriage here becomes almost a punishment for the hubris of the Cambridge graduate who "because she had been to a good school . . . thought she was God" (236) and therefore exempt from the lot of women, that is, marriage and motherhood.

The ambivalence about women's education that laces all Wallace's work is nowhere more obvious than in her first novel, appropriately entitled *A Little Learning*, published in a limited edition and usually left off the list of her works. Elizabeth Slack, a novelist in Wallace's short story "Last Love," has "shouldered off the temptation to write that autobiographical first novel which almost all writers have to get off their minds" (*Going to the Sea*, 227). Though the melodramatic plot of *A Little Learning* is less obviously autobiographical than those of some of the later educated-woman-marries-farmer novels, this work is probably one of the books "about the women's colleges . . . by dissatisfied young persons . . . recently down from

Oxford" to which Sayers objected (*Titles to Fame*, 82). Whether or
not *A Little Learning* deals with autobiographical material that the
aspiring novelist had to get off her mind, it certainly contains all
the themes that permeate her later novels, especially that of the
ambivalent effects of education on a woman's life.

The novel opens with Olive Flowerdew's return to the family
farm, in a hired car, from her first term at Oxford—a return to "Father, Mother, and the kids, and the cramped surroundings" in
which "there was not room for Oxford" (7–8). The eight weeks she
has spent at college have unfitted her for life on the farm and sepa-
rated her from the rest of her family, who now must inconvenience
themselves on her account: "Olive had to have a room to herself,
even if it meant cramping the rest; her luggage took up a great deal
of space, and besides, she must have a table upstairs to work at"
(15). This physical separation is the necessary correlative to the
more serious intellectual and emotional separation, which her father recognizes as inevitable. "Us'll be far behind you soon. We
'oont mind. Someone must allus be left behind when folks get on"
(14). Olive leaves her friends behind, too. Ida has gone out to service and the two young women have nothing to talk about; Olive's
boyfriend Rowley, a kind, practical young man, does not understand why she will not agree to marry him. Her attempts to explain
do nothing to ease the situation. "Libraries, Rowley," she says, "You
don't know the smell of old book-bindings. You don't know the feeling of having books in your power; all other people's old knowledge
there for your brains to pick. All waiting. And I haven't had enough
of it yet" (62). Rowley, as might be expected, cannot sympathize.
He wants a wife to do the housework on the farm and to be a
mother to his children. His purposefulness and confidence contrast
clearly with Olive's vague desires for something more.

Though the reader, being her- or himself a person who knows the
feeling of having books in one's power, can see Olive's plight, her
snobbery and self-importance—"she felt she was entitled to her superiority because she, Olive Flowerdew, was actually somebody"
(45)—do little to enlist reader sympathy for higher education.
Olive becomes particularly intolerable when she compares Rowley
to Oxford men:

> If he had not the trailing aroma of stable always with him: if
> one could invest him with a Fair-isle pullover and a rose beige

shirt with an open neck, if he knew some good slang and did
not talk about . . . hogs; in short, if he could go to Oxford,
one might love him.

She concludes, "But things being as they were, one could not
dream of losing the world for a handsome face" (65). This flippant
treatment of a respectable and sympathetic young man seems a direct result of her Oxford-induced change in values. Hard work,
closeness to the earth, straightforward talk, and the purposeful
living of farm life seem at this point to the reader to outweigh
Olive's petty concern with bad smells and dirty clothes.

Just before her return to Oxford, however, an incident occurs
which shows another side of this life she is in the process of rejecting. Olive's brother Clem, who resents his sister's growing aliena-
tion from the family, makes fun of something she has written. She
slaps him and he attacks her murderously. She manages to escape
and, when she recovers, tries to talk to her mother about what happened. At the suggestion that Clem might be a bit dangerous, Mary
Flowerdew lashes out at Olive for provoking him and asserts her belief that it is good for a man to have a temper "to keep his women-
folk in order" (91). The violence lurking under a surface that seems
at first peaceful and harmonious, violence occasioned by a woman
writing and presented as a way of controlling women, is not only
tolerated but condoned. A writing woman's work cannot survive
here—and neither can the writing woman.

> It is, then, relief that accompanies Olive back to Oxford
> where there was no hatred and no fear; there was no gossip;
> there were no smelling rooms; no Grandmother Steggles with
> channels in the face like muddy creeks; no shame. There was
> instead mental aspiration and a great deal of fun; and, this
> Trinity Term, the river (103).

The juxtaposition of legitimate bases for relief and Olive's continued snobbery typifies the text's ambivalence toward Olive, who
prefers to be called "Olivia" at Oxford, and toward that education
she wants so passionately, an ambivalence intensified by Olive's
shift of emphasis, in Trinity Term, from work to love. She meets an
artist, Roger Dennison, cultured, smart, worldly and the brother of
one of her fellow students. He seems taken with her and she falls in

love. The superficiality of his affection for her and of the life he leads are revealed when Olive visits his home to sit for a portrait and must endure his and his family's rudeness. Charmed by her unsophisticated ways, Roger decides that he has been unkind to her and that perhaps he feels more toward her than he had thought. When she returns home after the term, he follows her and begins to see her life through his romantic-artist lens. "She turned out to be far from the dullard he had thought her: instead, with her handicaps, she must be considered a girl of unusual ability. Her mother could perhaps teach her to make rushes. The Hinnerys were pure joy and landscape painting was an enchanting new adventure" (191). The Hinnerys whom Roger admires so much are Mary Featherdew's brother and his family. Mr. Hinnery is a brute who threatens to kill his unmarried pregnant daughter and later tries to kill the baby. Again we see that however deplorable Olive's intolerance for smelly rooms and Grandmother Steggles, hatred and fear and violence and brutishness, from which Oxford is an escape, are equally part of the life she is leaving behind. Roger's romanticization of that life, however, illustrates the text's claim that Oxford breeds immature idealists.

Attempts to unite Oxford and the "real" world seem doomed to failure. Olive and Roger have a concrete example of the marriage of education to life on the farm in Olive's neighbor Laura Harden (whose story is told more fully in *God's Tenth*) who has tried to put her Oxford M.A. to good use for her husband Anthony, her children, and the farm community. Though Laura and Anthony have more money and more status than the Featherdew family, Laura cannot create a niche for herself. She tries, for example, to convince the Book Club, whose reading tastes run to romance, to read a Hardy novel. The response is "If we start letting the classics in, where will it end?" (101) The humorous question illustrates the impossibility of Laura or Olive's finding intellectual companionship or stimulation in the English countryside. Roger Dennison knew Laura in her Oxford days and was very much in love with her. He stays with the Hardens while he is in the neighborhood and quickly realizes that Olive suffers from comparison with Laura. He wants the latter to run away with him, an obvious step for her to take since she feels so alien to country life and since she, like Olive, feels herself above her neighbors and even her husband. She senses that Dennison's phrase "housekeeper or concubine" expresses well her relationship to Anthony. She thinks, "How degrading for a woman of gifts and education!" (217)

Unlike Olive, however, who would eagerly have taken Roger up on the offer, Laura has had personal experience of marriage and has, besides, used her powers of observation, honed by an Oxford education, to take in the experiences of others. To be "housekeeper and concubine," hard as it is to accept, seems to her the inevitable lot of women: "Considering the fate of the other married women she knew, she came to the decision that that was how wives did end, without exception" (217). Laura refuses Dennison's proposal not because she loves Anthony, not primarily because she feels committed to her marriage or even to her children, but because she knows that marriage with Dennison would not ultimately make any difference. When Dennison asks her if she has never "pined" for him as he has pined for her, she replies, "For a long time now . . . I have pined for nothing but freedom" (214). Dennison finds this rejection difficult to accept and renews his pleading. This time Laura's response is even more explicit, "My dear Roger, you, like all men, find it impossible to believe that a woman can do without a man's love . . . Believe me . . . if any cataclysm did separate me from the children and good old Anthony, I wouldn't take up with a man again, ever. I've had enough of man in his maleness, and all the responsibilities that one accepts along with him" (228). While, then, country life for the educated woman means entrapment, isolation, and deterioration, marriage itself—in the country or out of it—means precisely the same.

Ironically Laura recognizes that she can do without a man's love only because she has already married and had children. Like Audrey, educated women are betrayed into believing in the heterosexual romance by the bodies that Oxbridge has neglected in favor of the mind and by the social expectations that, muted in the women's college environment, emerge more forcefully in its absence. Olive Featherdew is no exception. Although she refuses to marry the country boy, marriage remains a goal, a trap, and an inevitability. Even the horrors that occur between the visit from Dennison and her going down from Oxford result from the romantic plot that every level of society assumes. As Dennison walks away, rejected, from Laura Harden, Olive's brother Clem, thinking that Dennison has jilted his sister, kills him. The uneducated Clem, taking to himself the role of protector of women, acts out this plot unthinkingly but the educated men and women in the novel participate in it just as thoroughly. Only Laura questions it and does so only after years of living with its murdering ways.

In spite of the ensuing scandal, Olive returns to Oxford where "the Elizabethans saved [her] from a nervous breakdown, without a doubt" (244). Befriended only by the devoted Claire, Olive studies on in isolation, seems assured of a First, and continues to assume that marriage rather than education will remove her from home. The ground is laid for Olive's marriage, but Laura, the married, educated woman, again realizes its risks. She almost dies after the birth of her third child. Like the brutality of farm life itself, marriage threatens not only her intellectual life but her physical life as well. The only solution is to reject, as far as possible in her circumstances, the marriage relationship. She says firmly to Anthony, "I don't care what you intend to do about it: I shall sleep alone and lock my door—nothing else is safe. I will not be put in peril of my life again" (257).

When Olive returns to Oxford for the last time, she studies hard and alone, Claire by this time having made other friends, and she ends up not with a First but with a nervous breakdown. When she goes home for good, Dick Chomley, a bank manager, a thoroughly decent sort, saves her life and wants to marry her. In her weakened state she has nothing to say to his argument for the romance plot, appropriately phrased in economic terms:

> You'd be giving up something, of course, but all bargains have two sides to them: You'd be getting a livelihood without having to work for it, and the certainty of proper attention if you were ill, and of never being cornered by circumstances. . . . Have you ever considered the hazards of your intellectual life if you are to stay single and work for yourself? (263)

Olive, beaten down by circumstances, agrees to the marriage, registering without reflection the appearance of Laura Harden with her three children. She tells Dick, "Mrs. H. was at Oxford—I don't know which College—and got a First" (276). Neither Dick nor Olive recognizes the relevance of this comment to their situation. She buries her face in Dick's Harris tweed "to escape his kisses," and their physical contact jolts her out of her "disembodied" state.

> Life was coming back. Pricks of doubt and tinglings of the old ambition worked painfully in her reviving brain. But she was

strong now with some of her mother's brute strength: she shed
no tears. She looked instead into a future that stretched away
as long and dull and out-of-the world as Ousedale Street, and
accepted it. There was no going back (288).

Awakened, then, by the jacket if not the kiss of Prince Charming,
Olive awakens as well to the limits she has accepted. Dick's offer of
the certainty of "never being cornered by circumstances" becomes
especially ironic. Olive has been cornered by circumstances from
the beginning and effectively corners herself for life, like Laura, by
accepting the proposal. But, as both Dick and Laura realize, there
are no alternatives. Wallace's women continue to have no alternatives, and efforts to find them in independence or in art are
swiftly punished.

Though women inevitably fall into marriage, there is nothing
particularly attractive or pleasant in Wallace's novels about life with
men, who are portrayed as physically too demanding at best, physically repulsive at worst. Laura decides, in *God's Tenth*, that "It was
the man who was so dependent on the physical side of marriage:
how Anthony could find time and energy for it, Laura did not
know" (70). Mary, in *So Long to Learn*, "had taken in her stride,
with philosophical endurance, her husband's physical demands on
her. . . . The bodily contact of marriage was tolerable . . . it was
even rather comic when she thought about it afterwards . . . it
seemed to mean so much to Bartley and meant so little to her" (34).
Jessie in *Woman with a Mirror* found "it" less amusing. Her husband
Adam "was the essence of maleness, he stank of it, you could wash
and wash his clothes without washing out the characteristic male
odour" (68).

Even the least physically repulsive males, however, have more
serious drawbacks in these novels than unattractive bodies. They
are uncontrollable egoists who genuinely feel threatened by intelligence, education, and the least sign of independence in the women
they marry. *Latter Howe's* Katherine gives up her university lec-
tureship to marry Lanty, who thinks not at all about her sacrifice.
"In his view Katherine was to be unequivocally blest in the gift of
Lanty as husband and Latter Howe as home" (53). Such convictions as the seventeenth-century John's in *Land from the Waters* that
God "created women for cooking, cleaning, and childbearing and
little besides. Argumentation is a man's business" (156) are predict-

able enough given the historical setting, but they change little over the centuries. In *The Spring Returns* Richard thinks it is only right that his wife Hester, a successful commercial artist, "should give her time to the house, servant or no servant," because "a woman was born to manual labour. But a man was not" (54). Educated, intelligent, successful women are either relegated by their menfolk to housekeeping and childrearing or they are not chosen as wives at all. The doctor in *Even Such Is Time* says categorically that Somerville women (especially the ones with Firsts) "aren't good mothers, and the children are delicate or dotty" (178). Not all rejections are on such eugenic grounds. Like Lord Saint-George in *Gaudy Night*, who thinks Oxford women "too grubby," Wallace's relatively sympathetic Lawrence in *The Time of Wild Roses* chooses, instead of a Somerville student, the lovely Anne whose "Daddy wouldn't let me try for college—he can't abide blue-stockings" (25). When she turns out to be idle and uninterested in his farming problems, he resents her, but when she decides to write a novel, he is furious: " . . . a novel seemed to him the strongest insult she could throw at life" (349).

Men not only repel and demand, they hate their wives' outside interests, especially writing. Far from being proud of his wife's lucrative novels, Raymond Slack in "Last Love"

> hated her writing. She got lost in it. . . . Once, and once only, she refused to go with him to a political meeting at which he was taking the chair. She had work to do, she said, meaning writing. As though you could call that work! Novel-izing, inventing. . . . He made her understand on that occasion . . . how deeply he was hurt at her putting mere writing before the interests of her husband who loved her (*Going to the Sea*, 238).

It is Raymond, too, who articulates the basis of his fear and hatred: "[Writing] was the job of sex-starved spinsters, to weave wish-fulfillments" (239). The writing woman calls into question the ability of her man to satisfy her on every level.

Most of Wallace's aspiring women writers and artists do not, in the end, create very much. For one thing, their men hate their work; for another they simply do not have the place or the time. In *God's Tenth*, for example, Laura recognizes that she can do little without a room of her own "with a door that will lock" (147). Yet claiming a room most often means inconveniencing others; Olive's family, as we have seen, must crowd themselves to provide her with work space; we doubt that her husband will be willing to make such a sacrifice. In *God's Tenth,* Anthony Harden has a stroke and Laura goes into the field, leads the neighborhood rebellion against the tithe. When she becomes physically and politically active, she realizes that "the old nagging consciousness of something other, something better, waiting to be done if only there were time, had left her. She forgot that she had ever wanted to write" (267). Too busy to put pen to paper, she again relinquishes any intellectual or artistic life. While Wallace's women writers and artists are hemmed in by men's fears and the demands of the household, they cannot create, finally, because they and the texts themselves are not at all convinced that the intellectual life is a valid one. Hester, for example, the commercial artist in *The Spring Returns,* wonders if one is not more alive when the sensuous pleasures of country life take precedence over "reading Shakespeare or watching a Shaw play and living with the brain. . . . It was the urban life, so deadly for the senses—with its stinks and bustle and tiredness and noise—that had forced those who lived it to create artificial interests, to make up in some measure for what they lacked" (261). Art as compensation for the sensuous and the sexual, then, is a notion that troubles not only the men but the women as well. Elizabeth, the successful novelist in "Last Love" writes as austerely as she does so that no one could "accuse her of taking to novel writing as compensation for a love affair gone wrong" (227), which she herself fears is the case. Like education, like the intellectual life itself, art complicates a woman's life, makes her restless and dissatisfied and not altogether attentive to the simpler pleasures of nature, home, husband, and children, just as opponents of women's education predicted. Laura's experience as head farmer suggests further that when women have real and meaningful work their need for artistic and intellectual productivity abates. Interestingly, this "real" work is in these texts equated with men's work, which women take over out of duty and loyalty and which they often perform better than their husbands. These texts seem then to concur in the characters'—both male and female—sense of art and the intellectual life as compensatory for the "real."

Though women in these texts are, for all these reasons, seldom productive artists or writers, they are almost always either artists

manquée or art objects, or both. The sharp, observant Laura recognizes this about herself, "There's nothing I enjoy more than being
a great writer manquée" (*God's Tenth*, 136). Viola in *The Faithful
Compass* is explicitly described as "artist manquée" (288). Reenie,
the femme fatale in *Woman with a Mirror*, if "really stumped for occupation . . . would give herself a home hair-do or change the
colour of her nails and would take as much interest in this as though
she were engaged on a work of art (as perhaps according to her
lights, she was)" (113). This sort of art, the making of oneself into
an art object, is, of course, approved of by men; they reward Reenie
with constant attention and gifts. Margery in *The Time of Wild
Roses*, no longer young, must use such art to make her way in
the world of men unsympathetic toward aging women. "Over the
lengthy process of making-up, she did not have to look at anything
but the detail of each piece of face; it was a work of art, not a person, which she scrutinized" (188). The process of making herself
into a work of art is especially necessary because not only is she
aging but used—a widow and a mistress—and, as one of the bitter
mothers notes in *Daughters*, "You can talk equality all you like, but
you don't alter the fact that a man, however rotten and used up,
wants a wife who is young and if possible chaste—and can get her,
too" (190). Olive Featherdew has great hopes of securing the artist
Roger Dennison when he asks her to sit for him. This agreement to
become an art object, which coincides with her desire to become
Dennison's sex object, effectively marks the end of Olive's own aspirations to write.

Art object, housekeeper, concubine, child-minder, these are the
roles to which men confine women, in order, most often, to preserve their own territory and guard their own egos. The result—of
both confinement and of attempts to avoid it—is inevitable death
for the woman, intellectual or physical or both. We have seen
Olive's death-like resignation to her marriage with Dick, and Audrey's "surrendering unconditionally the Intellectual Woman" when
she realizes that she must marry (*Barnham Rectory*, 282). In *Latter
Howe*, Katherine, who gives up being an Oxford don for marriage,
dies of consumption brought on by childbirth. Another victim of
consumption is Becky in *Even Such Is Time* whose too rigorous
schedule as a performing musician has brought on illness and,
simultaneously, marriage; her sister-in-law Marjorie Ambrose, an
Oxford woman who "looks down on her poor old father" (67), dies

in childbirth. Bridget's daughter Betsy, too, dies in childbirth; just when Bridget herself has some hope of a freer life, she must be mother to her grandchild. Reenie is killed trying to escape from an admirer who has just raped her. Laura Harden, at the end of *God's Tenth*, asks "Wasn't every normal man the enemy of every normal woman?" (274) In these texts, this seems indeed to be the case; resignation and death for the woman follow from this enmity. Men win the war.

Despite men's misogyny, however, women cannot escape the heterosexual romance: their coupled fate is not simply individual but is required by the species, and not only for reproductive purposes. Kate in *Woman with a Mirror* opines that

> There always were these silly, childish, destructive males. Each . . . generation has had this disease of maleness and survived it somehow. People and animals die in millions because of men, cities and civilizations die because of men; [but] if a world-matriarchy relegated men to begetting and breadwinning, and permitted no more killing, the world would soon be even more madly overpopulated than it is now (120).

Kate here perhaps directly answers the nurse in Sayers' *Even the Parrot* whose "world matriarchy" poses a solution to the problem of war. Both assume the relationship between large-scale violence and what the narrative voice in *Woman with a Mirror* calls natural "male blood-lust" (355), itself closely related to that sexual lust which we have seen in Wallace to be so constitutive of the male being and generally rather foreign to the female. Women as servants and art objects are the fated victims of this lust and violence.

Unlike Sayers' texts, Wallace's offer no female community to absorb and transform this conflict and offer no other concrete vision of change. Laura Harden hints at a possibility in *God's Tenth*, first rather whimsically when her third child is born and she notes disappointedly, "There's nothing new or different about Jane. . . . now if Jane had been a hermaphrodite" (147). This brief reflection indicates a kind of hope, made flesh in a vision of a child belonging to neither sex or to both, for a way women could escape their fate. She makes this hope more explicit later, at the end of the novel: she has successfully taken over the farm and accomplished what Anthony has failed to accomplish, when Anthony recovers from his stroke and wants to take charge again. Laura resents the intrusion into what she has come to consider her work; again what has become a satisfaction is denied her. She thinks,

> The time will come when men cease to despise women and women cease to resent men. They won't be enemies anymore; but they will be less warm lovers. It's the differences that keep men and women desiring each other, not the similarities. And when the differences are smoothed out and a sort of mid-sex arrived at—well, it will suit me excellently (274).

Laura Harden, née Campbell, M.A. Oxon., thus finds hope in the "mid-sex," a creature she here imagines to be only of her fantasy but whose lineaments come, perhaps, from her own experience at Oxford. This source is suggested by the juxtaposition here of the hermaphroditic fantasy with a wish for a bigger house so she "might have some of the old gang to stay," the old Oxford gang who, unlike her, have things to talk about beyond "infant diet and child management and servants" (147). This "mid-sex" which would suit Laura excellently seems an idea she associates with her college days and college friends. But she sees the futility of this wish; she would have nothing to say to them.

Other educated women, too, look back to college for ideas of what life could be. But these glimpses are brief, insubstantial, ironic, and without power to have prevented the fall into marriage and domesticity which is the fate of these women. In *Daughters*, for example, Isabel Pearce rejoices when her daughter goes off to college because then she will have room for visitors,

> mostly old college friends, who talked and talked, just as they had at college and renewed the youth of all concerned. Nearly all the friends were unmarried and still actively engaged in work at one University or other. . . . sometimes [these] friends made them sigh for their old haunts, where the newest thoughts of the best minds were being expressed every day (107).

The diction here—"just as they had at college," "old haunts"—and the ironic tone of the "newest . . . and best" impute a certain unreality to this life and imply that its adherents have not quite grown up, exactly the opinion about her writing and lecturing mother which the young Judith Pearce holds (15). In none of Wallace's texts does a vigorous intellectual life remain central to a woman's existence—at least not without rendering her incompetent (Isabel Pearce) or intolerable (Harriet in *Elegy*).

The suggestion that college life represents an imprisonment in immaturity is constantly reinforced by reference, almost always negative, to the female/female relationships that flourish there. If male/female relationships are marked by enmity and disgust, the alternative, the text suggests, is simply childish. When her father encourages her to teach in a large public school for girls, the eponymous protagonist of *Carlotta Green* realizes that he "had no idea how the very idea of a community of females revolted her . . . the pashes (or raves or schwarms), the pi-jaws, the petty rows, the turning of the old girls, by means of exaggerated responsibilities, into deaconesses before their time" (7). We have seen that Walter Campbell in *Elegy* attributes lesbianism to the thwarting, by women's colleges, of "normal" sexual development. In "Going to the Sea" Marie Lambert misses her "lover" when she comes home from college and is "sure that she needed nothing but the friendship of Celia to complete her life" (140). According to the text, she is of course wrong, as she discovers when she falls in love with a man, wrong because college has inhibited her development, as it has Audrey's in *Barnham Rectory*: "Like most young things devoted to learning . . . Audrey was late in developing physically. She knew a great deal at second hand about sex, because it was all part of learning, but she felt nothing, yet—had laughed at her swains, and on the whole preferred women" (159). Once she does experience heterosexual passion, she succumbs immediately, "surrendering unconditionally the Intellectual Woman" (282).

Katherine, the don in *Latter Howe*, thinks she must be somewhat attractive because "several of her girl-students had developed passions for her" (39) but, in her academic environment, she knows "about the sexual reactions commonly known as love" only "theoretically" (38). When she meets the young farmer Laity, however, she falls quickly in love and gives up her intellectual work. This theme is developed at some length in the earliest novel, *A Little Learning*. Olive's best friend at Oxford is Claire, who is "jealous of anyone who stared at Olive, like a man with his sweetheart" (77). But Olive, who has never before "been segregated from men, in a girls' boarding school, as has Claire" (59) is, at nineteen, more properly, the text implies, attracted to men and properly uncomfortable at "memories of being kissed by Claire" (19). When Olive comes back to Oxford after her brother has murdered Roger Dennison, only Claire befriends her, and "the two of them were left in an isolation made conspicuous by the sidelong looks of those who mistrusted young women of Claire's type" (250). Eventually Olive withdraws even from the attentive Claire, and Claire takes up with one of the younger students. Olive's hesitations about Claire, her discomfort over kisses and effusive letters, make clear that the relationship was never overtly sexual. Few of these "pashes" seem to be, unless like the "Piers set," the women continue in their sexual immaturity and do not make the transition to heterosexuality, which failure is the apparent danger of such female/female romances.

Martha Vicinus suggests that it was during and after World War I that the discourse of the sexologists, who gave an explicitly sexual vocabulary to the phenomenon of raves or pashes, began to impinge upon and then replace the prior discourse which, assuming asexuality, accepted and even praised romantic friendships (621). These Wallace texts make clear the sexual undertones of these relationships and deplore them accordingly, though almost all the girls involved eventually experience awakening to "normal" sexuality and marriage, after which, ironically, for most of these women sex becomes a mere formality or, if they are lucky, a source of amusement. For Wallace's women, then, female/female relationships are not alternatives to marriage but at best preambles, at worst hindrances, to adult—that is, heterosexual—relationships. Women, however, are then caught, imprisoned, oppressed by the marriage and motherhood that replaces romantic friendships, which, in Wallace's texts, do not endure. Marriage effectively separates women from one another and their only subsequent relationship becomes one of rivalry. The three young women who go off to London as flatmates in *Daughters*, though they are friends of a sort, establish no bonds but busy themselves in pursuing relationships with men. The adviser/advisee relationship between Margery Greene and Anne Blaythwaite in *The Time of Wild Roses* is based almost solely on preparation for marriage; it becomes superfluous after their respective marriages take place. In the late novel *Woman with a Mirror* there is something of a community among wives, though even there the topic of conversation is generally men or Reenie, the femme fatale.

Reenie is the uneducated woman, "so beautiful and so devoid of

brains" (123), who systematically wins the affection of all the husbands and forces her own husband "to move every few years to get
Reenie away from Men" (28). Helen Barraclough, described as "the
feminist," occasionally shifts the blame from Reenie "for the upsets
caused by beauty," but her friends tend to think that the men "can't
help it, poor things" (123). At the end of the novel, when Reenie is
dead, Helen feels guilty. "She and all these others had helped to kill
Reenie. A woman of right feeling might have guided the silly creature, or at all events tried to, long ago. But the women stood aside
because of jealousy" (189). Even this admission of guilt is not based
on any sense of female solidarity; Helen chides the women not for
not taking Reenie into their circle, but for not reforming her flirting
ways. When there is, in these texts, a group of women, it is unsuppor-
tive, superficial, and wholly unable to prevent death in its midst.

According to Wallace's texts, marriage oppresses and deadens,
but it is inevitable; relationships between two women indicate immaturity and must be abandoned; communities of women are insubstantial. What, then, is a woman to do? Doreen Wallace writes
novels, something most of her female protagonists are incapable of.
But even she, as subject of the autobiographical *In a Green Shade*,
longs for "the quick thrust-and-parry of good talk, the joyful recognition of a point of agreement, the keen hunt along the track of a
new line of thought, one talker helping the other. I have scarcely
ever had the opportunity of this exhilarating mental release, since I
came down from Oxford more than thirty years ago" (136). For
Wallace the female academic community provides the model for a
vigorous intellectual life but such a life can, for a woman, be only
temporary. Like her female characters, who are betrayed by bodily
desire into heterosexual relationships, the gardener-writer of *In a
Green Shade* falls into marriage "because no one could help marrying the Master's long eyelashes" (151). Hard work cures her and
other women if not entirely of bitterness at least of immature long-
ings: "We are living the lives of prisoners; we are too busy to repine"
(20). Though this autobiographical work is ostensibly about gardening, those operations Wallace performs in the garden are analogous to the operations she performs on her unruly self, the one that
looks back to Oxford or forward to independence. She complains
that the garden is too large—"I shall become a character long before I have succeeded in disciplining it in every part." She looks
forward here to old age when, like the garden, she will grow more

unruly: "a hobbing witch, passing my time between cobweb-hung house and bindweed-tangled garden, careless of disorder, doing nothing about it . . . save occasionally to pursue with eldritch screams some infant rabbit" (81). The present solution seems to be constant effort to eliminate the weeds along with resignation and patient waiting for a time when age makes such weeding super-fluous, when she can allow the lurking witch free reign. Bridget in *Land from the Waters* says, "it is obvious that to be happy in this life, all one needs is a narrow horizon, a world bounded by house and garden" (288). It is the only answer that the seventeenth-century Bridget can, on the basis of her own frustrating efforts to live an intellectual life, produce. Centuries later, after decades of women have worked for emancipation and freedom, Wallace's women, in-cluding her own persona, can offer nothing more hopeful. The al-leged Doreen Wallace character in *Gaudy Night*, Catherine Bendick, has the same sense of futility: "One's rather apt to marry into some-one else's job" (44), she tells Harriet Vane after describing her life as a farmer's wife: "Slumps and sickness and tithe and taxes and the Milk Board and the Marketing Board and working one's fingers to the bone and trying to bring up children." For Wallace's women "rather apt" is an understatement. There is really no escaping it.

Wallace's constant use in *In a Green Shade* of "the Master" to re-fer to her husband emphasizes this fatality: *He* is in control, not only of the farm, not only of his wife and children, but of the course of human life, especially when that human life is female. Bridget not only ruthlessly narrows her horizons or accepts the narrowing of her horizons but offers such narrowing as a prerequisite to hap-piness. She does so, however, "with an ironic twist of her beau-tiful, thin lips" (*Land from the Waters*, 288), an irony present perhaps in the use of "Master"; in the gardener's cheerful sacrifice of "travel, . . . elegant clothes and a fast car" (81); in her correction of herself when she says she has a farm: "at least, it is the Master's farm" (81). Even that enterprise around which her life revolves is the property of another, a job she, like Catherine Bendick, married into. When Harriet asks her if it was worth it, Mrs. Bendick replies, "Worth it? . . . Oh yes . . . the job was worth doing. One was serv-ing the land." Harriet infers the completion of the sentiment ". . . a service harsh and austere indeed, but a finer thing than spinning words on paper" (43).

We have seen that for many of Wallace's women, writing or art is indeed an almost superfluous activity, the need for which diminishes if one is involved in good, hard work on the land. The biographical blurb on the jacket of *In a Green Shade* claims that Doreen Wallace's "over twenty novels" and "several non-fictional works are written in odd moments, when work in house, garden, and fruitfields permits." The comment, which has the mark of being Wallace's own, combines well the distanced, practical attitude toward art and the intellectual life that permeates the novels and the edge of bitterness that, like the weeds in her garden, takes her unaware. At fifty she admits, in *In a Green Shade*, to being a heavy smoker (78), to being too tied to the farm even to seek relief from her arthritis (81), to finding hard her middle age, "that featureless tract of time when one has ceased to be active and attractive" (81), to knowing farms where "the cows are treated better than the wives" (75). This life, which on the one hand seems to her more "real" and valuable than the life of an intellectual or an artist, on the other hand takes its terrible toll even on the more prosperous of farm wives. Despite the toll, *Latter Howe's* Katherine thinks that motherhood has "something sweeter about it than donhood" (60). Bridget cries, "And oh, my little children, I'd not be without you! Who would choose between children and wit?" (*Land from the Waters*, 156) Laura forgets about writing when the farm work absorbs her and when she finds meaning in "the signs of earth and sky" (*God's Tenth*, 267). Tied down, worn out from childbirth and farm labor, old before their time, these women see the rewards of their situation as well as its inevitable self-destructive consequences, and, much as the life of the mind attracts them all, they think a more practical involvement must come first.

The chapter began with Wallace's impatience toward the modernist innovators: she wants to "get on with the story"; she wants something to happen. What Richardson and Woolf do not make happen is precisely the heterosexual, couple-based romance—harsh, inevitable, and death-dealing as, like Wallace, they sense it to be. But unlike Wallace's getting on with the story, women modernists' technical innovations not only break the story, as Rachel DuPlessis points out, but impute a certain value to the text itself and to its techniques. Stream-of-consciousness, as Wallace understands it, implies a validity to the meanderings of the mind and to its fictional correlative which Wallace does not admit. What she must do as a part-time writer, someone who sandwiches art between more urgent, more real concerns is to tell a story, in fact, to tell, again and again the story of the inevitable victory in women's lives of earth and body over mind. The very telling of the story, however, belies this, because, in good fairy-tale fashion, it keeps the teller alive—keeps her mind working and her sense of irony active on the one hand, and prevents her from being "a wife as a kept woman" (*In a Green Shade*, 151) on the other. Besides keeping her self and self-esteem alive, she must tell the story because it is the truth as she sees it. Its very repetition becomes a warning; its very insistence on the narrowing of one's horizons incites dissatisfaction with that narrow world "bounded by house and garden" and promotes recognition of its roots in a social system where the Master rules.

One of Wallace's women in *Even Such Is Time* admits that women cannot be "impersonal for five minutes together." "Is it because we have always had so much to do with the providing and scheming side of life, and with birth, and with laying-out the dead, and all that? I don't see any hope of change if that's so" (239). Though Wallace's women and perhaps Wallace herself see little hope of change, the repetition of the circumstances, the telling of the story of inevitable romance, alerts the reader to the problem and sends her in search of another story—the non-story of the modernists, perhaps, or the utopia of Sayers' community of women or the visionary tale of Jaeger's female savior. The excessive insistence on the "real," and its constant repetition, calls attention to the problems inherent in the story as surely as technical innovations and alternative genres, because it asks the central question, rhetorical as it is in Wallace's work, about the boundaries of a woman's life. Wallace poses this question most directly, most desperately, not through her fictional women but in her persona of a gardener dismayed by the proliferation of nettles and weeds in her plot. "But what," she asks, "can one woman do among acres of strong, malignant enemies?" (74)

7 Margaret Kennedy's
"Roundabout Way of Telling Things"

In a reworking of her pre–WWII journal, published in 1941 as *Where Stands a Wingèd Sentry*, Margaret Kennedy—that aloof Somervillian—describes a party at which

> there was a charming little person with a face like a kitten and very pretty curls. . . . She was one of those women who are like a nosegay of flowers in a room. I don't think she can have been under forty, she gave an impression of maturity and experience, but at the same time had an innocence, a naive, almost childish, freshness, which was quite delightful. I don't suppose she is a bit clever, but she succeeds at the job of being a woman (198).

She refers to this woman further on in the passage as "kittenface" (200). The puzzling mixture of disdain and admiration is underscored by the comment, "She is the kind of woman I would marry if I were a man" (198). Since she admits that in the conversation among the women at the party, "We . . . were slightly inclined to laugh at men" (198), it is difficult to assess the tone of the former statement. "If I were a man" might well suggest a condemnation of male preference, yet there is palpable pleasure in the "delightful" juxtaposition of "maturity" and "freshness" that Kennedy perceives in this not-a-bit clever woman.

Kennedy's best-selling novel of the late twenties, *The Constant Nymph*, likewise evinces pleasure in the innocent, the naive, the fresh. The text pits Teresa (Tessa), the charming little nymph, against Florence, the clever, the educated, the civilized. The two women love the same man, a careless, amoral musical genius, Lewis Dodd, who, momentarily blinded by admiring desire, marries Florence and then runs off with "constant" Tessa, who has loved him since she was a small child. The flight is fatal to the consumptive nymph, but the text lays the blame for her death not on Dodd, who has failed to notice her deteriorating health, but on Florence, whose cruelty toward her wears down Tessa's determination to be loyal to Florence and drives her to become Dodd's lover. Although Kennedy later characterized, wrongly I think, the conflict in her novel as one between "Art and Culture," she admitted that "Florence was not an effective advocate for culture" and that she, Kennedy, ended up spending "a great deal of time and pains, upon Florence's father, Charles Churchill, "who was called in to state the case [for culture] fairly" (Roberts, 49).

While Lewis Dodd may state the case for Art—as this text understands it, a kind of instinctive expression of natural genius—the educated woman cannot do the same for culture and education. The reader is left to puzzle over Florence's transformation from a sympathetic, if slightly officious, young woman to a woman so unjust and hostile that her own father is shocked and uncomprehending at her behavior. Although the two male adversaries, Lewis Dodd and Charles Churchill, pose for Tessa the "alternatives," Art and Culture, and indeed fight for her soul, in the end they become uneasy allies; it is Florence, the educated woman, who destroys her. Like Mary Whittaker's excessive violence in Sayers' *Unnatural Death*, Florence's excessive unkindness to the loyal, innocent Tessa suggests that the text has less to do with its purported subject and more to do with anxiety about the educated woman.

Unlike the female worlds of Sayers' texts or even the very doublesexed worlds of Wallace's, *The Constant Nymph's* milieu is remarkably male: the women run households in support of art and culture, but the patrons, the artists, and the scholars are men, whose bonds of sympathy extend to one another more strongly than any claims of love for or kinship with the female characters. The focus of

Florence's father's concern shifts easily from the happiness of his daughter and of Tessa herself to the future of Dodd: "If he had married little Teresa she would have made a man of him, whereas mated with Florence he was nothing but a calamity" (229), an observation which implies the ubiquitous fear that the educated woman emasculates. Like the charming woman whom Kennedy would have married, Tessa is, unlike emasculating Florence, "little" and naive. She poses no threat to male hegemony or the primacy of male bonds, both so much a part of her childhood, unconventional as that childhood appears on the surface.

Her father, the great musician and composer, Albert Sanger, jokes that he will "initiate a disciplinary system" to keep the female children in line. "I'll thrash all the girls for half an hour every morning." He develops his plan by including the male children as fellow thrashers: "If the men of the family cooperate, we may manage to introduce a little order into the household. Caryl shall beat Kate" (50). He is not seriously proposing such a regime, but the assumption of male rule and solidarity makes the joke possible. The Sanger household, presented as charmingly bohemian, has become, though isolated and nearly inaccessible, a gathering place for the lights of the musical world, all of them male. Lewis Dodd, the composer, is Sanger's protegé; Jacob Birnbaum, who seduces one of the Sanger girls, a patron; Trigorin, a sycophantic, rich admirer. The children, born to a large number of mothers (now absent) and known collectively as "Sanger's Circus", had all received "a good, sound musical training" (3), but only the sons inherit Sanger's musical genius. The daughters are acceptable singers and discriminating listeners but devoted to the men rather than to the music.

Though the girls are fond of one another, like other women they, in this text, never question their eventual separation from one another and eventual attachment, however inexplicable, however self-destructive, to a man. Sanger's last "wife," Linda, wholly isolated in her stupidity and placidity, has "a sorrow," a vision of herself as "an enormous old woman, starving to death" (60). In spite of their valuable functions the females of Sanger's household have no future and no security. Their attachment to the men is fated rather than a matter of choice, is unquestioned and unquestioning. The wives have no funds, the daughters neither funds nor genius. Linda is simply there in the first part of the novel. Sanger has no interest in her beyond a possessiveness that manifests itself as "insane jealousy" (24), and he disdains their child, Susan, a "plebeian-looking brat, pink and formless as a wax doll" (24). Yet Linda has continued to live with Sanger for eight years completely without emotional nourishment, that is, "starving to death." The most important male-female attachment in the novel, the constant love of Tessa for Lewis Dodd, is equally inexplicable. Early in the novel, she laughs at Lewis's ill-treatment of Trigorin. "Teresa's mirth, however, was a little forced; she found herself wishing, absurdly, that Lewis had been kind to the poor fat person. . . . As if Lewis was ever kind to anybody!" (21) She fears him, "yet she loved him very completely—better than anyone else in the whole world. . . . She was inclined to regard these uneasy qualms [about Lewis's character] as peculiar to her age, like . . . growing pains" (21). Teresa cannot help loving Dodd, though she knows well that he is thoughtless at best, cruel at worst. Even when they are together, he is virtually absent and absorbed in his art. When she runs off with him, the stewardesses on the Channel boat ask, "Mademoiselle is alone? She has no friends?" (301) Not only has she been alienated from Florence on account of her constant love for Florence's husband, but the union with Dodd itself leaves her isolated.

Even the rational Florence's attraction to Dodd is inexplicable. Like a Wallace heroine she succumbs to the "pleasant languor" (176) of her sexual desire for him, which results in "a new uncertainty, a sensation of never knowing her own mind about anything" (164). Although Florence is at first fond of all the Sanger children, her love for Dodd soon puts them out of her mind and eventually make her turn on Tessa. When Dodd leaves Florence the first time, her friend Millicent listens to Florence's attempt to cover up for him "with a little smile," obviously enjoying Florence's discomfiture, as these women always seem to enjoy one another's small pains. While the men in the novel have a certain understanding of and respect for one another, a certain cameraderie, the women, in their isolation and single-minded devotion to their men, see one another primarily as rivals and treat one another with hostility.

The educated, rational woman, though as thoroughly indoctrinated as her uneducated sisters with the lessons of the romantic plot, disrupts this male-centered world. When Florence arrives at the Sanger household to take charge (after Sanger's death) of the children, some of whom are her cousins, she finds "the young Sangers quite charming" (100) unlike her Uncle Robert who thinks

that they are barbarians and that Sanger was as "a perfectly unculti-
vated savage"—thus implying the alliance of art and nature (81).
Florence's reply, that she likes "children of Nature" (81), is indicative of the tolerance with which she at first accepts the chaos, the
family, and the unkempt, awkward Lewis Dodd. But Florence is
a reformer. Though she finds children of nature attractive, she,
graduate of Cleeve College and resident of Cambridge cannot but
believe in education and civilized behavior. Her own relationship
with Lewis Dodd is a model of such behavior. Her attraction to him
may be irrational, but she meets him just after she had decided, rationally, that the excitement of post-college life "had gone on long
enough" and that "she would settle down to some serious work, or,
if she could find a man to her taste, she would marry" (82). Unlike
the naive nymph whose love for Dodd is constant, unexamined,
and uncalculated, Florence is prepared to enter a new phase, prepared to marry and settle down—prepared, that is, to fall in love.
The irrationality of that state is thus circumscribed by rational decision and preparation even though she can resist the artist as little as
Wallace can resist the Master.

Unlike Teresa, whose realizations of Dodd's unkindness seem
to her as natural and irrelevant as growing pains, Florence must
actively suppress her qualms about "his essential hardness, [her]
knowledge that this man who held her so close was indeed no
tender lover but a stranger, as cold as ice and harder than a stone"
(143). Florence's own hardness, associated, as we will see, with her
education at Cleeve, intrudes on and is incompatible with Dodd's
hardness, which is emblematic of the intransigence required of a man
in service of art. As Florence's father perceives, such hardness requires the infinite pliability of Teresa's innocence and unquestioning
devotion rather than the assertive dominance of Florence's experience and conscious devotion. The characters in the novel without
exception excuse, as the reader is invited to excuse, the hardness of
Sanger and Dodd on the grounds of their genius. Florence, on the
other hand, is condemned for her hardness. After Teresa's death,
Jacob is "amazed and a trifle shocked at [Florence's] composure"
(321); he meets "cold competency where he had expected distress
and indignation, he was relieved but not happy" (322). Jacob's
shock and unhappiness at finding hardness in Florence incline the
reader to judge her harshly and indicate, again, the sort of disrup-
tion the educated woman represents.

Florence, educated and civilized, does nothing, not even fall in love, with Teresa's unconscious fervor. Significantly, Florence, product of Cleeve College, sends Teresa there to be civilized, to learn, that is, to become conscious. Cleeve was, appropriately, founded by "a hard-bitten lady who apparently believed that a uniform and most desirable type can be produced by keeping eight hundred girls perpetually upon the run. . . . Miss Helen Butterfield, her successor, modified the syllabus and shortened the hours of work, but the girls still ran" (197). Florence's decisiveness and energy reflect Cleeve's influence and contrast sharply both with the lethargy of the stupid Linda and the casual unconsciousness of Teresa. To teach Teresa to run is to unsuit her to what the text implies is her fate as Dodd's partner, to give her a hard edge which will not easily conform to men's needs. Dodd is thus jealous of Teresa's affection and admiration for Miss Helen Butterfield. He dislikes the "new, thoughtful hardening about her eyes and mouth" (198) and is delighted when she runs away from Cleeve.

In the novel, then, two kinds of hardness appear: the hardness that nature bestows on male geniuses to keep them faithful to their art, a hardness that requires pliability and wholehearted submission on the part of the women who love them; and the hardness that civilization and education develop in women, making them, who are not themselves geniuses—genius in women this odd text will not allow—unfit even to serve genius. The "hard-bitten" foundress of Cleeve has passed on hardness to her successor, Miss Butterfield, who, like Florence, "whatever happened to her . . . would always know exactly how to behave" (194). Miss Butterfield has passed it on to Florence and, almost, to the constant nymph. What the female community, such that it is, does in this text is to harden, to make less malleable, to spoil. Instead of the light "windblown locks" which Dodd "used to twist and play with" (199), Tessa comes home from Cleeve with a "horrid braid that slapped her back" (198) and even when she loosens her hair it now looks "sleek and heavy" (199). From lightness to heaviness, from pliability to hardness, the half-educated Teresa has changed as a result of her months at Cleeve, the school which formed Florence and which Florence finds so congenial. Now married to Florence, Dodd refuses, in spite of Florence's insistence, to send Tessa back. He prefers her uncivilized ways, ways Florence's father notes carefully. He thinks she fits in "almost like Lewis's belonging"; furthermore, she "nicely" performs the role of his wife; she makes tea for his guests, she fetches lunch; "her chief business was to minister to them", though her hospitality has no "polish" (228) like that of the civilized, educated Florence. Daily contact between the two women turns the initially sympathetic Florence away from her young cousin. Florence becomes jealous of the obvious bond between Dodd and Tessa; she is not "going to be cut out, in her own drawing-room, by an unformed schoolgirl" (230). In the presence of Tessa's "natural" behavior, Florence becomes more adamant in her efforts to civilize her genius-husband. Dodd revolts against such efforts, against, that is, his educated wife's increasing hardness.

The complicated relationships in this triangle and their shifting grounds are illuminated when Florence's father begins to pay attention to Teresa and to sympathize with her plight. Like Dodd, he prefers to his daughter the charming nymph, the "virgin soil" (226) uncorrupted by Cleeve, that place he suspects "was full of earnest, cultivated women who read Robert Browning and wanted degrees" (225). Teresa, on the other hand, has eschewed this female educational community and turned to Florence's father for her education. She wants him to give her "a thorough classical grounding" (225); she is eager to please him. When she orders his breakfast, she asks for the big cups because "Men always like them" (220). So pleased is he that he gives her money, a belated birthday present, to buy herself "something pretty" (220). She buys an orange luster bowl, which Florence admits is very beautiful and good" (248) and which suggest Tessa's taste for civilization, developed during the months at Cleeve. Charles is pleased but taken aback by the object because it seems to him "strange . . . that Teresa should ever own anything so concrete as a bowl" (248). Dodd is simply annoyed by the purchase. This hard yet female object embodies his fear of the Teresa who went to Cleeve College, the Teresa who has, temporarily at least, achieved distance from him and offers resistance to him. She has refused at this point to run away with him. Dodd breaks the bowl— "Charles could never quite make up his mind if it was an accident" (249)—because "Bowls lead to houses" (248). The bowl, though round and feminine, is nevertheless a hard thing which will lead to other hard things, larger, more angular and symbolic of stability and civilization. But perhaps the most threatening aspect of the orange luster bowl is Florence's admiration of it. Critical of and nasty to Teresa though Florence has become, the bowl both signifies and creates a bond between the women, who appreciate its shapely feminine beauty. Dodd's breaking it not only puts a definitive end to Tessa's pretensions to education and culture but damages irreparably the already fragile relationship between Florence and Teresa. Florence eventually recognizes that she has been unfair to Tessa. The possibility frightens her: she thinks she may leave the house which "had witnessed too much of the wreckage, the gradual disintegration of the old, civilized self, and the emergence of the untutored creature who talked as she had just been talking" (239). The use of "untutored" here implies the difference between Charles and Lewis Dodd's attitude toward education for women and Florence's. Though on opposite sides of the art versus culture debate, they agree that the female educational community corrupts and hardens, divests a woman of that naiveté and spontaneous self so charmingly devoted to men. Both men have come, therefore, to prefer the fresh, unspoiled nymph to Florence. For Florence, however, the unconscious, unformed self, far from being charming and fresh, is dangerous, irrational, and out of control. It is tutoring which creates the civilized self, the self which is kind, rational, and competent. Florence's jealousy of and resentment toward Tessa erupts finally in a scene so nasty and primitive that Tessa refuses to tell Dodd about it. The last vestige of her female loyalty, gained, one imagines, at Cleeve, prevents her; she will not tell "Because . . . women oughtn't to . . . to tell men . . . about each other" (311). But the scene has convinced Tessa, too, that education is a bad thing. "Uncle Charles might prate about the merit of civilized life, but there was no safety in it. If Florence, who had seemed so beautiful and good, was really like this, there was no safety in it" (286). Teresa, unused to "controlled animosity" (285), finds Florence, "this horrible woman who looked like an angel and talked like a devil" (286), incomprehensible and frightening. The cruelty in Dodd and in Sanger, her father, she can accept as natural—they are, after all men—but this emergence of cruelty in the ostensibly kind Florence terrifies her. The luster bowl, broken to slivers, has like Pandora's box unleashed evil, here Florence's, uncontrolled and uncontrollable. Her education has been as fragile and superfluous as the bowl, which Tessa does not replace in spite of the five-pound note Charles gives her for that purpose. Tessa thus acquiesces in Dodd's desire for a woman without pretensions or possessions.

"We must find a little coffin to put the remains in" (250), says

Teresa of the broken bowl. While the fragments are to be treated with respect, they will be buried, a fitting end for the pieces of a civilization which, on the one hand, traps and domesticates genius and, on the other, is ineffective in keeping the "untutored creature" at bay. Its destructiveness has, however, already affected the fragile Teresa. Florence's hard words, her "stony, vindictive head" (285) drive the nymph to rescind her refusal to run off with Lewis Dodd. Like the poor victims of Medusa, whom Florence so resembles in her fierce attack, Tessa cannot withstand the gaze, and the first night the couple spends together, in Brussels, Tessa dies. This casting of the educated woman as mythical monster suggests again the fear implicit in the Oxford debates and there, too, often expressed in mythical terms. But unlike *Gaudy Night*, which buries Harriet's "ancient dread of Artemis" and of shrews, this text shares those fears of the monster who drives the nymph—the natural, light, charming, unthreatening woman—to her death.

Dodd responds to Tessa's death by being inconsolable and irrational, a response which points to the source of the educated woman's monstrousness: her rationality. Jacob Birnbaum, who has accompanied Florence to Brussels in pursuit of Dodd, sympathizes with Dodd's irrational behavior, the more so when he remembers "the inordinate rationality of the lady upstairs" (325). Florence, though shocked by Teresa's death, takes charge of the situation, acts when no one else can, and plans for the future. "You'll think I'm hard," she writes to her father. Florence's hard, monstrous rationality triumphs over Tessa's fragility, but by such hardness the educated, civilized Florence loses the sympathy of every character in the novel and, presumably, of most readers as well. The novel ends with Jacob's wishing himself at home with his wife Tony, Teresa's sister, who when she hears his news will "sob and cry and turn to him for comfort" (326). For all her spite and immaturity, Tony is at least a woman who turns to her husband for consolation, who breaks down in the face of tragedy, who relies on men to provide the hardness necessary to carry on. Florence does none of these. While Jacob had envisioned himself as "the only practical person at hand, dealing with doctors and policemen" (321), it is, in fact, Florence who takes over. In all her competent efficiency, she is a threat to the male world into which she inserts herself so resolutely, in which she demands accommodation. Unlike Teresa, whose "chief business" at the tea party is to "minister" to men, Florence wants men "to consider her as one of themselves" (230). They bestow this favor on the unassuming nymph but refuse it to the confident, hard woman. Admission to this world is, for women, by invitation only. The educated woman, then, is less suited to life in the (male) world than the uneducated one, who at least succumbs gracefully to its demands for self-effacement and pliability.

The text's attempt to contrast art and culture fails, in part because art and culture are strange opponents and art and nature strange allies. Neither the opposition nor the alliance can be logically or philosophically sustained. Even for those "natural" geniuses Sanger and Dodd, musical education and the musical world itself, such an obvious product of civilization, have made their work possible. This failure is, however, made worse by the difference, unacknowledged by the text, that gender makes *in* the text. Florence cannot properly present to Tessa a case for civilization because as a woman Florence is inevitably involved in the rivalry of heterosexual romance, seen here not as ideological construct, but as nature—and thus inimical to civilization. Sanger and Dodd cannot properly present the case for Art to Tessa because she, as a woman, has only a secondary role in that world. Florence marvels when Tessa dies that Tessa has "escaped from life so easily" (323). Without conferring on her the hardness of either genius or education, the text loses her, in her soft malleability, altogether, and leaves us with Florence, named for a center of art and culture, intent on a kind of sinister artistry as she resolves, with the inconsolable Dodd "completely in her hands" to "build upon wrecked love a monument of worthy achievement" (323).

Kennedy's text is not, then, so much about the conflict between art and culture as about the conflict between the natural and the unnatural woman. Much less ambivalent than *Unnatural Death*, however, *The Constant Nymph* for the most part allies itself with the natural woman—envisioned here as a nymph, so close is she to nature itself. And nature, in this text, includes the heterosexual romance, that is, the natural sequence of a woman's life. So long as this sequence is perceived as part of nature, so long, that is, as the heterosexual romance remains the unquestioned center of women's existence, the educated woman must be enemy to it, must seem unnatural. We have seen that nature in this text includes art, which holds the same place in the lives of genius-men as romance does in the lives of women. So long as art remains male territory, the educated woman must remain enemy to it, too. Driven by forces she does not recognize and could not change even if she did, the educated woman, the text illustrates, tries to trap and mold the artist just as she has trapped and molded herself.

In Kennedy's later novels, however, women themselves become artists and no longer serve simply as artists' wives, lovers, and servants. With this serious consideration of the female artist comes the inevitable recognition that the heterosexual romance is not destiny, not fulfillment, but burden and that the fictive scripts, far from being the "true" stories of women's lives, are monolithic lies men tell to protect themselves from female power. Nicola Beauman, in her introduction to the Virago reprint of Kennedy's first novel, *The Ladies of Lyndon*,[1] notes that "there is an element of contempt, certainly not of sympathy, in her descriptions of subjugated women. It is the rebels, the Sangers . . . of this world, who have her sympathy" (xvii). When, however, the Sangers, the rebel artists, become female, the texts' sympathies become much more engaged with the "subjugated woman," and the basis of the subjugation becomes a focus of attention.

In *Not in the Calendar*, published in the sixties and dedicated to a Somerville friend, the heroine, a deaf-mute, is an incipient artist. Carrie, her only friend, interprets her sounds and gestures. One day as the two girls play by a pond, Carrie "translates,"

> I can almost hear what you say. Little girls choose best sticks. Not so impatient. Put them in carefully. Girls boats sail away. Boy boats sink. That makes boys angry, They throw stones. Sink girl boats. Say not real boat. Only girl boats. Men say that, when we do anything (110).

Such analysis, which earlier texts use ironically and thereby imply the relative triviality of such complaints, becomes poignant in the words of a girl whose physical handicaps mirror her isolated status as a woman artist. The subtitle of this late novel is "The Story of a Friendship." Not only has the woman become an artist, she has become an artist nurtured by another woman, Carrie, the only person with whom Wyn can relax enough to make herself understood.

Even more dramatically different in both theme and sympathy from the earlier novels, *The Heroes of Clone*, published in 1957, portrays not only the struggles of a woman artist, here a writer, but also the misunderstanding and misreading her work engenders precisely because she *was* a woman. In this novel, a British broadcasting company (B.B.B.) has planned to film the life of Dorothea Harding, a nineteenth-century novelist whose childhood creation of a fictional world, Clone, asserts her relationship to the Brontë sisters, whose name recalls the similarly exploited heroine of *Middlemarch*, and whose personal mystery suggests kinship to Emily Dickinson. Poet/critic Alec Mundy, the playwright Adelaide, and Dorothea's descendants all have different versions of her life and work. Mundy has framed an elaborate scenario in which this author of "prissy books for kids" (12) has a passionate affair with her sister's husband. Mundy's book, the young filmmaker Roy says, "explains what poets really mean and how they get to write their poetry. He got hold of this diary and wrote a book proving that D. Harding was only able to write poetry because all this happened to her" (12). Mundy has little respect for Harding's work and subscribes to the theory that women write out of frustrated love and inhibited sex lives. He sees, therefore, the mysterious "G." of the diaries as Harding's brother-in-law Grant. Adelaide in turn becomes fascinated with Mundy's romantic story and writes it up as a screen play. So long as she envisions Harding's life as a romance narrative, she can weave her superficial fictions of romantic love. But as she begins to identify with Harding as a writer, her suspicions that the story is not true increase. When she suggests to Mundy, for example, that there had never been any such affair, he exclaims, "My dear lady! Passionate love poems. A perfectly inexperienced woman could never have written them" (230). A perfectly inexperienced woman herself, Adelaide senses the falseness of his assumptions. Like Dorothea Harding, she is, she realizes, an object of Mundy's scorn. When he says to her, "I had no idea . . . that you took yourself seriously" (232), Adelaide feels "as though he had spat in her face" and while she admits his right to think her work bad, she's sure that "nobody . . . nobody at all . . . has the right to say that!" (232)

Two problems of the woman artist emerge in this conflict between Mundy and Adelaide. Mundy, representing the male literary establishment, refuses to take the woman writer seriously. He does not believe that either Harding or Adelaide takes her own writing seriously, an assumption which leads directly to his misreading of a central text in Harding's poetic canon:

160

Kennedy's Roundabout Way

A ghost stands o'er the bridal bed
Of every wedded maid.
And, like a wail above the dead,
It cries: I was betrayed.

Her broken vows, her ravished truth
Lie in the grave with me.
I was the first love of her youth,
And my creator she.

Because of his conviction that man and not art is the center of a woman's life, he takes the seventh line literally and concludes that the "first love of her youth" was Grant. The discovery of some letters, however, makes clear that it is the eighth line which is to be taken literally. The G. of the diaries is not Grant but Gabriel, the hero of Clone. Like her sister, who abandoned her early creativity for marriage and family, Dorothea betrayed art to domestic duty and in the poem expressed regret for her betrayal of that art, represented by the ghost.

Mundy does not, furthermore, take the works themselves seriously. He scorns the prissy novels as he scorns Adelaide's popular and romantic screenplays. In doing so he overlooks any merit the books may have and overlooks as well the nature of the strictures which encourage women to write in popular genres. A letter from Harding's cousin Effie to her husband, who a hundred years before similarly criticized Dorothea's novels, reminded him that he "allowed that parts of The Children's Crusade are very striking . . . you exclaimed over it when you read it. . . . You said then that parts were so good as almost to compensate for holy little Ulrica converting so many Turks" (240). Mundy's literary snobbery makes him unable to appreciate the striking, the vivid parts of Harding's work and it insures the continuation of Harding's reputation as second-rate.

A more serious impediment to discovering the "truth" about Harding's life is Mundy's refusal to acknowledge the conditions under which she wrote, under which nineteenth-century women wrote. Framed by the narrative of contemporary events (that is, the intrigues involved in the filming of the screenplay) in this text is another narrative, which tells the nineteenth-century story of Dorothea and her family. There we discover that Dorothea started out as a poet and storyteller, perhaps of the first rank, but that events conspired to convince her to give up poetry and to tell prissy stories. Unlike most female children, Dorothea had considerable freedom as a child. She and her sister Mary "did as they pleased, unharrassed by warnings concerning all the prison bars awaiting them with womanhood" (69). The prison bars, nevertheless materialized. Mary had to give up her creative activity to take over the household and when she married, these duties—which included serving as literary secretary to her father and waiting on her brother Philip, his wife Selina, and their child—fell to Dorothea. At first she rebelled at the prison bars. She tried to explain to her brother Bob the injustice of her position. Women, she argued, "could support ourselves if we were given the opportunity; if the professions were open to us. Cottage women . . . have more freedom than we have, I think, and more self-respect. . . . It is only ladies . . . you keep us, yes! As you might keep animals" (126). In an attempt to wrest some time for herself and her work, Dorothea had left the house one day and returned to find that Katy, her spoiled and probably retarded niece, had disappeared, and that Selina, Katy's mother, had been so distraught that she had had a miscarriage. Since Selina had supposedly left Katy in Dorothea's charge, everyone blamed Dorothea for the turn of events. In response, she sacrificed writing to her housekeeping duties.

Suspicions about the effects of Dorothea's poetic activity had, however, begun long before the disappearance of Katy and her subsequent reappearance, unharmed in a closet. No one approved of her writing. Bob, though he liked her verse, was convinced that "women can't write poetry" (106) and Mr. Winthorpe, the local clergyman, thought "that this poetry, more than anything, is likely to come between Thea [Dorothea] and God" (106). Winthorpe's increasingly severe judgments on Dorothea's attempts to write were, like Bob's, gendered judgments. Dorothea, first of all, wrote verses which clearly rivalled his own and so threatened his assumed superiority; second, she "inspired sensations which he could not feel to be entirely pure and [she] affronted him by her innocence" (136), and, finally, she failed to evince any interest in him as a man, a possible husband. His response to this provoking situation was "the desire to crush her, subdue her, see her at his feet"—a desire shared in one way or another by Dorothea's father, brothers, and even sister-in-law, whose own prison bars made her resent any small freedom of Dorothea's. That "Thea," the female god, should overcome the man of god disrupts the "natural" hierarchy of his world. In the end, however, Dorothea agreed out of guilt and a sense of

duty to give up her writing, to "do everything I can for poor Selina
and little Katy" (140); she furthermore came to regret having allowed Mary to do all the household work. "I ought to have helped
her more, and then perhaps she would not have married at all"
(139). Dorothea recognized, rightly, that Mary married Grant, in
part at least, to get away from the Harding house and her duties
there. Even in this submission to her duty, then, Dorothea's motives were not the "proper" ones that Winthorpe hoped for. Instead
of taking over the household to ease the burdens of men, she did it
to make the women's lives less burdensome. Mr. Winthorpe realized
angrily that although she finally agreed to give up "men's" work,
"she sought guidance from no man and was governed by the dictates of her own lawless heart" (140).

When Bramstock, the family estate, was in danger of being lost,
the males changed their minds about Dorothea's writing and convinced her to return to her work—in order to bring in enough
money to save their home. Mr. Winthorpe "practically stood over
her while she wrote" (169); he told her not to read reviews lest they
make her vain but used to pass on any adverse criticism which he
thought might be good for her. He even scolded her "for wanting to
take too much trouble over her work, and not being satisfied with
it. He said if her books were written in good English, and had a
moral, and were marketable, they had justified their purpose. . . .
They must never be an end in themselves, or they might tempt her
to vanity and self-indulgence" (171).

Dorothea saved Bramstock with her prissy novels and was scolded
in the process for wanting to write them well. Cecilia Harding,
Dorothea's great niece whose Oxford career hinges on the sale of
the rights to the screenplay, has, like early Kennedy texts themselves, little sympathy for the subjugated woman and is unmoved by
the "Victorian . . . orgies of priggishness" (171) which influenced
Dorothea's prissy texts. Mundy, the biographer, understands so
little of these gender-based economic and moral forces that he
adopts the same attitude toward Adelaide's work that Winthorpe
adopted toward Dorothea's. Cecilia's judgment that the Victorians
"were like that, in those days" (171) overlooks the similarity of the
contemporary situation in which the literary establishment, represented by Mundy (the likeness of whose name to *mundi*, "of the
world" in Latin, suggests that this attitude is not confined to the
literary establishment) still attempts to explain away the writing

of women of the past and to scorn the writing of women of the present. That Cecilia must depend on Dorothea's story to finance her education results from the same attitude toward women's work and education: her family has not hesitated to squander money on trifles and on her sister's season in London but has nothing left for "the only clever one in the family" (223).

The person who sympathizes most with Dorothea is the struggling film-maker Roy. He uncovers fragments of her story, including the explanation of "G."; he defends her to Cecilia. He does, in fact, identify his own struggles with hers and sees himself "swimming, sinking, fighting for life in the same inclement ocean" (174). What appears to be a welcome diminishment of gender polarization here ultimately is not, because he cannot see the difference that gender makes. Although he scolds Cecilia for her condescension toward her great-aunt—"I daresay she'd have liked to go to college. But she seems to have spent her life doing chores, poor girl" (173)—he has no understanding of the gender-based difficulties of Cecilia's own life. Roy's aunt, May Turner, does. Cecilia, she says, was "sent to a silly snob school, where the teaching was wretched. Any education she's got she's given to herself; can you wonder if she's a bit conceited and egotistical? She got that [partial Oxford] scholarship by sheer determination and hard work" (223). Like her sister, Cecilia has been schooled for charm. Even the Victorians Dorothea and Mary had a better education: "Not only could they read French, German, and Italian, they knew Latin and Greek. Their father, who had been preparing to write a book on the Homeric Age . . . wished them to learn the classics, in order that they might be useful to him" (169). The times, the text suggests, have not changed so much from those of Milton and the Victorians. Women of Cecilia's generation are educated to make them attractive and helpful to men just as Victorian women were. And, of course, the rhetoric bears significant similarity to that of the degrees-for-women debate of Kennedy's college years. Ironically enough, it is Adelaide's screenplay, which embodies assumptions of women's limitations, that is supposed to pay for Cecilia's Oxford education.

The screenplay, however, is not to be. Once Adelaide, Dorothea's other champion, begins to see the falsity of Mundy's theories, she refuses to release the play. Adelaide, says Roy, "puts us all to shame . . . I haven't heard her say one word about how hard it is on her. She's so keen to get it put right, and the picture stopped and the truth published, she even talks of giving back all the money she got for the rights" (281). In her refusal to tell a false story, Adelaide refuses to compromise women's art, either her own or Dorothea's, and refuses besides to tell again the romantic story with which she has made her reputation.

Roy, for all his artistic pretensions, for all his innate feeling for the Harding story, does not have Adelaide's integrity. "It's always better," he says, "not to stick your neck out" (281) and he has little interest in Dorothea's writing; he is interested in Dorothea only to the extent that she mirrors *him*. He begins one of her novels, but "the form of the narrative had irritated him. . . . In the course of far too much time, this person [the consumptive narrator] obligingly confided the story of his life to the invalid, who confided it to the reader. Such a roundabout way of telling things struck Roy as unnecessary" (233). Roy's sentiment here is most obviously an impatience with the common nineteenth-century frame. But Dorothea's indirect, framed narrative has another dimension. Framed herself, she could not be direct; assured that her writing came between her and God, that her duty was service to the household, she renounced the fictional world which had been her creation and her life; told to write for money, to ignore the demands of art, to make her work moral, she used a frame structure and Gothic conventions not only to cater to the demands of the public but as strategies for haunting her text with fragments of the story she wanted to tell. We have seen that these fragments worked, that there was life, energy, and vividness in her books that transcended the moral tales Winthorpe and failing finances forced her to tell. Cecilia, critical as she is of her great-aunt's life, appreciates the literature: "Her Sparta is completely convincing. . . . And the battle! It's terrific. You hear the shouts echoing from the cliffs. You smell it. You see the sort of steam from sweating bodies hanging in the air above it" (167). Roy, in love with Dorothea Harding because she embodies his own struggles as a young film-maker, is distracted by the roundabout narrative and his own narcissism from hearing, smelling, and seeing Dorothea's work, while Cecilia, herself a master of indirection, has access to the work's vitality.

Roy's impatience with Dorothea's strategies is paralleled by his impatience with Cecilia's. Torn between not wanting Mundy's sordid tale about her great-aunt made public and needing the money to supplement her hard-earned scholarship, Cecilia tells Roy stories which are not always perfectly true, and leaves out important stories which are. "Trust her," Roy thinks, "not to play anything straight" (280). Though he himself suggests that Cecilia's uncle tell a false story about how he acquired Dorothea's letters—a false story designed especially to avert Roy's employer's wrath—Roy leaves the Harding house without saying good-bye to Cecilia, who has fallen in love with him, because he judges her a liar. He leaves Bramstock thinking not of her nor even particularly of Dorothea but of what "story" he should tell about his part in the whole affair: "Should he be recalled to London he must have some plausible story ready, or suffer for it" (290). Annoyed by the indirection of Dorothea and of Cecilia, he plots his lies and so leaves the sympathy of the reader more with the women, artists manquée, than with the clearly talented male artist, so similar to the artist-heroes of Kennedy's early texts.

The reader has, however, been predisposed to sympathy for Cecilia by May Turner, Roy's initially doting aunt, who begins to realize that Roy, being male, has had many more advantages than she, than her companion Alice, even than Cecilia. Roy complains to May about how little he earns at B.B.B. When May gets home, she asks Alice to guess his salary. "Ten pounds?" The answer is twenty-five. "Never in the course of their hard and useful lives, had May or Alice earned as much as this" (219). Annoyed at this discrepancy and slightly piqued that he has borrowed money from her, May regrets that, in a hasty moment, she informed Roy of one of Cecilia's half lies (222). She sees Cecilia suddenly as "a vulnerable young creature, hovering perhaps upon the brink of destiny" (224), irrevocably hurt by the accusation. May's increasing sympathy for Cecilia and decreasing sympathy for Roy are indications to the reader to judge likewise. The Florence-like Cecilia, then, far from becoming excessively hard and heartless, becomes, though ostensibly "hard as nails," "rather touching, somehow" (222) in her confusion over the film, her affection for Roy, and, most important, her personal struggle for education.

Like her great-aunt Dorothea, Cecilia tells her story in a roundabout way. At first mistrustful of Roy, later wanting his approval too much, herself caught between the promises of Oxford and the good name of her family, Cecilia does not always tell the truth. At first unsympathetic to her problematic relative Dorothea, Cecilia believes Mundy's version of Harding's life and professes to think little

of her work—"unutterable rubbish, but full of vitality" (35). But
Cecilia, unlike Roy, has read the novels; she can quote the poems;
she has no respect for Mundy's critical acumen: "If he reads a line
like: 'My heart leaps up when I behold/A rainbow in the sky,' he
thinks it's evidence of some remarkable abnormality. *His* heart
doesn't leap up in that maladjusted way" (38). Like Roy, Mundy
reads texts and people only through himself. Cecilia respects her
aunt's critic even less than she respects her aunt's fiction, but in admitting the latter to be full of vitality and in her appreciation of her
aunt's poetry, she is open to Roy's discoveries about Dorothea's life.
What she loves most about Roy, in fact, is his passionate defense of
her aunt. After he tells the Hardings what he has discovered about
this remarkable woman, Cecilia goes to her room and lies on her
bed, "sobbing, not from grief but from sheer intensity of feeling.
Roy's voice, when speaking of Dorothea, had been too much for
her" (284). This hint of female bonding parallels and revises the
male bonding so pervasive in *The Constant Nymph*. The sympathy
between Cecilia and her great aunt, along with May's increasing
sympathy for Cecilia's plight, again suggests a significant shift in
Kennedy's vision: the world of *The Heroes of Clone* is decidedly
female-centered.

In spite of Cecilia's snobbery about Dorothea Harding, she evinces
a certain sympathy for her all along and comes more and more to
seem a modern counterpart. Roy defends Dorothea to the family in
terms that could easily apply to the niece as well—"She never
wanted to write all those stories, she was forced into it, because
they needed money" (276). Without money of their own, women
must tell stories, especially their own stories, in roundabout ways.
Roy can understand this about Dorothea, but he cannot forgive
Cecilia for feeling the same. He can identify his own struggles with
Dorothea's: "And I know," he tells the Hardings, "how hard it is for
anybody young . . . to be young and want to do your own work,
when the whole world seems to be saying: 'You can't. You never
will!' And she was very young. She was only a girl" (276). Roy does
not, however, see that things were even worse when she got older.
Unlike him, she had no future to look forward to. Nor can he identify Cecilia's struggles with Dorothea's, though she, too, is "only a
girl." Aunt May alone recognizes Cecilia's snobbery and cynicism to
be a result of her struggle to do her own work.

Dorothea had died, "crying for Clone, and calling herself a traitor" (276). The only thing left of Clone is the vividness of Harding's writing and a picture of "Fountainhall" which her sister Mary painted and which Cecilia finds in a portfolio in the library. When Roy shows the letters and narrates the new Dorothea story to Cecilia's father, the latter is bewildered. He cannot believe Fountainhall is not a real place, because "We've got a picture of it" (282) and Mary, who painted it, "was a very sensible sort of woman. *She* wasn't a writer" (282). "Mary Baines," he calls her, using her married name. Mary was sensible because, unlike Dorothea, she married and gave up her art graciously when called to new duties. Dorothea's view of Mary's renunciation was quite different: she saw it as a betrayal, as "broken vows." And from her death wail, it is clear that Dorothea passed the same judgment on her own renunication and, when forced to write, compromises. Not one of her contemporaries understood, not even the co-creators of Clone, Mary and Cousin Effie. Roy finds in one of Effie's letters: "I never learned Latin. Thea did, and Greek too. But she never had anybody to explain anything to her. I do not think a great education is of much use to a woman unless she has a husband. And if she has a husband she does not need an education. She can ask him" (246).

   In Dorothea's diary was an entry which Effie read and questioned her about. It noted Bob's opinion that women cannot write and followed it with a line in Greek, a quotation from Sappho. Dorothea translated it for her cousin: "But I sleep alone" and said she wrote it there "Because Bob says women can't write poetry" (114). The quotation accomplishes two things: it proves Bob wrong by quoting a woman poet, and it indicates Dorothea's own consciousness of the relationship between the romance plot, her own life plot, and the story of the woman artist. Though Winthorpe seems to have had considerable influence over Dorothea, she never agreed to marriage. To do so would have been to betray Clone, her created world, symbol of all that she desired and cared about. By insisting on asserting her intelligence, Dorothea rendered herself unfit for the romance plot, unfit for wifehood. By sleeping alone, Dorothea avoided at least some of the compromises women make. Even if she renounced art, which she eventually did, she renounced it not for men but for women, not for marriage or duty to the Father, both urged on her by Winthorpe, but to make up for wrongs done to Mary and to Katy, the latter also destined, for other reasons, to sleep alone.

The line from Sappho who, Dorothea knows, did without men altogether, suggests further the extent to which the Clone characters are Harding's attempt to explore her own psyche. She tells Effie that Mary ought not have married Grant because she does not love him the way she loved her Clone hero. Dorothea tries to remain faithful to her hero, Gabriel. But it is not as men that she clings to these heroes. Rather, as her proud "I sleep alone" in conjunction with Bob's accusation emphasizes, Gabriel and the other Clone characters represent independence, power, and choice to someone dependent, powerless, and silenced.

Although Cecilia has the advantage of being a modern woman and of anticipating an Oxford education, she has had to struggle and to compromise for her relative independence and power. Yet like all the women in Dorothea's life, she succumbs, at least temporarily, to the romance plot. She falls in love with Roy, and her feelings for him are described in the romance plot's conventionally hyperbolic rhetoric: "complete despair," "calamity" (287), "state of euphoria" (284), "too happy to move" (285). So pervasive and persuasive is this plot that it makes the life of the modern woman as problematic and contradictory as it made Dorothea Harding's. Cecilia realizes "that the focus of her existence had now shifted" (215). When Mundy reads the romance plot into Harding's life, Adelaide Lassiter, herself a single woman who has never been involved with a man, is inspired by the story. Only Adelaide's integrity as a writer prevents her from making use of the romance, which she gradually realizes is false. Significantly, however, she never suggests rewriting the play to tell the truth about Dorothea's life and Roy never suggests that B.B.B.—which controls the media's representation of women and disseminates the fictive scripts that control women's lives—would be interested in such a project. Without the romance between Grant and Dorothea there is no story, because the story of a woman who writes second-rate novels for money and regrets all her life her betrayal of her talents as a poet is not an accepted plot.

So unaccepted and unacceptable is this story that the text itself cannot tell it directly. The most roundabout narrative is not one of Dorothea's novels or one of Cecilia's fibs or one of Roy's cowardly versions of his own actions, but the text's own attempt to tell the story of the non-story that is Dorothea's life. The reader first gets Mundy's version of the story, then Adelaide's fanciful modifications.

Cecilia's reconstructions follow, then a fourth character insinuates "She was pathological. Why did she quote Sappho? Oogh! She never had a man. They're barking up the wrong tree! G. wasn't a man" (59). The context invites the conclusion that G. was a woman. Still another character then claims to have letters which tell something altogether different. Even the middle section of the book, set in Dorothea's own time, opens with Dorothea and her situation seen through Cousin Effie's eyes, then through Bob, who despairs of Dorothea's life ever following the correct narrative because "What man wants a wife who talks in words of five syllables?" (96)

The substitution of art for romantic hero/husband in the life of the educated woman, who speaks in words of five syllables, disrupts the traditional plot line of women's lives so thoroughly that other characters try to undo the effects. Selina, Dorothea's sister-in-law, tells Bob to find out "who it is that she meets when she goes creeping out . . . at night" (101). Selina's version of Dorothea's story—Selina who lives in the same house—is not unlike Mundy's. She cannot believe that it is her writing which takes Dorothea out every evening to "the old playhouse by the river" (105). Bob and Mary, having known from childhood Dorothea and her obsession with her writing, are sure that Selina's interpretation is false, but this resigns neither of them to the true story. Mary thinks Dorothea should show herself "much more fit to be a clergyman's wife" and marry Winthorpe (106), and Bob is sure that "women can't write poetry. They should never try" (106). Both attempt to make Dorothea conform to their frame of reference. To lighten the effects of her having to take over the household, Bob assures her confidently that the situation will not last long. "You'll marry." "No," she replies, and adds quietly, "Never, never." (126).

The final chapters of the nineteenth-century section are seen from Winthorpe and Effie's respective points of view, after which the text returns to its frame in the present. So roundabout, then, is this text which is ostensibly about filming the life of Dorothea Harding that neither narrator nor reader is allowed direct access to the subject except through her conversation and her letters. Although there is a certain objectivity in the nineteenth-century section, the story told there has its limitations, because the reader cannot see events from Dorothea's own point of view. Roy's intuition, the reader realizes, comes close to the "real" story when he tells Adelaide, "Can't you see? There never was anybody. It was her writing. She gave it up. They were too much for her. He [Winthorpe] had all of them behind him and it was too much for her" (192). Adelaide, however, though she begins to see that this is nearly the case, has a slightly different version, which she gives to Roy:

> Can't you see that Katy was the key to it all? . . . You, being a
> man, make too much of Winthorpe. Nobody but another
> woman would understand. That poor little creature . . . very
> ugly and unattractive . . . nobody caring for it and the parents
> ashamed of it. She must have felt Katy had nobody but her.
> She'd have stuck to Katy, even if a million Mr. Winthorpe's
> had told her not to (196).

Katy, Dorothea's niece, is portrayed in the nineteenth-century narrative as obnoxious, spoiled, and retarded. At three she howls and bites and cannot talk at all. Bob suspected that "there might be something very much amiss with Katy" (99), "some serious deficiency" (103). Mary denied it—"Not in our family" (103)—but Effie's letters and Harding family stories indicate that Katy did not improve and that there was talk about "putting Katy away" (245). Cecilia considers disconcerting the family "by coming out with the truth about Aunt Katy, concerning which there had been a tribal conspiracy of silence" (163), the "truth" being that she was " a congenital idiot" (103). Judging from the contemporary sources and Cecilia's remarks, Adelaide seems to be romanticizing Katy and the part she played in Dorothea's life. Even the fact that Dorothea left her small fortune to Katy could be explained by guilt induced by the closet incident and Harding's relentless sense of responsibility: she would make sure, by her legacy, that Katy was not put away. But there is a deeper "truth" in Adelaide's insistence on Katy as "key" that neither Roy nor any of the other reconstructors of Harding's life sees—a blindness induced by tribal conspiracy of silence which refuses to let women tell the real stories of their lives. The narrative hints at Katy's function in its mention of her alcoholic nurse and of her probable "Creole" background. Linked here with the mad wife in *Jane Eyre*, Katy plays a similar role as the heroine's double. Dorothea the dutiful, who gives up art for her family, fails finally in the eyes of the Hardings when she leaves everything to the family idiot. But Katy's howling gives voice to Dorothea's despair, Katy's destruction of Mary's wedding cake enacts Dorothea's anger at Mary's betrayal both of Clone and of her. And Katy obviously identified herself closely with her almost equally alienated aunt. After Dorothea's death, Effie wrote:

> She is busy dragging everything she can lay her hands on out of Thea's room to her own. Books, clothes, papers, odds and ends of rubbish! There is not much that anybody could want—all poor Thea's things so plain and shabby. . . . Katy said to me in her loud flat voice: "It is all mine. Nobody can have it but me!' (246)

Katy, then, saves Dorothea's manuscripts, which nobody else could want; it is thus through Katy, the key, that Dorothea's secret writing comes to light at all, that essential fragments of her life eventually emerge. And Katy's passion for Dorothea's possessions indicates a link beyond literal kinship between the almost dumb niece and the aunt who speaks in words of five syllables. Both evade the romance plot; both sleep alone. Katy's limited language skills suggest the silencing of Dorothea; Katy's ineducability suggests the state to which Winthorpe and the Hardings try to reduce the wayward writer. But by giving Katy all her money, Dorothea finally gained power. She compromised her artistic integrity to save Bramstock, but she had the last word about how the Hardings would benefit from their estate. Cecilia describes the situation:

> Bramstock had been preservered for them, with Katy permanently inside it. Nobody could turn her out, for if she went to live elsewhere she might take her money with her. Only so long as she stayed there would funds be forthcoming when the roof needed repair, or a bathroom had to be installed.
> For more than ninety years, through two world wars, she had made life hell for everybody. Generations of children had grown up under the shadow of that bulky old crow, whose continual idiotic remarks must always be answered with patience and courtesy, lest she fly into one of her rages (162).

The heaven that Mary and Dorothea tried to create by smoothing over all problems in the Harding household was succeeded by the hell of Katy's rule. Their intelligent conversation was followed by Katy's idiotic remarks, their controlled pleasantness by her rages.

Katy becomes the link between the past and present. In her ninety year reign, she tyrannized the Hardings the way they had tyrannized Dorothea. Not only, then, does Katy express what Dorothea could not, but on her aunt's death she becomes her avenging angel. Only Adelaide, the woman writer scorned by the literary world, senses this centrality perhaps because, like Dorothea, like Mary, she is not permitted to indulge her rage or her idiosyncrasies. Mundy, Cope, and Roy can all behave badly, can shout at one another, can employ physical violence—Roy punches Mundy in defense of Dorothea—but Adelaide makes peace, and she alone acts out of a sense of duty to Dorothea without regard for the harm she thereby must do to herself. Katy captures Adelaide's imagination because as idiot she can howl, as heiress she can dictate her terms.

Dorothea's Clone hero Gabriel was "amazingly wicked" (80), as was Laura, Clone's heroine. Actually, Dorothea explained to Effie, "There are two Lauras. One he [Gabriel] had thought an angel; he now sees that she was a mean, base, paltry creature. The other, now dead, he had believed to be entirely bad; he now perceives she was a kind of saint" (86). She also told Effie that "Gabriel . . . quite takes possession of me" (87). This confusion of good and bad, of female and male bewilders poor Effie, but Dorothea seems quite at home with it. This ability to explore ambiguity and, further, to delight in it, suggests the appropriateness of Katy as key. Katy remains throughout the novel a profoundly ambiguous figure. She is imperious, grasping, and malicious in her idiocy; she strikes out at those who have been good to her. Yet no blame can be attached to her howling, her destructiveness, or her violence. She does and does not know what she is doing. Dorothea's legacy becomes an experiment in unleashing semi-conscious rage, yet no one can judge Katy either base or saintly. What seems "amazingly wicked" nevertheless punishes the oppressors of Dorothea; Katy expresses her aunt's rage with impunity, not only because she is rich and must therefore be catered to but also because she is retarded and must therefore be excused. The Harding family cannot even decide whether Dorothea, in her adoption of Katy and provision of a legacy for her, was being amazingly wicked or a kind of saint. Katy serves as the embodiment of the good-bad confusion which occupied Dorothea from her earliest imaginative efforts.

It is finally not the powerful male Gabriel, the devil with the angel's name, who gives voice to the female artist but the idiot woman who preserves the manuscripts, who becomes queen of Bramstock and reigns for ninety years, illustrating to the Hardings and to the world the consequences of keeping women from a life of the mind. In a late Kennedy short story, "The Little Green Men," a group of women, like the women in Susan Glaspell's *Trifles*, conspire to prevent the arrest of one of their friends for the murder of her husband. One of the other husbands realizes that the friend "had been saved by the loyalty, the unscrupulous, irrational loyalty, of those idiotic women" (*Women at Work*, 87). Similarly, Aunt May, Adelaide, Cecilia, and the idiot Katy conspire across generation and narrative to preserve a woman's voice from oblivion.

The outcome of all this, however, is as ambiguous as Katy, as ambiguous as the role of the educated woman. Cecilia, bound for Oxford (the money now available from an uncle, a sign perhaps that the Harding family will begin to take its women seriously), is left with a broken heart. Her twisted tales have driven Roy away. The reader's romantic expectation are partly thwarted—Cecilia, at least for the time being, will sleep alone—but not altogether thwarted, because she has not chosen to sleep alone. The broken heart is as much an element of the romance plot as the expected couplings.

More significant than the broken heart, however, is the broken narrative. Like Dorothea, the text recognizes that the woman who speaks in words of five syllables cannot simply tell her story, so different from "the story," straight. The multiple points of view, the frames, the starts and stops, the multiple readings and misreadings of the woman artist's life, make room in this text for the educated woman. The conditions of a woman's life, assumed to be inevitable and rather trivial in the earlier novels, in this flexible text acquire economic and social bases and assume great importance. Here women have risen from the status of servants and helpmates of male artist-heroes to the rank of artist-hero. No longer are educated women a threat to art, a male province, because they have become artists and claimed that province for their own. Finally, the monster lurking under the educated woman's controlled surface is here displaced to the idiot, who is impossible to blame.

The multiple narrative strategies of this text remind us of the ideological filters through which we view, perhaps even construct, reality. Because they offer so many vantage points and perspectives, these strategies, like Dorothea's own framed narrative, can tell hidden stories as well as obvious ones, forbidden stories as well as permitted ones. Further, like the clue-finding and multiple reading demanded by detective fictions, these multiple readings call attention to the presence of these hidden/forbidden narratives, represented in part by raging idiots and raving villains, and keep us, as readers of the clues/tales, alert to the infinity of stories that every story, but perhaps especially the repressed story, contains. That *The Heroes of Clone* uses a frame structure to tell a story of a writer, Dorothea, who uses a frame structure to tell a story of a writer—herself—whose story has been repressed suggests this infinity. Such complex indirection becomes, then, like alternative genres a way *out* of the romance by focusing on it from a variety of angles of vision—a way to write stories of, rather than *the* story of, the lives of women, especially of educated women.

8   *All Men Are Mortal:*

Winifred Holtby's Plotting for Survival

In her introduction to the 1981 reprint of Vera Brittain's *Testament of Friendship*, Carolyn Heilbrun comments of the Brittain-Holtby relationship, "There was no script for young women which seemed written to their needs" (xxiii). Muriel Hammond, in Winifred Holtby's early novel *The Crowded Street*, has a similar complaint: "Read? All books are the same—about beautiful girls who get married or married women who fall in love with their husbands. In books things always happen to people. Why doesn't somebody write a book about someone to whom nothing ever happens—like me?" (219) In this bitter rejection of the romance plot, Muriel suggests the alternative this text has chosen. *The Crowded Street* is the story of a girl to whom nothing ever happens and of her friend Delia, to whom things do happen and who, ill and possibly dying at the end of the novel, acts with the self-confidence of Holtby's own brave verse, "We'll make the whole world go/My friends and I." Muriel, like Woolf's passive heroine Katharine Hilbery in *Night and Day*, loves mathematics and astronomy and has read the life of the scientist Mary Somerville—after whom, of course, Somerville College was named—a woman to whom things did happen but not the things Muriel's mother and Marshington society think important. It is Mrs. Hammond, acting with the tacit understanding and approval of the whole village, who discourages Muriel from pursuing her intellectual interests and who, like her literary predecessors, Austen's Mrs. Bennet and Woolf's Mrs. Hilbery, wants for her daughters only a good marriage. Muriel, therefore, stays at home instead of going to the university, while the vicar's daughter Delia sets off for Newnham College at Cambridge and then dedicates herself, like Mary Datchet in *Night and Day*, to political work. Like Mary, too, she reminds her passive and conventional friend that there is another plot besides the romantic one. Unlike Mary, however, Delia, the educated woman, directly alters the plot by giving Muriel the words with which to reject the romance that has begun, like Elizabeth Bennett's, at a dance and that ends with the inevitable, if belated, proposal of marriage. These clear references to other women's texts invite the reader to see this text as a retelling; Muriel's complaint about romantic texts suggests that this retelling is also a revision.

The novel opens with a prologue which describes Muriel's first party, an event whose essence eludes the young girl at every turn. For one thing, the party operates by confusing rules. While, for example, "To sit quietly in the drawing room at home was a virtue, the same conduct [at the party] was an undesirable combination of naughtiness and misfortune" (16). What she is expected to do, it seems, is not to enjoy "the music, the people, the prettiness—all this counted for nothing. It was not the Party" (16), but to attract partners. She dances clumsily with Godfrey Neale, corralled by her mother, and she tries to avoid the constant embarrassment of an almost empty program by filling in the rest of it herself. Armed with this testament to her adherence to the rules, she slips into another room and takes a sweet from the supper table. The hostess catches her at it and nearly accuses her of "stealing all the sweets" (18). Muriel returns home humiliated but having learned her lesson well: to act for oneself, to reach out for a sweet, is to violate the code. One must, if one is a girl, look pretty and wait. For Muriel, however, the promised reward for good behavior does not come. For dances she gets no partner, for life she gets no husband.

In the first chapter, Muriel's lessons continue. She goes happily off to school because "school was a place where one learnt things" (27). Thinking that she will at last be able to study mathematics and astronomy, Muriel approaches Mrs. Hancock, foundress and head, who explains to Muriel that there are "some things that it was not suitable for girls to learn." Astronomy, "a very instructive pursuit for astronomers and professors" (29) is one of them. As she earlier acquiesced in the rules of the dance, Muriel resigns herself "to the wisdom of Mrs. Hancock," even though she is "certain that fate [holds] for her something more exciting than dressmaking lessons" (29–30).

Yet in spite of her external conformity to the expectations of Marshington, Mother, and Mrs. Hancock, Muriel cannot always control her mind and heart. She cannot, for example, "stop herself from loving Clare, though passionate friendships between girls had been firmly discouraged by the sensible Mrs. Hancock. Their intimacy, she considered, was silly and frequently disastrous. If carried too far, it even wrecked all hope of matrimony without offering any satisfaction in return" (41). Not only is Muriel expected to give up her intellectual interests, she is to be deprived of friendship as well, for the sake of the glorious future which awaits her and every girl: "To serve first your parents, then, I hope, your husband and your children, to be pure, unselfish and devoted," as Mrs. Hancock tells her graduates this and every year (42). She adds a little meditation on the school motto, *Leata sorte mea*: "Happy in my lot. God will, I hope, give you happiness, but if he chooses to send you disappointment and sorrow you will, I hope, resign yourself to His dear will" (42).

This is Muriel Hammond's education. She continues to love Clare because, in part, Clare, the unconventional child of a writer and an actress, represents the elusive party. She is bright, fearless, impulsive, beautiful, and talented. Unlike Mrs. Hancock's ideal graduate, unlike Muriel herself, Clare resigns herself to nothing and is not pure, nor unselfish, nor devoted. The music, the people, the prettiness of Muriel's ruined party are unquestioned constituents of Clare's life. She is a girl with a voice. Not only does she have a lovely soprano singing voice but she has control over her own life and a voice in her future. Even Clare, however, absorbs some of Mrs. Hancock's lessons. She accepts marriage as the basic plot of her life and at first, therefore, sees no need to exert herself. "It's not so easy as I thought," she remarks, "to become a great prima donna. They want me to work" (65). Clare's vitality, though unchanneled and undisciplined, attracts not only Muriel but Godfrey Neale, whom Muriel has been taught to worship and to hope for. Mrs. Hancock's dire predictions about the evils of passionate friendship come to pass in an ironic way: it is Clare who twice ruins Muriel's hope for marriage to Godfrey Neale.

In the course of the novel, however, both young women, their early "education" increasingly shown to be less and less adequate preparation for the realities of a war-torn world or their own growing needs, reject Godfrey for lives less restricted than the one Marshington can offer. While Clare's unconventional family allows and even encourages her to reject the marriage plot, it is only Delia, Muriel's educated alter ego, who, though she cannot bring Muriel her party, can at least offer her a vital, practical alternative to the role of perpetual wallflower. Delia is, first of all, the only character in the novel who has no particular stake in Godfrey Neale; she treats him, not as an eligible man who may deign to make her his wife, but with a slightly patronizing friendliness. In spite of the almost universal respect Godfrey inspires as "squire of Weare and Marshington and lord of the Marlehammar property" (258), he—handsome, confident, charming, and kind—is as parochial as Marshington itself. He quarrels with Clare, to whom he has become engaged, because she was "spoiled by all this singing and publicity and having her photograph in the papers [and] wanted to fill the house with damned foreigners and Jews and things" (251). Though Muriel thinks early in the novel that Godfrey is "a little stupid" (13) and asks herself "Who is Godfrey, that here we all are with our lives centered in his?" (131), it is only Delia who acts on such reflections.

Delia first appears in the novel at a tea party. When she asks for a bun with sugar on top Godfrey says, "There is only one bun with sugar on it, and I want it for myself." "Then you can't have it," she replies. "How like a man to think that he has an indisputable right to the best bun" (48). Her outspoken critical ways shock Muriel— "Fancy anyone daring to talk to Godfrey Neale like that!" (48) The scene points to the difference between the two women: in the prologue Muriel takes her sweet but is defeated by the hostess's accusations and spends the next twenty years of her life unselfishly giving up everything potentially sweet in her own life in order to please her mother and Marshington; Delia, on the other hand, takes her sweet, ignores Marshington's accusations, ("Well, I think it distinctly lacking in a sense of duty, that Delia should go gallivanting off to college just now when her father's getting old" [46]), and lives for what she has decided is important. Instead of centering her hopes on Godfrey Neale, she finds significant work in London and a congenial love in the short, stocky, humorous Martin Elliot, who also shocks Muriel: "It was incredible that a man should really want to talk to her about herself" (105). Delia's ability to resist Godfrey's looks, charm, and wealth stems from her larger view—the result, the text implies, of her education, first at the hand of her liberal-minded father, then at Newnham College, Cambridge.

Her university education gives her the perspective necessary "to think that service of humanity [is] sometimes more important than respectability" (87) and thus to be free, unlike the other women in the novel, to think her own thoughts and speak them. Muriel, who "had never been to a college debating society" finds Delia at first rude and impertinent. Because she cannot herself think and speak freely, Muriel becomes defensive and refuses to hear Delia's important judgment that "There's only one thing that counts for a girl in Marshington, and that is sex-success" (88). The emptiness of Muriel's own life and the tragedy of her sister Connie—who, desperate for "sex-success," becomes pregnant, is forced to marry a man she does not love, tries to kill herself, and dies before the birth—later forces Muriel to recognize the truth of Delia's rude words. "'The only thing that Marshington cares about is sex-success.' Delia Vaughan had said that. It was true enough, quite true" (227).

With her wider perspective and superior judgment, Delia, even though she appears to have a relatively small role in the novel, serves as a model for what Muriel, educated, might have been. Muriel herself recognizes that Delia functions as her double:

> It was as though Delia in her London office, looking up from the work which her brilliant, courageous mind directed, might think of Muriel in Marshington, living her drab ineffectual life among tea parties . . . and might say to herself, "There, but for the grace of God, goes Delia Vaughan." Most successful people . . . have a shadow somewhere, a personality sharing their desires and even part of their ability, but without just the one quality that makes success (102–103).

Though Muriel is clearly intelligent and insightful, she displays here the passivity to which she was bred. She implies that the "quality" is a temperamental one, which comes from "the grace of God," but the text suggests a more sociological explanation.

Connie's temperament, for example, is more like Clare's and Delia's than it is like Muriel's, but without perspective on the pervasive ideology of Marshington, repeated relentlessly in all the books they read, that what matters for women is "marriage, marriage respectable and unequivocal, marriage financially sound, eugenically advisable, and socially correct" (226), Connie, too, succumbs. "I wanted to chicken farm," she says during her suicide attempt, "I wanted to go away and do just anything. But mother wouldn't let me. It was just men, men, men, and make a good match" (199). Connie dies trying.

Earlier in the novel Connie repeats the Marshington rhetoric in judgment of Delia: "It's surprising really that she's caught anything. She must be over thirty and that skinny figure of hers and then all those stories about her being a suffragette and going to prison. It's just the kind of thing that all nice men hate" (102). This repetition illustrates Connie's thorough acceptance of the romance plot for women, even though she is, like Delia, a spirited young woman with a sense of humor and of her own needs. Muriel, on the other hand, "drab and ineffective" has a different response to the announcement of Delia's engagement. She feels "strangely excited, because of the . . . insistent feeling that there existed between her and Delia some tie" (120).

This tie, this doubling of the two women, suggests that it is education rather than "the grace of God" which explains their difference. Clare, brought up in Bohemian fashion by her artist parents and herself an artist, intuits but cannot articulate or analyze the fallacy of the Marshington commonplaces as Delia can. Clare attributes her problem with Neale to his nationality rather than to his gender. "How very English you are, Mr. Neale, that proprietary instinct. You want everything for yourself, land, ladies, music. You would like to put up a notice on me like you put up on your woods, 'Trespassers will be prosecuted'" (66). She eventually breaks their brief engagement, in recognition perhaps that the "proprietary instinct" was more deeply rooted than she had thought, and goes on with her artistic, flamboyant life. Though Muriel loves her and admires her vitality and independence, Clare cannot effect change in Muriel's life. It is only Delia, whose work with the women's movement attacks the real source of Marshington's death-dealing assumptions and whose debating skills eventually penetrate Muriel's rather slow intelligence, who can offer Muriel an alternative to the Marshington plot.

Before she proposes this alternative, however, Delia performs another important function for her passive, indoctrinated double—she prods Muriel to speech. At first, Muriel speaks to defend herself from Delia, who, Muriel admits to Godfrey, is "like the Day of Judgment . . . I always remember all my misdoings in her sight. I—I'm terrified of her" (52). When Delia urges her to see Marshington as a trap, to resist, that is, the plot it has laid for her, by leaving the place and becoming an educated woman, Muriel, in her first attempt to talk back, replies "stiffly": "I certainly am not going to college, because my mother needs me at home. I am not unhappy here. Some of us have to stay at home. I have my duty too" (88). Delia rightly infers the reproach: "Am I being properly called to order for pursuing my selfish ambitions while you are following the path of virtue?" (88)

Rather to Delia's surprise, Muriel here defends her own choice to stay at home and prepare for marriage, but the defense itself is a departure for the passive young woman, and she follows it with a small but significant act of rebellion. "That night she stood before her bedroom window and pulled back the curtains that Mrs. Hammond liked her to keep drawn" because "It looks so bad . . . to see an uncurtained bedroom window" (89). With this gesture, Muriel indicates her willingness to look, at least, out into a larger world than her bedroom. Mrs. Hammond's stricture underscores the importance to Marshington of appearances ("It looks so bad") and indicates its hypocrisy: the very sex success it advocates is something to hide behind the bedroom curtains lest anyone infer some sort of sexual activity. Thus, as a direct result of her contact with Delia, Muriel both speaks and acts in ways which threaten the accepted conventions of her upbringing.

Later in the novel Delia incites Muriel to break her passive silence permanently. This time when Delia accuses her of cowardice for not going to college, Muriel agrees and begins to talk volubly with, for the first time, some sense of her own worth and abilities. "I never could stand up on a public platform," she says, "But I do believe I should be able to tell your audiences things you never could" (234). Delia is gleeful: "I might have known," she thinks, "that when Muriel really did begin to talk we should hear some surprising things" (234). A college debater, Delia has learned not to take things personally; she appreciates Muriels' attack rather than resenting it; instead of defending herself she urges Muriel on. Again Muriel's talk surprises, again it is followed by an act of rebellion,

this time definitive: Muriel decides to go to London and work with
Delia. When Godfrey meets her there, he is taken aback by her
new-found powers of speech. Asked if she does not like Marshington, she replies, "I loathed it with all my heart and all my soul and
all my spirit" (249). That Muriel should loath Marshington with
the Christian formula for the way one should love God emphasizes
the extent of her rejection of its discourse. After this outburst,
Godfrey, himself a god included in her reversal of the formula,
stares at her "in amazement that so guileless a creature should show
such emphatic disapproval of something that he had always quite
taken for granted" (249).

Though it is through Muriel's eyes that we see the whole action
of the novel, it is not until the last "book" that the novel properly
belongs to her. "Clare," "Mrs. Hammond," "Connie," "Delia" are
the names of the first four books; respectively, they indicate the persons around whom Muriel lives her life. But women's education
begins to have effects beyond those on the woman who goes to college, and finally, after living in London with Delia, Muriel begins to
live for herself. On a visit home she amazes her mother and, for the
first time, attracts the interest of Marshington inhabitants. "Her
manner had changed. She was more sure of herself. She expressed
her opinions with . . . assurance" (259). Mrs. Hammond is triumphant, not because of the change, but because, with this new
assurance and composure, her daughter is more popular and has
clearly attracted the neighborhood god, Godfrey Neale. But Muriel
has learned her lesson well. She will not accept Marshington's
plot—neither Weare Grange, the plot of land Godfrey offers when
he finally proposes, nor the romance plot that has, to the reader of
romance, seemed inevitable from the scene at the party in which
his offering his hand as a dancing partner saved her from humiliation.
She refuses to marry him. She knows that life at Weare Grange is
not what she wants for herself; she recognizes that Connie's story
represents the "Marshington way . . . carried to its logical conclusion." She acknowledges her debt: "If it hadn't been for Delia, I
should have died—not with my body, but my mind. . . . She let
me see . . . that there were other things in life" (269).

Though part of Muriel's decision to go to London is based on
Delia's *need* for her, and though her role there is a womanly one of
housekeeping for her politically active and possibly dying friend,
Muriel's refusal to marry makes clear that she has not merely sub-

stituted Delia for a husband. In fact, she is quite confident of her ability to carry on *without* her friend, who is "probably . . . going to America soon anyway" (270). Muriel has "an idea" for her life. She does not rule out marriage altogether, but she knows she cannot marry Godfrey, and her arguments here are firm, logical, and persuasive. In learning from the educated Delia how to speak, she gains powers heretofore absent—the power to attract, the power to refuse, and the power to create a life for herself, which, she realizes, is what she has always wanted. And she has wanted this life in the context of a community.

After viewing a film called "Triumph of the Mating Instinct," Muriel wonders, "Why did everything always conspire to mock and hurt her, to show her how she sat alone?" (136) At the time, of course, being alone meant, as the film asserted, being without a man, but later in the novel, when Delia prods her to speak, she sees that her desire for company was actually something quite different: "I didn't so much want marriage. I wanted to feel that I had not lived unloved, that there was nothing in my nature that cut me off from other women" (233). Muriel acquiesces for thirty years to the Marshington way not because she accepts the romance plot for itself but because she thinks its playing itself out in her own life will unite her with other women. She does not want to find herself "left alone in a dull crowded street" (232).

Delia notes the passivity inherited in the image and scolds Muriel for trying to "wriggle out of responsibility by a metaphor" (232). Life for Muriel is a crowded street, or alternatively, a party or dance "where the girls had to wait for men to ask them, and if nobody came—they still must wait, smiling and hoping and pretending not to mind" (267). Delia's ability to identify the metaphors and see the destructiveness inherent in them seems, again, a result of her education, and it is this identification and insight which finally persuade Muriel to decide and to act. Muriel herself recognizes Delia's advantage. "You know, you are very lucky, being so clever and going to Newnham like that. It must be frightfully nice—" (231). Muriel does not finish the sentence, but in the context of her revelation of what she has really wanted all these years, the reader may supply what Muriel thinks Delia has gained from her education: articulateness, detachment from the Marshington way, a healthier view of the "mating instinct," and, especially, solidarity with other women that is not grounded in romance. In this scene Delia has just reminded her father that in becoming engaged to Martin she was not being inconsistent, because, "it isn't marriage I object to—only marriage as an end of life in itself, as the ultimate goal of the female soul's development" (230). Newnham College has provided for Delia a concrete experience of an alternative. A woman's educational community, like Newnham, like Shrewsbury, like Somerville, undermines by its very existence the Marshington plot, which insists that life is nothing for a woman without a man.

Muriel's recognition of this, indicated by her mention of Newnham and by the possibilities implicit in her unfinished sentence, enables her for the first time to distinguish between her apparent acceptance of the Marshington ideology and her personal variation, which is a kind of subversion of it. "I often used to think," she tells Delia, "that it would be lovely to have a little house all one's own— only again the necessity of sharing it with a husband was an obstacle" (235). The perquisites of marriage—a house of one's own, inclusion in the couple-based world, a commonality with other women—which Muriel desires are not, she finally sees, inevitably linked to that institution. Further, a husband can, as Muriel has recognized, actually undermine these perquisites. A house shared with a husband who owns it is not a house of one's own; a husband can impede rather than promote solidarity with other women. A husband like Martin Elliot, Delia and Muriel feel, who takes women seriously, who is unprepossessing and therefore, perhaps, unpossessive (in contrast to Godfrey who hangs a "No Trespassers" sign on his women), can, like Peter Wimsey, offer a new kind of marriage. But the text itself undercuts this optimism, and by Martin's death, a gratuitous death, as the characters themselves admit— "knocked down by a motor lorry in Amiens station. Just the sort of idiotic thing that would happen to him" (142)—the text claims that it is the absence of men that truly allows women to be free. At the time of Martin's death, Muriel, though she envies Delia's having been loved more than she ever envied her engagement, is still locked into the romance plot. She assumes, like Casaubon, that Delia has an obligation to carry on her loved one's work. Delia, however, revises Dorothea Brooke's story and refuses to be so trapped. "Don't be a fool," she tells Muriel, "It was his work. He wanted to do it" (142). Martin's death makes possible both Delia's wholehearted involvement in her own work and eventually the living together of Delia and Muriel, which is salvation to them both. Delia would have died if someone had not taken care of her (Martin, in-volved in his own work, was an unlikely candidate for the job) and Muriel, as we have seen, would have died—in her mind—without Delia's intervention.

Holtby's text further emphasizes the importance of men's absence for women in two juxtaposed sentences about Clare. Muriel's exu-berant schoolmate, whom the text leaves early in the novel without the motivation and discipline to become a singer, had contracted a romantic marriage. In a ladies' magazine Muriel reads that "All so-ciety is speaking of [Clare's] beautiful soprano voice. It will be re-membered that her husband was killed about a year ago in a tragic motor accident in Chile" (129). Signor Alvarado's death seems, in this passage, to be responsible for Clare's resurgence as a prima donna. When she becomes engaged to Godfrey, her career, her voice, is again threatened: "I wanted to marry a wife," Godfrey tells Muriel, to explain the broken engagement, "not a p-prima donna . . . I wanted someone who'd be a companion, who'd take an interest in my work. A man in my position wants someone to be his—his hostess, and look after his home and all that sort of thing" (251). His use of "prima donna" makes clear Clare's predicament. He describes by the epithet Clare's wanting her own way; he links her beautiful soprano voice to the voice she demands in running her life. He will tolerate neither. Having regained her voice, then, by the death of her husband, Clare is eventually clear-sighted enough to refuse to have it taken away by Godfrey.

Clare's marriage would have resulted in the death of her voice; Connie's forced marriage results in her literal death. Muriel sees that if she accepts Godfrey's proposal, she, too, will die: " . . . if I married you I'd have to give up every new thing that has made me a person" (270). Though Godfrey protests that that would not hap-pen, Muriel is adamant in her refusal of the end toward which Marshington and the readers' expectations are pushing her. "If I married you, I'd simply be following the expedient promptings of my mother and my upbringing" (270). The fates of Delia, Clare, and Connie subvert the text's explicit rhetoric about marriage, voiced by Delia to her father, as we have seen, and by Muriel to Godfrey: "A perfect marriage is a splendid thing, but that does not mean that the second best thing is an imperfect marriage" (269). The experience of the characters suggests, on the other hand, that at best a perfect marriage is highly improbable and at worst, it

results on some level in death for the woman. It is only men's death/
absence which gives women a chance to pursue their own interests.
In fact, World War I, which constitutes the background of the
novel, effects women's freedom by its requirement of men's absence/
death.[1] Thus, though marriage and family are held up as good, the
text can find no way of making those goods concrete. All the
women in the novel are better off on their own, preferably with one
another, and that condition is invested with a sanity and "naturalness" that marriage is not.

In the middle of the novel is a strange sequence which illustrates
this. Muriel and her family are in Scarborough and Godfrey, sta-
tioned there, dines with them. Muriel is wearing red for a change
and, "conscious of the flame of her bright dress . . . feeling like a
princess in a fairy tale suddenly released from her enchantment"
(117), she realizes that Godfrey will probably ask her to marry him
"someday," not because he loves her but because he loved Clare and
Clare was Muriel's friend. She knows she will accept the proposal
because marriage to Godfrey would be "a splendid triumph, the end
of her long years of waiting and feeling that she was a complete failure" (118). But when she gets into bed to indulge this pleasant fantasy she lies "limp and unresponsive between the cold sheets" and
shrinks from the thought of further intimacy with his bodily perfection and his limited mind" (118). Suddenly big guns go off and in a
dense fog the whole family runs for safety toward the Seamer Valley.

Elated rather than frightened by the fact that something is actually happening to her, Muriel watches the villagers passing before
them on the road—"a grotesque and unending procession" (123),
part of which were students from a girls' school who "came trotting,
two and two, in an orderly procession, laughing and chattering as
they ran" (123). Her exhaustion, the fog, and the swarms of people
lend a dreamlike quality to the scene. "Everyone was a little fantastic, a little distorted." Part of the distortion is the sudden appearance of Godfrey "very tall and clear against the hills." Muriel
perceives the apparition as "her lord and master, Godfrey Neale,"
(123) with whom she now, in this time of disorder and distortion,
imagines she is in love and imagines it in rhetoric suited to the romantic plot: "Here at last she had found all that she had been seeking. The fullness of life was hers, here on the threshold of death.
She knew that it must always be so; and she lifted her head to meet
love, unafraid" (124).

Two significant elements emerge in this sequence. First, it is only the imminence of death which convinces Muriel to accept the Marshington plot and its discourse. She is no longer afraid to love Godfrey, because she is going to die—that is, she does not have to face a life of "further intimacy with his bodily perfection and his limited mind." This association of romantic love with death does not here simply repeat the romantic cliché nor precisely fit the logic of the Freudian coupling of sex and death. Rather it emphasizes the practical conclusion of this and other Holtby texts that marriage is death-dealing to women. That the bombing and confusion follow directly on Muriel's acceptance of Godfrey's expected proposal reinforces this conclusion. The rhetoric of romance—"all that she had been seeking," "fullness of life," "threshold of death," "always be so," "meet love, unafraid"—is the culmination of the nightmare, an orgasmic acceptance of love/death, but, lest Muriel or the reader be tempted to take it seriously, it is effectively subverted by the immediate sequal: "It seemed to Muriel just part of the futility of things in general that there should have been no invasion after all" (124). "Very cross and tired" they all are, but in no danger; in fact, there has been no danger in the first place, and the lord and master Godfrey later appears at the door "in mud-splashed overalls" (125), the antithesis of the romantic hero of Muriel's brief fantasy.

Second, in the midst of the description of the dreamlike escape is the jarring perception, presumably Muriel's, that "Nothing was quite normal except the girls' school" (123). The simple language which describes the girls' school contrasts with the inflated rhetoric of Godfrey's almost ghostlike appearance; the normality of the laughing, talking pairs contrasts with the unreality of the Muriel-Godfrey drama. The girls process in an orderly way, without panic, without, in fact, any departure from their usual behavior. It is they who perceive the truth: that there is nothing to worry about, that the attack is spurious. Muriel's family exhaust themselves in vain; Muriel and Godfrey indulge in a melodramatic rescue scene which is wholly unnecessary and seems silly the next day. But the girls' school remains untouched by irrational fears and misperceptions. That the schoolgirls' trotting in pairs, laughing and chattering, should be the only normal element in the scene implies the hope that women's education holds out, not only for order in confusion and for humanity in an inhuman war, but for sanity in the crazy conspiracy that constitutes the Marshington way. Muriel and Clare,

Muriel and Delia—these are the pairs that endure, that keep Muriel, in her lethargy, from succumbing to certain mental and emotional death. The perception of the fundamental normality of this female-female pairing, of this female educational community, allows Muriel, in the end, to choose life with Delia over life with Godfrey, not as a substitute for marriage but as a revision of the Marshington plot, as an experiment with alternative endings.

Both these themes—that traditional marriage means death (either death to the woman who cannot survive the physical and mental demands of a husband or death to the man so that the woman may live a productive life), and that the female educational community offers hope and life play themselves out in a remarkable way in Holtby's next novel, *The Land of Green Ginger*. Like Muriel, the heroine, Joanna, is not only not an educated woman but a woman who had refused to be educated and who suffers the consequences.

Like *The Crowded Street*, *The Land of Green Ginger* creates a situation in which the man must die in order for the woman to live. The particular oppressiveness of the male is, however, more thoroughly developed here. For most of the novel the reader sees the dynamics of marriage and the playing out of the ideology that underlies it. Joanna's mother Edith was an adventuresome child, encouraged by *her* mother to marry early because she showed such dangerous tendencies as eschewing needlepointing and "devouring unladylike literature" (11). One of Edith's books was *A Voyage up the Amazon*, the sight of which made her mother, having heard of only one kind of Amazon, panic and marry her daughter quickly to a missionary. This fear of strong, independent women revealed in Mrs. Entwhistle's panic, appears over and over in the novel.

Edith loved Africa, though her relationship with her husband was little different from her relationship with her "preoccupied priest" father (16). An early vision of the South African landscape suggests her situation and predicts her daughter's:

> She saw the bushes of prickly pear crouched in fantastic attitudes, thousand-armed, pulpy-breasted, like the lascivious goddess of the Ephesians pictured in her Bible Concordance. She saw the cool, transparent cup of the evening sky warmed at the rim by burning hills, and the goats, with bearded, provocative faces, mocking her from their grim banquet of thorns (15).

Ironically, it was not the Amazon book, so wrongly feared by her mother, which gave Edith her female myth, but her Bible concordance. Though the goddess is "lascivious," the "cool, transparent cup . . . warmed at the rim" suggests a positive female sexuality mocked by the male sexuality of the bearded goats. And this male sexuality was Edith's downfall: she died of puerperal fever, having given birth to Joanna, who appears later to her young suitor "like an immature young goddess" (30), and who, too, is mocked constantly by male sexuality and freed only by its absence from her life.

After her mother's death Joanna returns to England to be raised by her conventional aunts near a street called The Land of Green Ginger, a name which excites her imagination and comes to stand for her hopes of adventure and for a life not bound by convention. The aunts, however, Joanna's socializers, refuse to take her onto the street, and Joanna forgets about it until the hearse carrying her husband's corpse turns onto the street to avoid a truck. Again, the text associates a life of freedom and adventure for women with male death or absence. Only Teddy's hearse can allow Joanna finally to see the Land of Green Ginger and take advantage of its promises.

Joanna meets Teddy during the war in a nursing home where she has taken a job after deciding against a college education. She spends her hours there dreaming about having adventures in exotic places, especially the South Africa of her birth, and weaving fantasies of Queen Elizabeth and Sir Walter Raleigh. Teddy Leigh, a dashing, amusing, young soldier, appears suddenly, like a character in one of Joanna's fictions. Not surprisingly she falls into her own romantic plot and quickly agrees to marry him. Her school friend Rachel, an ardent Jewish feminist and student at Somerville, objects, "Why you hardly know him." Joanna replies, "That's the lovely part . . . Our marriage will be one long voyage of discovery" (31). The educated woman scorns this romantic sentiment and predicts that marriage to Teddy will be "the only sort of voyage you'll ever make then" (31).

Rachel's laconic prediction almost comes true. As soon as Joanna marries Teddy, she begins to realize the oppressiveness of the demands, physical, mental, and sexual, that marriage and men will make on her. First of all, they cut her off from "the world which she had known before her marriage" (51), that is, the world she shared with Rachel and Agnes, her other school friend; marriage takes up

all Joanna's time and energy. Teddy turns out to suffer from tuber-
culosis, a condition he had known about but concealed from his
future wife. By the time she finds out, they have two daughters, and
one of them has inherited her father's lung weakness. The family
farms because that life is best for Teddy's health, but Joanna must do
most of the work, must nurse Teddy, and must take care of the girls.
One day she finally has a moment to write to Agnes, but just as she
begins to join herself again to "the world she had known before her
marriage," the Letherwick clergyman, Mr. Boyce, comes to ha-
rangue her, because she is "one of these modern young women who
think that they can get on all right without organized religion"
(39). He later sums up the Letherwick case against her: "She wore
green stockings, and said smart, uncomfortable things, and brought
up her children badly, and proved herself no housekeeper" and had,
worst of all "that dangerous levity of manner . . . as though her business of a wife and mother were somehow not quite real to her" (171).

Thus, besides cutting her off from her former world, men also
criticize her for doing her job badly. They expect from her feelings
she does not have and work she cannot do. When she manages
to send the girls off for awhile to avoid infection from Teddy, he
objects,

> cherishing a thought common to many men that mothers pos-
> sessed a standard of values unknown to husbands and spinsters
> which made the presence of their children essential to their
> happiness. . . . He was . . . shocked at Joanna's manifest de-
> light in the prospect of a period of less work instead of more
> maternity (96).

Other male expectations, too, oppress Joanna. "Men are always
wanting to be listened to. They feel tragic and want to be com-
forted. They feel humiliated and want to be grand again. You've all
the time got to be nursing their vanity" (119).

Even the distant, exotic Paul Szermai, whom the family takes as
a boarder to augment their income, begins to tell Joanna the sad
story of his life, expecting sympathy and, eventually, sex. "They
pressed about her. . . . They besieged her, the miseries of these
men. They entered with their incessant demands the secret for-
tresses of her mind. She had no place of refuge from their clamorous
sorrows" (189). Their desire to enter her fortress is, of course, physi-

cal as well as mental. When Paul makes advances, though she feels "no emotion, but surprise and sorrowful repulsion" (193), she believes it must be her fault, that she somehow "led him to believe that she cared for him 'that way'" (206). Added, then, to her oppressive role as protector, comforter, and confidante of men is her assumption of responsibility for the fact that men find her attractive, but her only ground for self-reproach is that she hoped "that because he was strange and foreign and had so wild a story, he might in other ways be different from the men she had known" (206).

But he is not. He expects from her what Teddy expects from her—sex and service. The willingness of the villagers to believe that she is his mistress emphasizes the misjudgment bred of these male expectations. Even Teddy, whom she serves constantly and without complaint, misunderstands her completely. Not only does he believe that she is in love with Paul, but he defends her to his pub cronies in the most offensive way: "Joanna's a good woman, a good woman, a good good woman, but very—stupid" (142). In fact, Joanna is not, according to his and Paul's and Letherwick's standards, a good woman, nor is she in the least stupid. She is simply bewildered by the betrayal inherent in her marriage and is therefore unable to figure out wherein her accountability lies. Paul is aroused by her; she feels she must have brought it on. When she indulges in small pleasures, tragedies occur: the night she and Teddy attend a party, their prize pig dies; the night she and Paul go dancing, the Finnish camp burns down. These are consequences the nature of which she has learned early: she "measured her iniquity in going . . . by the extent of her desire to go" (56).

Her attendance at the dance with Paul is, in fact, the reason the camp burned down. Fearful that the foreigners are stealing their women, the villagers burn the migrant camp of which Paul is the foreman, to get them out. But Joanna has not been stolen and it was Teddy who, feeling himself a martyr, insisted that she go to the dance. Men's expectations are, to Joanna, confusing and sometimes contradictory. Finally, when Teddy forces her after the dance to have sex with him, she understands the rape as a type for the reality of her imprisonment and oppression. "Fool, fool," she accuses herself, "to feed upon the fantasy till the life of the flesh betrayed you . . . to measure the frail integrity of imagination against the stumbling passion and craving needs of men" (241).

What she most resents about men is their intrusion upon her

imaginative life. "Is there no end, no end? Must you take my dreams?" (190) she asks earlier in the novel, when, in the midst of a fantasy, she is interrupted by Paul "bearing with him his unbearable memories" (189). Real men are facts of life for Joanna but figure only negatively in her imagination; they are all alike. She imagines, for example, a letter from Agnes which says "Did you know I had a husband? I forget when I found mine, but I expect that he is much the same as yours, so really there is no need to bother you with the details." The letter continues excitedly about a woman she has met "who has discovered the fourth dimension" (124). As Virginia Woolf said of herself, women alone (with the early exception of Sir Walter Raleigh) stir Joanna's imagination, and in interfering with that imagination men again interfere with a world of women.

Although, as in this passage, Joanna dismisses men quite casually in her fantasies, when the fantasies turn to dreams their symbolic presence assumes a threatening tone. In the midst of a meditation, only half-conscious, in which she sees love, "which she had thought would transfigure life" (290), instead bringing chaos and disappointment, Joanna falls asleep and conjures up again her friend Agnes, who tells her,

> Chameleons are not as we thought them in our innocence. They do not emulate the odours of grass, nor transform themselves to match the brick-red earth. . . . I caught my chameleon near a bed of salvia, deep salvia flowers with flaming scarlet mouths. I set him on a square of emerald lawn. But did he turn green? Not a bit of it. He grew black with indignation. He stormed at me. He twisted his head over his shoulder and rolled his furious eyes and hissed rude things at me in a small, venomous voice. He had no sense of gratitude (291).

In her dream, the phallic chameleons stand not only for men but for the romantic expectations associated with them. Like love, which has not done what she hoped, the chameleon is a disappointment and, worse, a hostile force. Love and men promise a life of variety, adaptability, and adventure, but taken from the "scarlet mouths"—an obvious symbol for female genitalia—set down in a pastoral, nonsexual landscape, they do not, in fact, adapt themselves to it but become angry, with "rolling eyes and fierce protruding tongues" (292). The romance plot is a fraud. Its promises are not kept, its expectations are dashed, and, further, it turns on the believer.

The dream continues with the appearance of Rachel, the educated woman, who is, appropriately, reading a book. Without taking her eyes from it, she puts the problem in perspective. "You spoil them. Discipline is good for the human soul. Still more so for the Protean soul of a chameleon" (29). Romantic love and men need to be controlled, and, further, *can* be controlled. This possibility diminishes the threat posed by the hissing chameleons and implies the power of women to change the plot. Joanna intuits this power from the beginning of her marriage. We have seen that, scolded for her indifference to religion, a reinforcer of the plot, she thinks about writing to Agnes, from whom she wants a letter "more than anything in the world right now" (39). The chameleon Teddy having turned out to be both bore and burden, Joanna longs for the world of her school friends, who have resisted the plot. "Agnes was now in China and Rachel in the Transvaal, lecturing in economics at the University there" (51). They represent for Joanna the adventurous life upon which she thought she was embarking with love and marriage, but which love and marriage effectively ended.

But these women represent more practical things, too. In the sequence above, Joanna thinks twice, once in the thought sequence preceding the dream and once in the dream itself, that her "tongue will not speak the language" nor can she understand the speech of the people in the village. She has gradually lost the power of speech because what people say and think are so foreign to her. Teddy, Paul, and Mr. Boyse's expectations, for example, make no sense to her adventuresome mind, nor do they conform to the promises of the romance plot. Agnes and Rachel, however, hold out the possibility that things could be different. After all they "had scolded and teased and petted and understood her" (119). They had spoken the same language and might be expected to do so still. Joanna craves just a little of the kind of attention she must constantly expend on the men in her life and looks to her school friends to give it to her. When she is feeling entirely overwhelmed by male demands, she tells herself severely that the problem is "that you know so few women" (119). She thinks it may be wrong to want a woman friend when she has Teddy and Paul, but she knows that men "just won't *do*" (119). Her school friends represent a shared language, a little attention, and friendship as well as adventure.

At one of the few social events Joanna attends, she meets Lorna
Levine, a sculptor. "Joanna knew by all the signs of her small expe-
rience that she was in love again. She did not want to part from
Lorna Lavine." Lorna sympathetically listens to her talk about
Agnes and Rachel, and holds out hope of adventure and of connection with other women. "Why, I believe that I may be going to
China and I'll look out for your Agnes" (67), she tells the infatu-
ated Joanna, who is so absurdly grateful for a little attention. Later
Lorna becomes a part of Joanna's dream of reunion and ends up
offering real hope for it. But what establishes this brief relationship
in the first place is that Lorna speaks the same language as Joanna.
Their conversation, so satisfying to the two women, is interrupted
by a man "who considered that Lorna had listened to other people
for long enough" (62). Again, men want to be listened to, not to
listen. And they want the women to do the listening—to them but
not to one another. The sharing of language that occurs between
Lorna and Joanna, between Joanna and her school friends, was
Joanna's expectation for her marriage. But once Joanna proves herself to be not what the men in her life expect a woman to be, their
language changes.

The diction of the text in the two scenes in which men assert
their sexual needs and expect Joanna to fulfill them is illustrative of
this language change. When Paul decides that he cannot go on
without possessing Joanna, he asks himself "Why not? Why not?
Should she not offer herself, her soul and body, to be a reasonable,
holy and lively sacrifice unto God?" (212) This diction, borrowed
from Christian scripture, starkly indicates the difference between
female and male roles. Joanna is to be a sacrifice; Paul is the god
to whom she should sacrifice herself. When Teddy starts to rape
her, she tries to reason with him. "No, no, Teddy. Not here. Not
now. Not like this." He shouts at her "triumphantly," "Yes, now,
now! . . . the zeal of the Lord of Hosts shall perform this" (238).
Again the language of traditional religion becomes the language of
male violence. The god Teddy will force Joanna to do her duty as
his wife in spite of the danger to her health and his—and that of
any child that might result from their intercourse. Mr. Boyse's
efforts to interest Joanna in religion fail because religious language
belongs to men, is used by them to justify violence toward women,
is understood only by them.

It is Teddy's language that originally attracts Joanna to him. The first time they meet for example, he tells her that he has been given the world to wear as a golden ball (29); he uses a kind of figurative language that she understands. But once the courtship is over, the language changes, just as the relationship does, and becomes the literal language of duty, responsibility, and conformity which Joanna finds so bewildering. At the end of the novel, when Joanna realizes that Teddy's rape has made her pregnant and that everyone believes her child to be Paul's, she feels herself "astray in an alien country whose speech she did not understand. The familiar words and speech and habits of men had grown grotesque; they assumed fantastic meanings" (290).

There are, of course, women who speak men's language rather than their own. Joanna's aunts, many of the village women, and even the pregnant, unmarried Bessy, who also believes that Joanna's child is Paul's, do so. Joanna does not attempt to set Bessy straight because to do so seems "a piece of priggish superiority which she could not tolerate" (286). She does not, that is, want to separate herself from another woman who suffers equally from men's expectations, society's requirements. What Joanna dreams is that the use of language will unite rather than separate. Had she as much money as he, she tells a neighbor, Sir Wentworth Marshall, "I'd want to send hundreds and hundreds of cables to all sorts of people in all parts of the world. Just imagine inquiring after the Shah of Persia's kittens! . . . Or sending Valentines to Mussolini and Christmas greetings to Trotsky" (298). Having recognized the difficulty of understanding men and being understood by them, Joanna here asserts a confidence in the power of her own language to effect communication with men, even men in power. But the fact is that she does *not* have as much money as Sir Wentworth nor does she know "how to behave" or "what things are dangerous" (300). Her choice for the future is to live with women; she wants to go with her girls to South Africa to be with Rachel. Sir Wentworth tells her that Lorna Levine did not find Agnes in China but heard that she had gone to South America or maybe it was South Africa. Joanna accepts this message from Lorna as a sign of the reunion of the school friends: "Why, don't you see, don't you see, we all may meet there, all three again" (303).

From their first meeting, Lorna has been a symbol to Joanna of the possibility of women's friendship and with it a shared language. Though Sir Wentworth cannot remember if Agnes was in South

America or South Africa—a distinction unimportant to him, vital
to Joanna—Joanna's faith in Lorna's power to effect such friendship
fuel's Joanna's hope. A young married woman on the ship to Africa
emerges from a brief encounter with Joanna with her fears gone and
with "a sense of confidence and freedom" (306). Significantly, she
remarks to her husband, "I believe she's going to meet her husband.
She looks like that somehow. It's as though she were expecting
something splendid" (306). The irony here is apparent—Joanna
did, of course, expect something splendid from her marriage and
found it a nightmare; this young woman, just starting out her married life, and starting it out, like Joanna's mother, in Africa, cannot
predict the suffering in store for her. But with this irony is the suggestion that what Joanna goes to now *is* something splendid and
that the something is not marriage but female community, fostered
by a shared language and based on the female educational community where Joanna, Agnes, and Rachel met and became friends.
Joanna is not going to Africa, however, in search of an elusive, idealized past. She goes rather with a practical plan for supporting herself and her daughters and for fulfilling a need in South Africa. This
plan, too, emphasizes Joanna's interest in and commitment to female community: she is going to start, having heard from Rachel
about the lack of accommodation in Johannesburg, a paying-guest
house "for young women earning their own living" (297). That
Joanna will fulfill her earliest dream of return to South Africa and
that her plans are to settle in the city whose name she bears imply
her success and fulfillment.

   Like Muriel and Delia's menage in *The Crowded Street,* a female
world dominates the end of *The Land of Green Ginger.* This world
serves women; the world consists solely of them. Significantly, both
Joanna's children are daughters and she and the girls refer to the
unborn child as Pauline. Though Agnes may have a husband,
Joanna has already dismissed him in her daydreams as much the
same as others and therefore of little account. Rachel, the professional, seems to be one of the single women whose lack of accommodation she deplores. Joanna in her "tranquil dignity" (305) has
become one of the Amazons whom her grandmother so mistakenly
feared, whose power and energy Joanna here puts to use for the ad-
vancement of women and the establishment of peaceful female
community. Though Rachel appears only briefly in the novel, it is
she, the educated woman, who holds out to Joanna hope for return

to her city and to that adventurous life which constituted her infancy; it is Rachel, the old Somervillian, who promises Joanna and other women a new plot for their lives in a female world.

In *Women and a Changing Civilization,* Holtby narrates a conversation, which she says she overheard on a bus, between a middle-aged man and an eighteen- or nineteen-year-old girl "nestling beside him"; the bus passes a girls' school and the man remarks, "Awful. . . . Imagine a place like that. All those women cooped up together, scratching each other's eyes out. Women weren't intended for that sort of thing." The girl "coos," her response: "No. . . . They were meant to be companions of men, weren't they?" Holtby comments, "Her dovelike tones never revealed the docility or satire of her motive" (1). Like *The Crowded Street* and *The Land of Green Ginger,* most of Holtby's fiction argues against the sentiments expressed here.

Teddy dies before he and their marriage can completely cripple Joanna. In Holtby's last novel, *South Riding,* Sarah Burton's lover not only dies before there is any question of marriage but has a stroke just as he is about to have intercourse with Sarah for the first time. The adventuresome, clear-sighted, determined Sarah, afraid of nothing, in succumbing to the romance plot has become "vulnerable, afraid, disarmed before a hostile world" (257). Like Joanna's agreement to become engaged to Teddy, which Rachel predicts will be Joanna's only adventure, Sarah's invitation to Carne to come to her hotel room has the potential for destroying Sarah's independence, ending her career, and being itself her last adventurous act. When she blames herself for his stroke, she is at least partly correct: the blatant invitation to sex by the headmistress of his daughter's school might well have been too much for him, but, more significantly, Sarah's situation requires Carne's death; without it, the pride, vitality, and self-respect she has retained at forty because no wedding ring has sunk into her flesh become their opposites.[2] Sarah's plot is not romance but spinsterhood—"I was born to be a spinster," she says early in the novel, "and by God, I'm going to spin" (49)—and that in the context of the female educational community which she runs.

The novel opens with Sarah's appointment as headmistress of Kiplington High School for Girls. Though she had a secure appointment as a teacher in a good school where she was respected and effective, she chooses this mediocre school in a provincial area because it will be *hers*. The other detail of Sarah's past the text offers is that she has been engaged three times. One fiancé died in the war; the second's politics became increasingly unacceptable to her;

> the third, an English Socialist member of Parliament, withdrew in alarm when he found her feminism to be not merely academic but insistent. . . . When he demanded that she should abandon, in his political interests, her profession gained at such considerable public cost and private effort, she offered to be his mistress instead of his wife and found that he was even more shocked by this suggestion than by her previous one that she should continue her teaching after marriage (48).

Sarah's spinsterhood, then, is chosen, not imposed, is a result of, not a cause of, her dedication to educating women—a dedication which inspires her charges to similar independence and determination. Lydia Holly, for example, Kiplington's scholarship pupil, begins under Sarah's influence to triumph over her squalid and oppressive family life: "she cared for nothing, was afraid of nothing. Neither squalling babies nor a scolding mother, neither the crowded van nor jam smeared over her school books, could separate her from the glory that was hers now and which was yet to come" (113). The biblical diction of this apocalyptic thought underscores Sarah's redemptive role for the young women in her school and the strength of her influence on them. Lydia's feelings for Sarah, though they partake, as Sarah well knows, of *Schwärmerei*, enable the girl to assume some of Sarah's bold philosophy in which "resignation, acceptance of avoidable suffering, timidity, and indecision," are "contemptible" (161).

It is, of course, these very contemptibles which threaten to overtake Sarah when she falls in love, not like Lydia, with an inspiring woman, but with a man who is, though kind and principled, of the conservative and patronizing sort who oppress the very women they love. Carne's mad wife, as little sympathetic as Mr. Rochester's in *Jane Eyre*, is an inevitable victim. Parallels with Brontë's novel abound, but the differences are instructive. Sarah, in new-woman fashion, eschews Jane's scruples and volunteers to become Carne's mistress. But this departure from nineteenth-century morality does little to advance women's cause. Still a representative of male sexuality and its consequences, even an ill and chastened Carne cannot be a fit companion for an ambitious woman. Jane could find satisfaction in a shared life; Sarah must, in spite of herself, subvert such a happy ending. In her book on Virginia Woolf, Holtby remarks that "marriage, once the postage stamp fixed on any heroine of fiction to insure her immediate transport to felicity, does not necessarily secure that perception" (15). Holtby sees the rejected lover Mary Datchet in Woolf's *Night and Day* as "the agent for breaking the bonds of unreality" (96), and "the light in the solitary spinster's room . . . a sign of triumph and not of loneliness." Like Mary, Sarah does not wholly acquiesce in her spinsterhood, but the prognosis in both cases is more hopeful than that for a conventional marriage.

After Carne's death, Sarah herself almost dies in an accident in a small airplane. The physical threat restores her confidence and renews her dedication. She realizes that the kind of adventurousness, the "audacious unconventionally" (487) implicit in surviving an airplane crash is part of "the charm by which she drew the girls after her idea of the good life" (487). And this idea of the good life has no room in it for that "unnecessary domestic ritual and propitiation" (183) demanded by marriage, which causes even the public-spirited Mrs. Beddows, an alderwoman like Holtby's own mother, to waste "three quarters of her time and energy" (183).

The novel opens with Sarah's appointment as headmistress to a girls' school and ends with her renewed dedication to it. Sarah's spinsterhood is, like Mary Datchet's, triumphant rather than lonely. Like Mary, she has her work; like Mary's, it promotes the cause of women. Its greatest significance, though, is that it teaches girls to rewrite the plot of their lives. Though burdened with incompetent and unsympathetic teachers whom she did not herself hire, Sarah's school is far from the abhorrent place described by the man in the bus where women are "cooped up together, scratching each other's eyes out." Her graduates would not acquiesce, like the girl nesting beside him, in his romantic antifeminism.

Sarah sets out deliberately to change the assumptions of girls' education. Ironically, the school itself "owed its independent existence to masculine pride" because "thirty years earlier the county council decided that a daily train journey to Kingsport, suitable enough to grammar school boys, was unsafe for girls. Girls were delicate. Life imperilled them" (21). Sarah herself is the antidote to this assumption. She lives on her own, she travels freely, she pursues adventure, she is fearless. She takes to task one of her teachers who perpetuates the myths of feminine weakness and the importance of coupling. Miss Jameson, engaged to be married, is "always sneering at unmarried women. She seems to think that either we all envy her her wretched little fiancé, or that we're frozen and inhuman and all riddled with complexes" (251). Like the faculty women of *Gaudy Night*, Sarah's teachers labor under the stigma of spinsterhood, which implies a life of frustration and unfulfillment. Sarah wants her students to learn otherwise. She says firmly that Miss Jameson's reenforcement of this stigma is "not kind and it's not nice. And it's not good for the girls" (251). What is good for the girls is to see the single woman alive, competent, intelligent, free, and attractive. She does not, like Mrs. Hancock, the headmistress of Muriel's school in *The Crowded Street*, deprecate and fear *Schwärmerei*. She sees clearly its value in empowering her charges to reject compulsory heterosexual romance and assumptions of female weakness and dependence. Asked how she deals with this problem, she replies "serenely, 'I control them all by monopoly and then absorb them. It's quite simple. We needs must love the highest when we see it. I take good care to be the highest in my school'" (110).

Not content, then, with training her students' minds, though that is a primary concern, Sarah diverts the creative energy of schoolgirl romances to the students' own intellectual and emotional strength. Lydia Holly's crush on Sarah, immature and predictable as it is, enables the girl to write, to sing, to fight her circumstances. Mrs. Hancock imbues Muriel with her motto "Happy in my lot," and thus reinforces the socialization of Marshington and family; Sarah Burton tries to undo such miseducation.

> To choose, to take, with clear judgment and open eyes; to count the cost and pay it, to regret nothing; to go forward, cutting losses, refusing to complain, accepting complete responsibility for their own decisions—this was the code which she attempted to impress upon the children who came under her influence. . . . Resignation . . . she found contemptible (161).

Without Delia's Oxford women's-college education, without Sarah Burton's girls' school exhortation, young women are condemned, like Muriel, to a life of resignation, of taking what they get. Life becomes, as it became to Muriel, a party which promises fun and excitement but whose rules for women of cheerful, patient waiting for a partner, of not taking and therefore not getting what they want, entrap the partygoers in a kind of hell. And the "luckier" girls who, possessed of conventional beauty and educated to charm and submission, do find fun and excitement—that is, a partner—at the party, like Joanna, also eventually experience a hell, different in content but equally painful, destructive, and ultimately more difficult to escape. Though marriage or heterosexual romantic attachment become themselves an education in the erroneous assumptions of the romance plot, this education is not curative or restorative. Though, that is, the women experience an awakening to limitation, they have no power, bound as they are by ill-health, poverty, and duty to children, to break through the boundaries.

Sarah Burton's sense that she is responsible for Carne's death is, as we have seen, partly correct. Joanna, too, with her penchant for unconventionality, may well have hastened her husband's final collapse. But these deaths are, first of all, exigencies of the new plot with an educated woman as heroine, a woman who, though she may temporarily entrap herself in the romance plot, has a way out of it. With death of the male love object, she may return with no more than minor self-reproach to association with women and the understanding, encouragement, and freedom that provides. Like Delia's Martin, Carne dies before the marriage occurs; Delia and Sarah, Oxford-educated, cognizant of the trap, already committed to other women, escape the worst of the ravages, and their ability to recover quickly from their disappointment, to enter into their careers with renewed dedication and intensity, inspires and redeems the women with whom they associate and whom they educate. That Holtby's heroines triumph convincingly and unequivocally attests to the success of her strategy for telling in a traditional narrative the story of the educated woman: the systematic elimination of men from the lives of her heroines and from her texts. Although certainly a limited and limiting strategy, it is nonetheless effective for telling the story of the educated woman without either departing so far from the genre as to eschew the romance plot altogether or endlessly repeating the inevitability of that plot. With Sarah Burton and her two dead lovers, Holtby does what she has not done before and what none of these novelists has done—she presents unambiguously the possibility that the educated, unattached woman lives a more fulfilling and exciting life than her married sister.[3]

9 Vera Brittain's
Educated Women and (the) Romance

Vera Brittain was as scornful as her best friend of the promises of heterosexual romance, of the myths of the family and the supposed unfulfilled nature of the single women, of assumptions about women's role and women's place.[1] In her journalism, in her history *Lady into Woman*, and in her fiction she describes the woman's plight. Virginia, a character in her first novel, *Dark Tide*, who, like Brittain herself, interrupted her college career to do war nursing, explains to a fellow student:

> Men as a rule do everything at woman's expense from their first day to their last. They come into the world at our expense, and at our expense they're able to do whatever work they please uninterrupted. We keep their homes pleasant for them and provide them with all creature comforts. We satisfy both their loves and their lusts, and at our expense again they have the children they desire. When they're ill we nurse them; they recover at our expense; and when they die, we lay them out and see that they leave the world respectably. If ever we can get anything out of them, or use them in anyway that makes things the least bit more even, it's not only our right to do it, it's a duty we owe to ourselves (71).

Despite this brave and bitter rhetoric, however, Virginia, afraid of her ambition, gives up academic life for a humble nursing job. Despite Brittain's own rhetoric, her novels, while they frequently deal with that new phenomenon, the Oxbridge woman, cannot find a new plot for her. The texts, instead, devise thematic variations on the romantic narrative in which educated women can retain some measure of self-respect and heroism, but even these variations partake clearly of the romance plot's assumptions about women's nature and roles. The ideological demands of the romance have priority in these texts over the thematic plot and ideological demands presented by the use of the character of the educated woman.

Daphne Lethbridge, the main character in *Dark Tide*, is a student at Drayton College, like Somerville one of the few women's colleges at Oxford and, like women's colleges in Brittain's undergraduate years, without degrees. Daphne is both naive and ambitious. At the beginning of the novel she wants "to learn everything, and get the best degree in History that woman ever had, and then to write things which would make the name of Daphne Lethbridge a household word in English literature" (11). Unfortunately, Daphne is not a genius nor has she been well-educated in her middle-class, vulgar family; nor has she begun to realize the conflict between ambition and the traditional plot so thoroughly implanted in her by her mother. Her rhetoric is vaguely feminist—she argues with a guest speaker, for example, that degrees for women are not a privilege but "simply what women deserved—their due, their right" (60)—but her instincts are not feminist at all. When she and Virginia Dennison share a history tutor, Raymond Sylvester, Daphne criticizes her fellow students: "She seemed to have none of the graceful gentleness, the soft deference, the subtle admiration which Mrs. Lethbridge had taught Daphne that she should always show to men even when she despised them, because they would never like her unless she did" (101).

There is a part of Daphne that can criticize and mildly despise her tutor. She recalls with some humor, for example, one of his typical remarks to Virginia: "This is an excellent piece of work. You've really got a splendid brain—it's clear—acute—logical— more like a man's than a woman's. In fact in many ways it reminds me of my own" (89). She recognizes Sylvester's egoism, but this perceptive judgment cannot save her from the family plot: she falls in love with the egoistical tutor, and her ambitious desires and plans shrink in proportion to her growing adulation. No one seriously objects to this change in Daphne. Although Sylvester is a poor choice, falling out of ambitions and into love seems acceptable and perhaps inevitable. Virginia, older and more sophisticated, jaded even, from her years of war-service, sees him for the absurd egoist that he is and acts accordingly. When, during the last tutorial—which he has arranged so as to see the two students separately—he proposes marriage to her, she laughs at him.

Daphne, however, does no such thing when, minutes later, out of pique and wounded pride, he proposes to *her.* Instead, she reads not his real reasons but the romantic narrative; she thinks he has, in response to her more womanly charms, her deference, her open admiration, fallen in love with her rather than with Virginia, even though she knows he thinks less of her mind and of her essays. In her desire to please her husband-to-be and in panicked response to his coolness toward her, Daphne wears herself out studying for exams and ends up with a Third while Virginia takes her expected First, but Raymond consoles Daphne with his own version of the familiar plot.

> People like Miss Dennison, he said, had a kind of cleverness which made them successful at examinations, but they were not the sort of women men wanted to live with . . . It was, of course, a good thing for the wife of a coming diplomat to have an Oxford degree, but as for the class, that didn't matter at all; it conveyed nothing to anybody outside Oxford (15).

With this permission to value the degree in the service of one's husband over the degree itself Daphne enters wholeheartedly into the romance rhetoric. She looks back on her college days and wonders how she could have been so absorbed by such trivialities as grades and exams. "What, after all, did any of them count beside the supreme love which was the consummation of those two years, that love into which she was about to enter with the joy of every woman who comes into her natural heritage?" (151) She relegates Virginia to the ranks of those unfortunate intellectuals who, though perhaps sophisticated in their way, do not know "the great elemental secrets of love and marriage and birth" (152).

The secrets, however, turn out to be not quite what Daphne expects. She is, first of all, rather disconcerted by Raymond's "passion which had almost terrified her in Paris"; though she belonged to a sophisticated generation, "she had not realized that marriage would be quite like this" (159). But worse is Raymond's near abandonment of her on the honeymoon, reminiscent of Casauban's honeymoon treatment of Dorothea in *Middlemarch*. "Sylvester presented his wife to the thin middle-aged man with the walrus mustache, and then proceeded throughout the meal to help the archaeologist to forget Daphne's existence" (166). Later, left alone to amuse herself, Daphne enters a cathedral where in her exhausted and by this time pregnant state, she has a strange sense that the cathedral is

> less like a building than a being. . . . Daphne almost ex-
> pected to see the pillars move, as if they were the heaving sides
> of a great supernatural creature. . . . Above the arches the
> sculptured heads of the Popes seemed to lean over and look
> down at her . . . Gregory the Great—Innocent III—Clement
> VII—Pius IX—their familiar names chased one another
> vaguely through her mind, lulled into drowsiness by incense
> and fatigue.
> And then, all at once, she realized what they were doing
> there. Of course—this big place with the striped pillars was
> the hall of the Examination Schools where she was doing her
> Finals, and all these Popes were the invigilators (169).

The oppressively male and malely oppressive cathedral contrasts sharply with Daphne's passive and pregnant state; the male menace is both sexual and judgmental. The "being endued with strange life," the "heaving sides," her own shrinking, the men leaning over and looking down on her, describe more accurately than her con-scious thoughts that experience which she has assured herself is "perfectly all right when you loved someone like she did—only it must be rather dreadful for people who married for some other rea-son" (59). These elements of a sexual initiation that sound rather like rape become confused, in her half-dreaming state, with that other experience of male dominance and power to judge—the ex-amination at which she tried so hard and did so badly. A period of unnatural tension and excitement precedes both events; a de-pletion of energy and ambition follow both; both frighten, both demand, both find her unprepared, ill-advised, and without com-fort—a woman alone in a male world.

Daphne, however, ignorant still of the inauspicious circumstances of her engagement, continues to believe in the romance
plot. Though Raymond's obnoxious behavior during their honeymoon continues—he ignores her, criticizes her, mocks her—she
hopes that the coming child will make a difference and she continues to value even her miserable marriage over previous plans.
"Daphne's early dreams of a great career seemed to her like chimeras
vanishing into the dusk of remembrance. All hopes, all visions, all
ambitions had long been absorbed into the one aspiration of winning back her husband's love through her child" (213).

Daphne is not alone among the educated women in this novel
in allowing the romance plot to overshadow her ambitions and
dreams. Virginia questions this phenomenon in a discussion with
Patricia O'Neill, a tutor who is engaged to be married to a fellow
tutor: "Why does this one thing make all one's work and all one's
achievement seem dust and ashes, however much worthwhile it
really is?" (204) It is a question of desperation rather than astonish-
ment; she asks here not "How can women let this happen to them?"
but "Why is it always like this?" The difference between those
two questions seems slight, but is, in fact, significant. Although
Daphne's case may be extreme in that she succumbed too soon and
to a cad, even Patricia's more mature and appropriate choice in-
volves a significant diminution of her work and implies acquies-
cence to at least some aspects of the romance plot; she hopes, for
example, that if she has children, they will be sons. Because Patricia's marriage so deliberately contrasts with Daphne's, because
Patricia herself is the most balanced and sensible character in the
novel, the text seems to assume the inevitability that the romance
will take precedence over work. There is great value in work, of
course, the text assures, because it's there, as Patricia tells Daphne
later in the novel, "when everything else is gone" (267)—that is,
its chief value to the woman worker is as a last resort. Write a
novel, Patricia urges Daphne. Fill your life with something because
your marriage has failed and your child is a disappointment. Work,
she implies, is important for a woman because marriages fail and
children disappoint, but marriage and children continue to be what
women really want.

Daphne's persistence in adhering to her husband and the recognition and admiration her persistence evokes, confirms this. So little
does Raymond Sylvester love her that he takes up with another

woman and finally ends his relationship with Daphne by hitting her and then abandoning her altogether. The blow, unbeknownst to Sylvester, causes a serious fall which precipitates early labor. As a result, the child is weak and crippled; furthermore, it is a son—a disappointment to Daphne who, feeling after her failure with her husband that she cannot "manage" (184) a male, wanted a daughter. Now, Daphne realizes, circumstances have really trapped her: "Jack would be more dependent on her care than any daughter. Round this frail human creature her world must be re-created; she must spend the rest of her days in striving to atone to him for the injury which had incapacitated him through no fault of his own" (269).

This heroic rhetoric is convincing in so far as the reader acknowledges Daphne's responsibility for the child. But Daphne's next act of selflessness and the reinforcement it receives from other characters imply that the womanly role of self-sacrifice demanded by the romance plot is the ultimate heroism. Raymond has, in his absence from home, begun to make his way into politics. His main opportunity comes when he is asked to run as a Liberal Constitutional Candidate—on an anti-divorce platform. He must, therefore, return to Daphne to ask her not to divorce him, since such a scandal would obviously ruin his campaign. Daphne, adhering to the dictates of the true love plot, tells him, "I'm as much of a fool as most women and there's one part of me that loves you and wants you as badly as ever" (309). Though he assures her that he does not love her, never has, and cannot come back, she agrees not to divorce him so that, through his public office, he can do good in the world. Virginia Dennison, who has nursed Daphne through her injury and childbirth and in the process has become her best friend, admires and praises her action. "You're giving up a great deal for Raymond," she tells Daphne, "—your just retribution for the many wrongs he's done you, your hopes for the future, even in a way your own honour. He isn't worth it—and that's what makes your sacrifice a splendid thing" (319). Virginia, then, though she herself refused Raymond's proposal, though she has known all along the real reason he married Daphne, though she has experienced with Daphne his irresponsibility, cruelty, and brutality, acquiesces none the less in Daphne's adherence to the romance code.

Further, Virginia, though she has not yet met a man to marry, has in spite of her Drayton education begun to regard her intellect as temptation. Instead of entering academic life, which, with her acknowledged brilliance and Oxford First, she is well-qualified to do, she chooses to become a nurse, a profession at which she is competent but which does not engage her analytic mind. To Patricia she writes, "If sometimes what I'm doing disappoints you, remember I have only one great enemy and that's my own intellect" (216). Patricia defends this position to Daphne, thus giving Virginia's sacrifice status as Virginia has given Daphne's. Later in the novel, Virginia explains to Daphne more clearly why she has made this choice: "Haven't you realized that I'm one of those unhappy people whose own gifts are their worst temptation? Intellectual success goes to my head like cheap champagne. I had to give up all chance of ever achieving it before I could do anything worth doing, anything that wasn't simply a glorification of myself!" (284). Though Virginia acted snobbishly at Dayton, nothing in the text suggests a concrete reason for such renunciation. Enjoyment of success and assertion of self at the expense of another, even though that other has by his actions relinquished claim to consideration are, in this text, as unacceptable for a woman as in any traditional love story. That these women have a university education—that they have, that is, spent several years and enormous energy in training their minds—seems to gain them little freedom or happiness. Though Oxford seemed, while she was a student, an exciting and challenging place, Daphne does not know whether she would send a daughter there. Patricia says she would, but Patricia does not even want to have a daughter.

In spite of this rejection of Drayton, in *Dark Tide* as in so many of the other novels these Somervillians wrote, it is the female educational community and/or relationships with other women that endure. Just before Raymond Sylvester's furious attack on his pregnant wife, she faints at a party he has planned to further his political ambitions. This late-pregnancy fainting sequence parallels the early-pregnancy sequence at the cathedral. The same transition from distorted reality to dream occurs, but this time the imagery is quite different. During a conversation at the party about weapons, Daphne thinks that her teacup is growing,

> getting enormous, colossal, altogether too heavy for her to hold. . . . It was not a cup at all, but a huge abyss full of tea, yawning wide at her feet, ready to receive her when she could

> stand no longer on the quaking floor. . . . And she must fall—
> she couldn't keep her balance anymore with everything around
> rocking like a ship at sea. . . . She clutched out wildly to save
> herself, but there was nothing to hold except the hot, slippery
> sides of the cup. Frantically struggling, she toppled headlong
> into it. The tea rose up all round her, enveloping her in warm,
> black waves (233).

Instead of the heaving phallic pillars from which she shrank in the
early dream, here the teacup, associated in both shape and function
with the female, tempts her to relinquish the male world in which
she functions so clumsily. The teacup is "ready to receive her,"
it envelops her, it offers warmth and unconsciousness. Daphne
succumbs.

As though recognizing the significance of this dark baptism, Raymond is disproportionately and irrationally angry at Daphne's fainting in front of his guests. It is the subsequent argument which
occasions his blow and his desertion. On the practical level, then,
Daphne does indeed cease to belong to the male world, and she enters a very female one. Virginia, her former rival and enemy—she
had at Drayton hated Virginia Dennison and her "perpetual triumphs" (150) and Virginia had despised her—finds her fallen and
injured and comes to nurse her; after Sylvester's desertion Patricia
O'Neill, too, reappears to befriend Daphne. The only remaining
male in Daphne's life is the pathetically deformed and helpless child
Sylvester has left her, the male legacy. Even Raymond's mistress,
the opera singer Lucia, becomes a part of this enveloping sea of
women who understand and support Daphne. Lucia meets her and
thinks, "She had doubtless been through a very hard time—like
most women who expected men to be reasonable instead of treating
them as the spoilt children that they were" (294). Lucia, unlike
Daphne, knows how to function in the male world and promises by
her attitude toward men in general and Raymond in particular to
execute the "just retribution" which the selfless Daphne eschews.
True to her role of Carmen, which has made her famous and attracted Raymond to her in the first place, Lucia assures Daphne,
"One day I shall tire of him . . . I will love as it pleases me, but
I will not lose my freedom" (297). Even the "fallen woman" offers
to act for the battered Daphne whom life and men have dealt so
many blows.

While, however, this revenge which Lucia promises is on some level necessary for what little self-respect Daphne has, it is the educated women, the college-associated friends who try to help her construct a new life and who validate her self-sacrifice. What Oxford has given these fictional women turns out to be not worthwhile intellectual work, not self-esteem, not even the ability to make their way in the world. Daphne gets herself a husband whom "Oxford had given . . . her" (150) and who has ruined her life. Virginia gives up the intellectual life because Oxford has tempted her to self-centeredness and desire for recognition. It has, however, given them one another—no small thing, perhaps, in a world in which "men . . . do everything at women's expense" (71).

Though the text does not, of course, explicitly address the question of the value of education for women, the issue is everywhere present and everywhere confused. At the beginning of the novel, Daphne and her friends try to bait the older Virginia Dennison by asking her to argue the debate proposal "that a life of travel is a better education than a life of academic experience."[2] She agrees and loses the debate—not because her points are any less valid than those of the younger women. The topic then disappears from the story but the issues it raises continue to dog the lives of its women. When Patricia asks, "Is it to be a girl, Daphne—and shall you send her to Drayton?" Daphne replies, " . . . as for sending her to Drayton—I don't know" (215). She tries to explain her hesitation by vague reference to her own experience, "it seems to me that you ought to have learnt widsom before you ever go there, or else you find you're faced with problems that you've no idea how to solve" (215). Caught as they are between the romance plot and the taste of academic work and female community they get at Oxford, these educated women emerge from their university experience bewildered, restless, and less equipped to deal with the male world than their uneducated counterparts. The discrepancy between Daphne's early rhetoric and the implications of her life choices mirror the discrepancy between the implications of this text and the unequivocal sense of the importance of higher education for women on which Brittain insists in her prose.

This discrepancy does, however, disappear in Brittain's later fiction, in which there is sometimes an explicit comparison, as in Holtby's *The Crowded Street*, between the uneducated and the educated woman—to the latter's advantage. In *Not Without Honour,* for example, the intelligent Christine Merivale wants a career and independence but her family insist that she "come out" and lead a life of leisured sociability. When, as a result, she is flattered into an unsuitable attachment, an older friend tells Christine's father, "You must train her for an occupation; she's only helpless because you've allowed her to become so. Her brains are good and could be developed if she went to college" (267). In *Honourable Estate* the son of an uneducated but ardent suffragist writes a letter to his Oxford-educated wife:

> I do want you to know how much I love and admire you for the way you have cared for our children, in spite of your inclinations being political, like my mother's, and not domestic. I sometimes used to think that because you are so much better qualified intellectually than she was . . . you would resent the claims of the twins on your time even more than she resented mine on hers. But instead you seem to have given them more thought and care than they would have had from the usual domesticated mother with only her household and children to consider (514).

In *Honourable Estate,* however, the clear and unequivocal advantage of Ruth over her mother-in-law Janet is in service of the romance and family-life narrative. Ruth, unlike naive Janet, marries appropriately and experiences no conflict between a successful public life in politics and an equally successful private life as exemplary wife and mother. Furthermore, unlike the novels of Brittain's friend Winifred Holtby and unlike her own early *Dark Tide, Honourable Estate* sets forth a world surprisingly male, heterosexual, and monogamous; even Janet's passionate attachment to Gertrude Ellison Campbell seems a substitute for ill-chosen marriage and, in the end, even less sustaining.

The novel opens with scenes from the marriage of Janet and Thomas, a clergyman who believes firmly that a woman's place is at home caring for husband and children. Though Janet tries to be a good wife, she finds herself unable to settle down to the limited life of an unpaid curate which Thomas expects of her. In her frustration she turns to politics, especially to women's suffrage. In this work she

finds the words to analyse the deplorable situation she sees as indicative of the situation of all women. Thomas finds such analysis
in his wife's diary, which he believes he has a right to read:

> The woman question is the result of girls' education and the
> mistaken conception of marriage which they are taught. Girls
> should have perfect freedom to exercise their wills in the dis-
> posal of their lives, to use their brains and bestow their affec-
> tions. They should possess or make for themselves independent
> positions, so that love and loyalty to each other and each
> other's interest may be the keynote of marriage. With educated
> women possessing this independence, they would marry only
> men who themselves could rise to the highest conception of
> marriage (28).

Janet is conscious of what her "education" has done to her and sees
the remedy in education of quite a different sort. These reflections
horrify her husband, as do her resentful entries about her first preg-
nancy and her admission that she tried to terminate the second.
Their relationship deteriorates as Thomas becomes more dictatorial
and censorious and Janet less attentive. A parish-wide argument
over whether Miss Garston, the local teacher, should be allowed to
retain her post after marriage, an argument in which, predictably,
husband and wife are on opposite sides, precipitates Thomas's resignation of his parish and Janet's conviction that she can no longer go
on living with him.

Meanwhile, Janet has met the playwright Gertrude Ellison Campbell, who becomes her best friend and the center of her life. Campbell, too, is tied to a querulous and self-absorbed male—her invalid
brother—and the two women escape to London whenever possible
for theater and for days alone together. Campbell, who significantly
prefers the male name "Ellison" to "Gertrude," and Denis, Janet's
neglected son, convince Janet to stay in her marriage. With Ellison
Campbell's love, Janet finds this just bearable; and Ellison, jealous
of Janet's commitment to women's suffrage, breaks off their relationship and thereby deprives Janet of her only comfort and intimacy.
Janet then plunges even further into suffrage work, now heedless of
the consequences. She tries, at one point, to burn down her husband's church as an act of protest but is discovered and prevented by
Denis. The narrator's comment on Denis's bewilderment is that it

would take him many years to realize fully that "the energetic, gifted woman to whom society offers no outlet for her energy and no scope for her talents, invariably turns anti-social and may become anything from an Olympias to a Lucrezia Borgia" (160). Finally, Janet leaves her husband and child to live in London where "without love or companionship" (188), she dies of acute peritonitis. The melodramatic extravagance of both plot and rhetoric reinforces the text's insistence that such a life is typical of the uneducated or wrongly educated "energetic, gifted woman." She chooses a husband wrongly; she knows nothing about sex or birth control, so ends up unfulfilled and saddled with children she does not want; she does not recognize the motives behind Ellison Campbell's desertion; she cannot discriminate between effective and merely cathartic political activities. She cannot even survive.

Janet's daughter-in-law and modern double, Ruth Allyndene, offers a point-by-point contrast, in spite of the two women's acknowledged similarities. Both Denis and a now chastened, repentant Ellison Campbell notice how like Ruth is to her husband's dead mother—"the same dynamic energy, the same impatient vitality, the same refusal to be chained by circumstances, the same swift intelligent responsiveness to unspoken suggestions and half-framed ideas" (586). But Ruth goes first to Playden Manor Girls' school, whose headmistress is a graduate of Drayton College, and then to Drayton itself where, before she considers marriage, she becomes interested in women's rights and understands, therefore, as Janet did not, that what is at stake in contracting a marriage is her own dignity and independence. Janet's son encounters her by chance at Oxford where he, too, is a student and where he, too, has become interested in women's suffrage. He is walking down Walton Street (the site of Somerville) when he notices "that the heavy entrance door of Drayton, the most arrogantly intellectual of the Oxford women's colleges, stood invitingly open" (163). In spite of a certain nervousness about its "cloistered seclusion" (163), Denis begins to walk through the grounds and, spotted by a lovely student, stammers, "I beg your pardon . . . but can I get through this way to the Woodstock Road?" The student is, of course, Ruth, who, conscious of the worth of both herself and her college says only, "Certainly—if you don't object to using us as a short-cut" (164). Her reply indicates both pride in Drayton and wariness of Oxford males who are willing enough to use the women's colleges to their own advantage

214 Brittain's Educated Women

and unwilling to grant the colleges their due. Denis's own respect for Drayton and unresentful response to Ruth's contempt prefigures the eventual relationship between the two—a relationship of mutual respect, intellectual equality, and civilized consideration. Ruth's potential, then, for choosing an appropriate life partner is enhanced by her Drayton experience in that it informs her of the issues, teaches her discrimination and self worth, and exposes her to educated, like-minded men.

Ruth's Drayton experience is supplemented by an educational experience she shares in some way by most women of her generation—World War I. It is Brittain, of these novelists, who, perhaps because of her own years as an active participant in that war, most emphasizes its importance in the making of the modern woman. She "chronicled" this importance in her war diary, re-formed that material into her best-known work, *Testament of Youth*, and wrote about it extensively in her fiction. She sensed early that the war was not only a very different experience for women than for men but that such difference would come between (*TY*, 185) her and Roland, her fiancé, would put between women and men "a barrier of indescribable experience . . . a permanent impediment to understanding" (*TY*, 143). Though she seems to have had in mind primarily men's closer involvement and greater risks, she realized later that the war was a turning point for women, and that in very positive, exciting ways. We have already seen that one effect of the war was a lessening of the opposition to suffrage and degrees for women; both were frequently presented as rewards for good behavior and war service.[3] Sandra Gilbert in her essay "Soldier's Heart," maintains further that "as young men become increasingly alienated from their prewar selves, increasingly immured in the muck and blood of No Man's Land, women seemed to become, as if by some uncanny swing of history's pendulum, ever more powerful" (200). Brittain's texts, especially *Honourable Estate*, express this power as knowledge and express it in the rhetoric of education.

The war *teaches* Ruth, for example, about sex, passion, family planning and homosexuality—all subjects which the Edwardian Janet needed to know about, all subjects about which she was wholly ignorant, with an ignorance which cost her both love and life. Ruth's experience is, of course much different from her mother-in-law's.

Working as a nurse for the duration of the war, Ruth falls in love with an American soldier who had been with her beloved brother Richard when he died at the front. The soldier, Eugene, brings her a letter from Richard in which he explains that he intended to get himself killed in the upcoming battle in order to avoid a possible court-martial for his relationship with a friend; the two young men decided that, under the harrowing circumstances of the trenches, "The only thing to do was to be everything we possibly could to one another" (342). The letter makes Ruth understand and to some extent sympathize with a way of loving which had previously seemed unthinkable and contemptible. Again, she has learned something not available to Janet. After Ruth and Denis have married, Ruth reads Janet's diary and concludes that Ellison Campbell was in love with Janet. Denis says, "Of course nobody thought of such a thing in those days, least of all the people concerned" (594). The implication is that had Janet understood, had Ellison Campbell understood, the erotic element in that passionate friendship, the separation which took away Janet's will to live could have been avoided. That Ruth and Eugene can rationally discuss, if a bit circuitously, her brother's homosexual relationship testifies to the sexual awareness, the new tolerance, and the more casual relationships between men and women fostered by the war and by education.[4]

Moreover, during the war Ruth's status as an Oxford graduate— and the maturity and competence signaled by that status—secures her more privileges than her fellow nurses had, privileges which facilitate the new knowledge which the war can offer. Ruth's frequent meetings with Eugene, who as an American is *ipso facto* a rulebreaker, result from this greater freedom and, partaking as they do of the urgency and uncertainty of the war, these meetings foster an increasing fondness for each other despite Eugene's engagement to Dallas, a young woman back home. Unlike Janet, then, Ruth experiences sexual passion and longs for that physical relationship which Janet knew only as her husband's selfish way of getting her pregnant. Her ignorance of the physical side of marriage, she thinks later, possibly propelled her into marrying for the wrong reason— "the admiration of a man so much older than herself" (39) or her "feeling of desolation" (42) and loneliness just after her mother's death. Ruth, on the other hand, goes into marriage not only with knowledge about sex but with sexual experience, a fact which helps her make a reasoned, informed choice of a mate—interestingly enough, *not* someone she feels passion for but someone like-minded, interesting, and loving.

Ruth's decision to sleep with Eugene, "to give all I had to give and hold back nothing" (497), is precipitated by her acquisition of information about birth control. Such knowledge makes her marriage to Janet's son something quite different from Janet's marriage to Thomas. Like Janet, Ruth does not have a strong maternal instinct but she thinks having a child with Denis would be "worthwhile" (490). Denis, unlike his father, defers to her wishes in the matter, "It's entirely for you to decide, darling. I'd never condemn any woman to that ordeal against her will" (490). He defers, knowing that such deference does not necessitate absence of a sexual relationship. And Ruth's desire for "a year first of work and marriage combined" before she has a child is easily accommodated. Her mother-in-law, on the contrary, had become pregnant almost immediately and recorded over and over again her resentment that Thomas "has had *all* the say. It seems grossly unfair, while it is I alone who am to spend my health and imperil my life in childbearing" (26).

As we have seen, Ruth, like Janet in so many ways, makes a better mother. Ruth's explanation for this summarizes the differences in the women's lives:

> To begin with, I wanted the twins and we agreed about having them, whereas your mother was not only unready for a child and quite ignorant, but apparently was never consulted. She was also expected to know how to manage you without any instruction, as though the knowledge of a baby's needs could be acquired by instinct . . . Don't you see that it is just because I am better qualified than your mother and still able to go on with my work, that I care so much? (516)

Ruth *knows*; Janet was ignorant; Ruth gets *instruction*; Janet had none; Ruth is *qualified* to do a job; Janet was not. Though the text makes the war responsible in large part for "the new woman," the rhetoric of education pervades the novel, makes the "lessons" of war of a piece with the "lessons" of Oxford, and implies that education is the solution to the problems of women and that educated women, far from being unfit for motherhood, make the best mothers, a rhetoric familiar from early defenses of women's education. Janet worked for women's freedom and independence; Ruth, whose education has given her that freedom and independence, works for what the text identifies as the larger cause of world peace. The educated woman, then, can combine motherhood and careers and can improve not only the family but the war-torn world.

Ruth Allyndene, who, unlike Janet, has it all, has, however, no female community. Her closest relationship with another woman is her affinity and fascination with the dead Janet. Like her biblical counterpart, Ruth follows her mother-in-law and redoes her life work. But Janet is dead when Ruth comes to know about her, and relationships among women seem almost superfluous in this world in which women can have what they want. Even Ellison Campbell's attachment to Janet, though on one hand it seems rooted in Campbell's tendency to lesbianism, might on the other hand, the text implies, have been unnecessary in this new, modern, saner world. The aging Campbell notes that "Quite a number of young women seemed to imagine that it was possible to marry and have children and bring them up decently and yet occupy a leading position in some art or profession" (584), a situation as clearly beyond Campbell's imagination as her sacrifices are beyond theirs: "if she confided in them her belief that marriage and children would have vitiated her art," she predicts, they would "respond with some modern jargon about the best of both worlds and getting rid of your inhibitions" (584). Her choice of a male name implies her inability to be both artist and woman, that is, the woman of romance, incomplete without a man. As female artist before the war, then, Campbell must masculinize herself. Her lesbianism, the text hints, is simply the result of having given up marriage and children for her art, the result of feeling obliged to choose between them, the result of her nineteenth-century sexual inhibitions.

The only other woman in the novel is the "wronged" woman—Dallas Lowell, Eugene's fiancée. When Ruth goes to the United States on a speaking tour, she happens to meet Dallas and must confront again her passionate relationship with the American soldier. At first Ruth does not want to talk to her rival but finally agrees. The two women have lunch together and over food and cigarettes, symbolic here of their status as new women, they discuss their respective relationships with the charming man they both loved and their lives after his death. Dallas describes her work as

the manager of advertising for Eugene's father's newspaper, while
Ruth speculates on the advantages of the modern world:

> A hundred years ago, Dallas Lowell and I would have been
> among those lost war-victims, neglected and unrecorded,
> whose mainspring of life was permanently broken when the
> men for whom they were destined died. At least this century, if
> it did smash the world for thousands of women, has given them
> the compensation of work" (546).

The choice of words here is significant. First, a woman is "destined"
for a particular man. Dallas emphasizes this by her spinsterhood—
"it's never been possible to switch over to someone else" (544); second, work is, again, "compensation." Her work is important to her,
not for itself, but because of its association with Eugene: "I adore
my work, because I'm doing some of the things Eugene would have
done if he'd lived" (545); even Ruth's important political activities
seem often her way of compensating for the passion she had briefly
experienced with Eugene and knows she will never have again.

In a melodramatic farewell to Eugene's memory, Ruth exclaims
"Henceforth I mustn't think of you as the centre of my life and the
only source of all that's dear to me. I have made someone else the
axis round which everything I am and do will revolve" (500). Even
the liberated, educated, modern Ruth sees her whole life and work
revolving around a man, first Eugene, then Denis, with the apparent complicity of the text. Dallas's life might be useful and her work
important, but without Eugene both lack purpose, excitement, and
passion. Ruth, destined perhaps for someone else, is luckier, because she does have what the women in these texts seem most to
want—a husband and family as focus for a varied, active, semi-
independent life. Ellison Campbell, in renouncing marriage and
family, produced a lifetime of plays that were good, that brought her
fame and recognition, but that lacked emotion and relevance to the
modern world, qualities which, the text suggests, a richer—that is,
in the text's terms, heterosexual and romantic—personal life would
have conferred on her work.

Finally, education and women's consequent emergence into public life begin to erode that last remnant of women's subordination,
what Brittain calls in her journalism "the most enervating influence
that women have to contend with," the "inferiority complex"

(Berry, 113). Ellison Campbell, the eminent, prolific playwright, continues to suffer from her inferiority complex until her death. She does not see herself as the unusual presence she is, but as "plain, awkward and unimpressive" (578). The crowd's ovation astonishes her: "Never could she conquer the feeling that enthusiasm shown for her plays or her presence was somehow due to a misunderstanding. Once she had a dream in which she was tried and convicted for obtaining applause on false pretenses" (578). Janet might be said to have died of her inferiority complex. Ruth, on the other hand, receives matter-of-factly her election to Parliament and the "flowers and banners" (535) of the Philadelphia crowd.

What education and post war society make possible in these novels, then, are better, more confident wives and mothers, women who participate, also with confidence, in art and politics while they provide companionship for their husbands and superior care for their children. If for some unlucky women marriage is not possible, education and modernity provide compensatory work and consequently moderately worthwhile lives.[5] What these novels claim as the ideal for the educated woman is that she marry, have children, and have a career; that, further, education enables her to do all these things better than her mother's generation did them. Ruth's own mother admits that "Ruth does far more for the twins than I ever did for you children. I never pushed a pram, or baked or dressed you as she does Jack and Jill. Nurses didn't expect so much off-duty time in those days" (574).[6] Like, presumably, other children of such mothers, Ruth's children—one of each sex, generically named—benefit from the added contact and from the more interesting, independent lives their mother now leads and from her new enjoyment of them. Ruth believes that "the cruelest thing society can do to children is to insist on their mothers sacrificing everything for them. An intelligent and talented person simply gets to dislike the creature for whom she is expected to do that" (516). Given productive work, that hoped-for corollary of a good education, a woman fulfills not only herself but her husband and children as well and effects significant contributions to her society, without falling into any of the pitfalls of her predecessors: she neglects none of her obligations.

In this text, education serves as the foundation, for women, of numerous accomplishments, but no special significance attaches here to the female educational community; if it serves any function at all, it is, quite properly the text implies, left behind as a woman goes about the business of her life, husband, children, and a career, preferably one of public service. Brittain's own attitude toward such a community was probably similar. In 1939 she lunched at the University Women's Club and commented that it was "full of grim-looking desiccated spinsters in appalling tweeds." She continued, "Heaven preserve Shirley [her daughter] from an academic career" (*CF*, 339)! This association of the academic woman with spinsterhood was natural enough at the time, but the further association of spinsterhood with desiccation plays out the notion that the female community must be left behind if a woman is to lead a fertile life. While she acknowledged the problems of a gifted woman who must respond to the demands of a husband and children and admitted to feeling sometimes "that writing women oughn't to marry," she added that "when, like Phyllis [Bentley], they don't, the results in tenseness and repression seem almost as tragic" (*CF*, 103).

Lynne Layton suggests that Brittain's early dislike of and lack of respect for women dissipated during her "personalization of the war," which engendered "a shift from male to female identification" (82). While it is certainly clear that after the war and after (I think more importantly) Somerville, Brittain discovered the importance and pleasure of friendship with women, she continued to assert indirectly in both her fiction and her journals that what women most needed was men. At the same time, however, she functioned best with her husband across the Atlantic and with daily association with her women friends. Her long-term relationship with Winifred Holtby was not her only passionate friendship with another woman.[7] The stormy, short-lived "affair" (it was probably not sexual) with Phyllis Bentley, for example, bears all the marks of a romance. In 1932 Brittain said she gave one of her very best lectures "Because it was done in front of Phyllis, of course" (*CF*, 112). The next day she and Phyllis "talked about the queer way that we'd 'fallen in love' with each other" (113).

What I am suggesting here is that Brittain herself, as well as her fiction, wants and does not want to put women at the center, wants and does not want to explore the possibilities of women alone or women with other women, wants and does not want to admit her own sexual attraction to and attractiveness to other women. The easiest way to live out this ambivalence for Brittain and her heroines is to act one way and dream another. Like Daphne *Lethe*bridge,

Brittain and Ruth "forget" the power of the female educational community and move on to a "larger" world of men and heterosexual romance while Daphne's teacup dream, Ruth's dreamlike fascination with her mother-in-law[8] and Brittain's own "queer" attachments suggest the bridge over Lethe to be less sturdy than promised by the romance plot.

This plot is at the center both of Brittain's fiction and her autobiographical project:[9] the story of Eugene and Ruth supersedes the story of Ruth and Denis; the story of Vera and Roland supersedes the story of Brittain's non-romantic marriage to George Catlin in 1925. In fact, there is scant story of the marriage at all. Although Catlin was apparently responsible for not wanting to be portrayed in Brittain's work (just as he says little of her in his own—see Heilbrun, Intro. *TF*), nevertheless it seems significant that Brittain's first diary ends in 1917 and is not resumed for fifteen years. When she describes her wedding day in *Testament of Experience* she, seemingly compulsively, must mention "Roland, to whom, but for a machine-gun bullet in wartime France, I should now be married instead of marrying G." (18). Roland comes alive in the war year's diary as a character comes alive in a novel; their romance reads like fiction. But one can easily finish all three testaments and the diaries and still wonder who George Catlin was, or, more to the point, who Brittain perceived him to be, presumably someone different from Vera's husband described in Stella Benson's diary, "so excessively posed, so full of Bloomsbury affectations and Cultchuh." She adds, "He annoyed me dreadfully" (Grant, 251).

The Winifrid Holtby character in the testaments and diaries resists both the fictionalizing inherent in the Roland character and the marginalization of the Catlin character. But there is a point in the diaries at which Holtby does become a character in a Brittain romance plot. As Holtby lies dying in the hospital, Brittain, keeping silent about the severity of this final illness, arranges for an old and close friend of Holtby to propose marriage to her because she had expressed a desire for that security. The friend, knowing that Holtby cannot live, willingly makes the proposal, and she dies happy, according to Brittain, knowing that she was engaged and thus a potentially normal Brittain heroine. That this literal plot so closely resembles Brittain's literary plots makes the entire incident seem an almost deliberate attempt to deny the centrality to Holtby of her relationship with Brittain in the same way that Brittain's literary plots deny, on one level at least, the centrality of women's relationships to one another, relationships which must eventually give way to male-female relationships, preferably romantic ones. Similarly, Janet's women-centered concerns in *Honourable Estate*—enormously important concerns at the time but in Ruth's adulthood, the text suggests, nearly resolved—give way to the "real" work of societal reform which requires the labor and talent of educated, liberated women, much as Brittain's own impassioned feminism gave way to her work for world peace.

In spite of many likenesses between the novels and lives of Holtby and Brittain, those of the latter continue to place the romance plot, albeit with an educated woman as heroine, at the center. Ruth's "semi-detached marriage" (the title of one of Brittain's *Evening News* articles, Berry, 130) and political career fail, as I have claimed, to move either the reader or the heroine herself as does the passionate relationship with Eugene, which Nicola Beauman in *A Very Great Profession* describes as constituting "the most powerful part of the six-hundred-page novel" (262). Made possible, in part, by her education, this relationship, the text implies, gives meaning and impetus not only to Ruth's life but to Dallas's and indirectly to poor Janet's—Janet, who was so cruelly robbed of both education and romance that her misguided attachment to Ellison Campbell offered her the only comfort she had. Janet could not have had an affair with a Eugene because women did not know about sex and birth control, because women did not have independence and mobility, but given these advantages they can free themselves from precipitate marriages, twisted attachments, and unnecessary sacrifices. They can, as Ellison Campbell complains, have it all—romance, marriage, children, independent lives, and meaningful work, but the greatest of these, according to these texts, is still romance.

It seems fitting to end this study with the novels of Vera Brittain, first of all because her fiction, more intensely autobiographical than the other Somervillians', illustrates well the tendency of the romance plot to take over. But more interesting is its tendency to infect even the overt autobiographies. Pickering notices that *Testament of Youth* is built on the structure of romantic comedy, ending, after the years of grief and isolation, in the traditional comic conclusion of marriage (76). Yet Brittain's testaments are not simply (if there is such a "simply") autobiographies. They are, perhaps, like Sayers' detective fiction and Jaeger's parable and Holtby's absent-hero novels, one way out of the romance bind. While the romantic plot, because it writes our lives, cannot help writing even alternative fiction, the testaments allow, for Brittain, more variations, expose more explicit confusions, encourage more consistent questioning. Marvin Rintala complains that Brittain "mixed the most particular and the most universal experiences" (23); he quotes a passage from *Testament of Experience* to support his complaint: "I returned to find Shirley with a high temperature and the doctor advised a tonsils operation. I had just arranged for this to be done immediately after G.'s return, when Hitler marched into Prague" (*TE*, 196). But this juxtaposition of the concerns of war and peace is by no means an illustration, as Rintala implies, of Brittain's messy female mind and lack of literary gifts. Rather, it typifies the flexibility of the testaments to include the female experience outside romance. Novelists, including Tolstoy and Styron, can juxtapose the concerns of war and peace, that is, battle and romance, in their fiction without accusations of harboring trivial minds and lacking elementary writing skills, because romance and war share certain ideological presuppositions. Dealing with a sick child, however, and the implicit conviction that "G." should have to deal with the child as well, falls to some extent outside those presuppositions. Because autobiography can legitimately concern itself with details of its subject's everyday existence, even in the midst of worldwide crises, and does, in fact, almost demand such a personal approach to the political, it is a genre well-suited to chronicling the chaos of the educated woman's concerns. While it can not free itself entirely any more than women's lives can free themselves entirely from the demands of the romance plot, it can, nonetheless, offer more flexibility than the traditional novel. Brittain's testaments and, now, chronicles, offer us a protagonist at once passionately involved in the political and unavoidably immersed in the personal—a personal which moves beyond the compelling but predictable love-affair with Roland to the more daily, more surprising, more sustaining relationships with a less romantic husband, an intimate woman friend, a son and daughter, as well as a myriad of less intense relationships, mostly with women.

Critics usually agree that the autobiographical writings are Brittain's best works and most unusual achievement. Most of the work which has been done on her has rightly, I think, emphasized her autobiographical writings. This work, combined with a new interest in women's autobiography, promises increasingly sophisticated discussions of Brittain's journals kept, in part, because she believed that what she experienced and what she had to say about that experience was of universal significance. In a foreword to her diary, which she had hoped to publish in 1922, she wrote, "I belong to the few who believe in all sincerity that their own lives provide the answers to some of the many problems which puzzle humanity" (CY, 13). None of those nagging little inferiority complexes so hated by both Brittain and Holtby are in evidence here, none of the apologies for putting pen to paper or lengthy explanations for daring to think that her life would be of any interest to anyone which often characterize female autobiographical efforts like *The Book of Margery Kempe* or the works of Teresa of Avila.

What is of particular interest, however, to a discussion of Brittain's fiction is a comment she makes in the "Foreword" (1933) to *Testament of Youth*: "My original idea was that of a long novel, and I started to plan it. To my dismay it turned out a hopeless failure; I never got much further than the planning, for I found that the people and events about which I was writing were still too near and too real to be made subjects of an imaginative, detached reconstruction" (12). It seems to have been Brittain's painfully felt experience that the novel, which she had envisioned as a "detached reconstruction," could not contain her own educated and war-worn self. When she finally did feel able to fictionalize at least portions of this material, she wrote *Honourable Estate*, not a "hopeless failure," but by no means as powerful as the *Testament*. As I have tried to show, *Honourable Estate*, like many of the novels these Somervillians wrote, finds the supposed requirements of the novel too constricted and constructed to contain the educated woman. Without constant vigilance and effort, these requirements, these demands, simply reinscribe the romance rhetoric of the early century in general and the Oxford educational community in particular. What Brittain does with her testaments—that is, she abandons the fictional form altogether, insofar as it can be abandoned—is to make more room, to give the educated woman a room of her own.

Unlike Dorothy L. Sayers, Brittain considered herself an ardent feminist. Indeed, her feminist journalism (so precipitously condemned by Marvin Rintala as having "disappeared without a trace" [24]), recently reissued, sounds fresh and relevant sixty years later. Dale Spender in *Women of Ideas* passionately praises Brittain's lifelong feminist positions, especially her persistent argument "that men demand that women make their resources available to others, that men help themselves liberally to such resources, and then blame women because they have so few left for themselves" (629). Further, Brittain lived intimately with another ardent feminist for over ten years. Yet her fiction, unlike Holtby's and Sayers' and perhaps more than any of these Somerville novelists', repeats and reinforces the romance plot. Even the egalitarian marriage of Ruth and Denis seems to represent, as Christina Simmons asserts such companionate marriages do represent, "the attempt of mainstream marriage ideology to adapt to women's perceived new social and sexual power" (55). A satisfying explanation of this repetition and reinforcement would require exploring many more contexts—personal, political, linguistic, and psychological—than I have explored here, but this look at Somerville College and its women writers does, I think, suggest a reason not to ask for such an explanation. As we have seen, the Somerville experience had both shown these women that they could lead productive, independent, "manly" lives and urged them to ladylike and "womanly" behavior, which either explicitly or implicitly entailed the duty of using their newly acquired knowledge and skills in the service of mankind. Attempts to balance these lessons in life and, for the writers among them, in fiction quickly became the quandary of the university-educated woman. Without directly attempting, as I think Kennedy attempted in *The Heroes of Clone,* Sayers in *Gaudy Night,* Jaeger in *The Man With Sex Senses,* and Holtby in *The Crowded Street,* to sort out these conflicting discourses, even the most explicit advocate of women's rights would become confused in applying her convictions to her own life and her own novels, since both female life and the novel are so thoroughly grounded in the romance ideology.

Life and novel demand romance. The question we should perhaps put to these texts is not why an ardent feminist would reproduce these demands when writing in a genre so imbued with them but how any woman could *not* reproduce them. Virginia Woolf, that intrepid experimenter, after trying in her early novels to write a new story within a traditional novelistic form, learned to break that form, as DuPlessis illustrates. But few of Woolf's contemporaries knew how to read her texts. Winifred Holtby did and, further, recognized the relationship between Woolf's literary heritage and her fearless exploration of its conventions. Woolf the writer was, Holtby asserts in *Virginia Woolf*, "intellectually free, candid and unafraid" (18). Doreen Wallace's impatience with such experimentation was, however, a more common response. Simply injecting the educated woman into the traditional novel, as I think she and the other Somerville novelists tried to do, introduced the same sort of irritant to the genre as simply injecting the educated woman into a traditional society introduced into the script for her life. To realize this, to write about it, to prod and interrogate it, without Woolf's access to means of production, as it were, seems to me a remarkable accomplishment. The variety of strategies eventually evolved by Sayers, Kennedy, Jaeger, and Holtby testifies to their own intrepidity and surprises more than their less coherent (*Unnatural Death*) or too coherent (*The Constant Nymph*) early efforts, surprises more than the less coherent novels of Brittain and the too coherent novels of Doreen Wallace. I have been appropriately, consistently, and greedily surprised.

Notes

Introduction

1. The phrase "to come up," as determined American readers of British fiction eventually figure out, is a phrase meaning to take up residence at the university, to begin one's student life. "To go down" means to leave—either temporarily (e.g. for a vacation) or permanently—and "to be sent down" means to be asked to leave.

2. "Scholarships" and "exhibitions" are awards of financial assistance for entering students. They are based on examination results—an exhibition is the less prestigious. Both exhibitioners and scholars wore gowns different from those of the rest of the students, the "commoners." At the other end of one's university career, a "First" is given to the students who perform best on the final examinations.

Chapter One

1. Viscountess Rhondda, later a friend of Winifred Holtby, founded the feminist journal *Time and Tide* in 1920 along with Rebecca West, E. M. Delafield, and Cecily Hamilton. Holtby became a director in 1926; both she and Brittain contributed regularly.

Some of their pieces are reprinted in *Testament of a Generation*, and Dale Spender edited selections from the journal's first fifteen years— *Time and Tide Wait for No Man*. London: Pandora, 1984.

2.   The situation at Cambridge was, as Woolf suggests, comparable. The one exception to poverty-plagued women's colleges was Royal Holloway College, an independent institution founded in 1886 in the rather isolated community of Egham, twenty miles from London, by a rich philanthropist. It had "an endowment of nearly a quarter of a million pounds" and, "in sharp contrast to other impoverished and comfortless women's colleges of the day, was celebrated alike for its good living and excellent food. It had its own kitchen gardens, asparagus and strawberry beds, orchards and piggeries. Dinner in the great central dining hall was served by the butler and a line of starched maids off solid silver plate with specially woven monogrammed table linen" (Spurling, 129–131). In 1888 it became a part of London University.

3.   For a history of the women's colleges at Oxford, see Brittain's *Women at Oxford*. On Somerville itself: *Somerville College* by Muriel St. Clare Byrne (contemporary and good friend of Dorothy L. Sayers) and Catherine Hope Mansfield; *A Somervillian Looks Back* by Vera Farnell; and the Somerville centenary publication by de Villiers et al. The latter two publications may be obtained from Somerville College, Oxford.

4.   "Home students" are what my California college called, insultingly enough, "day dogs," that is, non-residents. The "Home Student" association at Oxford functioned as a sort of college of its own. The Senior Student was the student head of the association. Among famous Home Students contemporary with the Somerville group is Naomi Mitchison. Like them, she wrote in a variety of genres including novels, poetry, political essays, and drama. Most unusually, however, at the age of sixty-three she wrote her first science fiction novel, *Memoirs of a Spacewoman*. Even more unusual, it is, as the title suggests, feminist sci fi.

5.   There was widespread talk during this period about opening upper-crust Oxford to people from all social backgrounds. Although the women's colleges were more egalitarian than the men's, they were by no means available to working-class women. "Poorer students" were, for the most part, middle-class students like Holtby, Brittain, and Sayers—but there were many such, in part perhaps because upper-class women, like Lady Rhonnda, did not find the ascetic atmosphere congenial.

6. For a current analysis of the rhetoric of the battle between the sexes in a more general context, see Sandra M. Gilbert and Susan Gubar's first volume of *No Man's Land: The Place of the Woman Writer in the Twentieth Century*.

7. Miss Penrose "reigned" at Somerville from 1907 to 1926. She had herself been a student at Somerville, starting in 1889 at the age of thirty-one (Farnell, 31). Before becoming Principal at Somerville, she was Principal at Royal Holloway College (see note 4). The novelist Ivy Compton-Burnett attended Royal Holloway while Miss Penrose was Principal there.

I use the "Miss" for these women because that is the form of address the subjects of my study used and because it conjures up, I think, a certain vision of academic women in the early part of the century which is important in understanding the terms of the debate on degrees for women.

8. A copy of this play, "Bolshevism in Bagdad," and of Sayers' creation "Pied Pipings or The Innocents Aboard" are in the Somerville College archives. The "red rag" refers literally, of course, to "bolshevism," but its context and the substitution of "rag" for the expected "flag" suggest the menstrual "rag" as well.

A similar manifesto, a song sung by the women of Girton College, Cambridge, is quoted by Martha Vicinus in *Independent Women*:

You may say us Yea, you may say us Nay
But the tide has turned and we've left the bay,
We've crossed the bar and we've felt the spray
Where the winds and waves have their freest play—
We like it, good Sir, and we'll have our way (143).

9. The archives does not have a copy of this play, but some of the songs are quoted elsewhere, this one in the Log Book for 1920. Jan Morris defines "Convocation" as the "theoretical assembly of all Oxford M.A.s, whose only functions are to elect the Chancellor and the Professor of Poetry. Members must vote in person, on the spot" (384). The "Cherwell" is the river that runs through Oxford. "Isis" is an Oxford name for Thames.

These stanzas are amusingly prophetic: Dorothy Hodgkin, Nobel Laureate in chemistry, is an old Somervillian, as is Margaret Thatcher, as was Indira Ghandi; the Somerville novelists were all popular and Margaret Kennedy's *The Constant Nymph* was a genuine "best seller"; Vera Brittain's daughter, Shirley Williams, also a

Somervillian, is an outspoken MP, former member of the Labour Cabinet, and one of the founders of the Social Democrats. There are, of course, many other famous Somervillians, some of whom are listed in the back of Brittain's *Women at Oxford.*

10.   This historical making of a women's college into a hospital for men is an interesting repetition of the fictional "fair college turn'd to hospital" in Tennyson's *The Princess* (VII,2), although the Somerville women did not, of course, like Tennyson's women, do the nursing. Possibly any college so close to the Radcliffe Infirmary would have been requisitioned, but it is especially symbolic both of women's status at Oxford and of women's presumed more proper role as nurturer and healer that the college requisitioned should have been Somerville.

Chapter Two

1.   Sayers came up with the name. One of the members, Charis Frankenburg, recalls Sayers saying "that if we didn't give ourselves that title, the rest of the college would." Frankenburg also remembers that "when later we came together, one of us suggested that the initials now stood for 'Middle-Aged Spread'" ("Talking of Dorothy Sayers").

Taking into consideration the difference between men's and women's position in the university at this time and Sayers' delight in imitating him—at which she was reputedly excellent—I suspect Sayers' relationship to Dr. Allen could be more accurately described as identification than infatuation. Sayers' biographers would probably disagree—Janet Hitchman goes so far as to claim that Sayers' crush on Dr. Allen prevented her from finding a husband (33).

2.   The tendency of these women to address one another with male nicknames again suggests their willingness/eagerness to play the manly part, not only in their plays but in their own interactions as well.

3.   Most of the information about the close relationship between Wallace and Sayers at this period comes from Wallace herself. Since Hitchman's biography of Sayers is dedicated to Wallace, I suspect that she is the source of the unflattering view of Sayers in this biography. I am inclined not to trust Wallace's recollections entirely, especially in view of her later bitter estrangement from Sayers.

4. Again, any vision of the women's colleges as embracing the lower classes or even admitting them would be false. Brittain's assertion here that class made no difference can be only partly true.

5. The two women rented a roomy flat in an unfashionable area so that they could afford to "acquire space for a housekeeper who would shoulder all domestic obligations" (*TF*, 114). Brittain's unquestioning acceptance of this arrangement again indicates her obliviousness to the realities of class differences. Though she took pride in her parents being "robustly 'low-brow'" (*TY*, 18) and not at all rich, they were, as were Holtby's, solidly middle-class.

CHAPTER THREE

1. I use the word "lesbian" in a fairly broad sense to indicate a woman whose primary emotional and physical (though not necessarily sexual) attachment is to other women. Nowhere does Sayers describe an explicit sexual relationship between women; even the Whittaker-Findlater relationship can be interpreted as a nonsexual romantic friendship. On the other hand, there is nothing to suggest that these women's relationships are *not* sexual. "Lesbian" applies to either possibility.

2. Although Miss Climpson mentions Clemence Dane (a pseudonym for Winifred Ashton) she does not cite a title. The book in question, however, is doubtless *Regiment of Women*, published in 1917 and one of the early expressions of the increasing hostility toward romantic relationships between women. It is, significantly enough, set in a girls' school; the villain is a power-hungry, unscrupulous ("a shrug of her shoulders had toppled God off his throne; and the vacant seat was hers, to fill or flout as she chose" [97]) schoolteacher whose "perverse" love destroys a bright student and almost destroys a young teacher. The latter, however, is rescued by cheerful young Roger who asks her, "What has any friend, any woman, got to say to us two? We're going to get married" (314).

The suicide of the bright student is interestingly revised in the near-suicide of a student in *Gaudy Night*, there egged on, not by a "perverse" teacher but by a "womanly woman," who believes, like Roger, that marriage is a woman's true vocation. The title "Regiment of Women" comes (like Father Ernest's "monstrous regiment of women" on page 49) from the 1558 tracts by John Knox, *The First*

Blast of the Trumpet Against the Monstrous Regiment of Women. Queen Elizabeth was not pleased.

CHAPTER FOUR

1. Bruce Merry quotes Julian Symons' judgment that *Gaudy Night* is a "woman's novel full of the most tedious pseudo-chat between characters that goes on for page after page" (24). And Merry himself, though he is willing to make an exception for *Gaudy Night*, thinks that Sayers' novels "do not age well" (18). The recent television dramatizations of the Harriet novels and the many, constant reprintings of all the Sayers detective fiction call both judgments into question. But Symons is at least correct in seeing *Gaudy Night* as a woman's novel, not because men do not enjoy it (Symons being an exception, of course) but because of the rigorous woman-centeredness, which I elaborate in this chapter, and because the "tedious pseudo-chat" is indeed gendered discourse whose meanings and significances may well be more apparent to women readers. The "cheese-paring" conversation discussed in my introduction is one example.

2. The possibility of combining dedication to an intellectual community with marriage or with other non-celibate commitment is not seriously considered here. Carolyn Heilbrun (Amanda Cross), writing a detective novel set in an American women's college fifty years later, can create women who do such combining—in part because conditions for women have changed, but also because faculty residence has not been so much a part of the American college tradition and because women's colleges in the United States have not, except for the early seminaries, had all-women faculties. Their sense of community has, of course, been correspondingly less palpable. Members of the Senior Common Room at Shrewsbury not only work together but live together as well.

3. Although the gesture may appear at first glance simply to reinscribe the giving away of women, that is, to reinscribe women as property, it is important to recognize that the gender of the gesturer makes all the difference. In patriarchal culture a woman cannot own another woman. By giving Harriet away, the Head of Shrewsbury reminds us that the traditional gesture is a patriarchal one and, in effect, undoes it along with the paternal claims which underlie it.

4. Mann (169) and others identify Miss Lydgate with Sayers' tutor Mildred Pope.

5. Ivy Compton-Burnett's biographer, Hilary Spurling (herself a Somervillian), notices this tendency in her subject's writing: "It is perhaps worth noting that the two books which unmistakably make use of Holloway College as their setting both deal, far more insistently than any of the other novels of I. Compton-Burnett, with strong currents of feeling between women" (136). These two novels are *Dolores* (1911) and *More Women than Men* (1933).

Obviously the writers of the twenties and thirties had a knowledge of lesbian relationships beyond those associated with women's educational communities. But none of my subjects was particularly comfortable, as my further analysis will illustrate, with these relationships. None had the sort of easy familiarity with homosexual subculture as did the Bloomsbury crowd or the expatriate women in Paris. It is, then, understandable that for the most part their treatments of intense same-sex relationships occur in the context of female educational communities—the place where these writers first encountered the phenomenon and where the debate rhetoric so lightly disguised real fear of these relationships. That Shrewsbury is relatively free from this fear seems to me significant. *Regiment of Women* (see note 19) is an obvious example of a book set in a girls' school which excoriates lesbian relationships, but Josephine Tey's *Miss Pym Disposes* is an even more appropriate one here since, like *Gaudy Night*, it is a mystery set in a women's college (here a college of "physical culture"). Unlike *Regiment of Women*, this text does not overtly condemn or even much discuss passionate friendships between women, but it makes clear the destructive potential of such friendships. The whole horrible drama of the death of one of the students is set in motion by the usually sensible headmistress who, blinded by her love for one of the students, unfairly gives her a plum of a post which should have gone to a much more suitable and intelligent candidate. The murderer—though she probably did not intend murder—turns out to be, not the overlooked student herself as Miss Pym first concludes, but her romantic friend.

6. This is not to imply that detective fiction does not itself have legitimate and numerous claims, many of which Sayers herself enumerates in her essays on the genre.

7. Sayers did a great deal of research on Collins in preparation for a literary biography she planned to write. Her material is available in the Marion E. Wade Collection; the book was never written.

CHAPTER SEVEN

1.   In Kennedy's *The Ladies of Lyndon,* written just after *The Constant Nymph,* there is a male artist character, James, who is similar to Sanger and Dodd. Beauman's remarks indicate her recognition of the contrast between "women" and "rebels."

CHAPTER EIGHT

1.   For a discussion of female empowerment by the absence/ death of men in war, see Gilbert and Gubar's chapter "Fighting for Life" in *No Man's Land.* Most of the male deaths discussed there, however, are helped along by antagonistic women. Holtby's male deaths are relatively free from female violence and so do not call attention to themselves as battle-incidents in the war between the sexes. What they do call attention to, of course, is the texts' need for female space.

2.   This image comes from a passage in Holtby's 1931 novel *Poor Caroline,* which recalls the party trope of *The Crowded Street.* A curate dreams:

> On the floor three couples of young girls . . . dancing to-
> gether, their charming faces intent, their young, slim bodies
> moving with grace and precision. Their hair was waved, their
> lips scarlet, their dresses of cheap satin or mercerized cotton
> symbolized their youth, their pride, their vitality and self-
> respect. They danced with sensuous yet sober pleasure, proud,
> sweet, lovely, unbroken things. Against the wall sat a row of
> older women. Their wedding rings had sunk into the flesh of
> their crippled fingers. Their gray sagging faces drooped into
> slackened necks which slid into huge, shapeless bosoms and
> distended stomachs (170).

The "wedding rings . . . sunk into the flesh" of the crippled fingers of the older women make clear the text's vision of the parasitic and debilitating nature of traditional marriage. Ironically, a dance is the very setting which pairs off young men and women, which, that is, lures young women into the bargain that turns out so disas-trously for them. But the young women here are dancing with one another rather than with young men, which suggests perhaps that for these young "new women" the bargain might at least be delayed. Note, too, the normality of the female community implied by this new dance. For a similar use of the wedding-ring image, see Adrienne Rich's poem "Aunt Jennifer's Tigers."

3. In *The Astonishing Island,* a distopian farce by Holtby, the narrator queries an islander about the latter's claim that women who do not marry are frustrated. "Frustrated from what?" the narrator asks.

"From—er—their true selves. Sex. Husband, patter of little feet.—Homes and so on. Think of the life of the Frustrated Spinster. The years pass on. Youth wanes. Daily she hopes. Daily she is disappointed. Will he come? she asks. He does not come. Warped and embittered—"
"Why?" I asked.
"Because she has no home."
"Do only married women have homes?"
"Of course."
"Do spinsters have to sleep out then?"
"Not exactly. But what is home without a husband?"
"Well, what is it?"
"Well—I mean to say—it's not a proper home, is it?"
"Is it an improper home?"

CHAPTER NINE

1. See, however, Brittain's *Women's Work in Modern England* in which, arguing for allowing teachers to marry, she suggests that celibate women are often "neglected," "dowdy," and not particularly good models of the professional woman to their charges. Her rhetoric about Phyllis Bentley (see *Chronicle of Friendship*), too, suggests that, as Bailey concludes, "Vera had some faith in the theory that marriage was essential and celibacy highly deleterious to women" (44).

2. Brittain and Holtby engaged in a debate on this very topic, and Brittain felt that Holtby and friends had set her up, but she

thinks later that they had not set out deliberately to hurt her. The Daphne-Virginia relationship mirrors in other ways the early Holtby-Brittain relationship.

3. This, as Joan W. Scott points out, was, however, "the politicians' explanation," which she claims, rightly I think, was "a far better justification in their eyes than appearing to give in to the militant tactics of the suffragists" (24).

By connecting the lessons of war with the lessons of Oxford, I do not mean to underestimate the role of World War I in the creation of the new woman. As *Honourable Estate* suggests and as new research on this period confirms, the war had enormous effect on the lives of everyone and, further, this war was, as the editors of *Behind the Lines* claim, "a gendering activity, one that ritually marks the gender of all members of a society, whether or not they are combatants" (4). One of these "marks" was women's new power and exuberance—and subsequent guilt, described by Sandra Gilbert in "Soldier's Heart." But Oxford women saw these as marks of Oxbridge education as well—in part, as I have shown, because there are many ways in which the Oxbridge experience was for them very like the experience of war, in the increased visibility of women and in women's acting the manly part, for instance.

4. The tolerance is, however, tempered. Although Ruth includes both her own sexual encounter with Eugene and her brother's homosexuality in the category "unorthodox relationships" (472), it becomes clear that some relationships are more unorthodox than others. One of the reasons, for example, that Ruth decides to "give herself" to Eugene is a fear that "he might go the same way as Richard" (470), and Denis responds to this explanation by assuring her that "nothing you've told me about him [Eugene] suggests he was anything but completely normal" (470). When Ruth reads of her mother-in-law's friendship with Ellison Campbell, she judges Janet to have been "normal" if "thwarted" and "starved," although Campbell's "passionate jealousy" (593) suggests that she is rather less normal. Brittain's own attitude toward homosexuality is also a mixture of tolerance and pity. Her book on Radclyffe Hall clearly expresses this attitude—an attitude not unlike that of *The Well of Loneliness* itself.

As Hilary Bailey points out in her biography of Brittain, the attitude was "compassionate and liberal at a time when compassion and liberality were probably less available than they are today" (71).

Bailey uses this compassionate but "not partisan" attitude to dismiss "gossip" that Brittain and Holtby had a lesbian relationship. I agree that Brittain's detached tolerance makes it unlikely; what is disturbing, however, about Brittain's attitude is that it seems oblivious of Holtby's feelings toward her, feelings that (in spite of the fact—a fact for which we have only Brittain's word—that "Winifred died with Harry Pearson's name on her lips," Bailey 71) seem to me unequivocably lesbian. Thus there is a sense in which Brittain herself seems to have replicated Janet's mistake in *Honourable Estate*. If Brittain did, on some level, recognize the nature of Holtby's feelings, she systematically refused to acknowledge them, much as she refused for so long to acknowledge the severity of Holtby's illness and to acknowledge her own efforts to "replace" Holtby with Phyllis Bentley (see Bailey 87–91).

Holtby's view of homosexuality is, like her fiction, rather more radical than Brittain's. In the conclusion to *Women and a Changing Civilization*, for example, she writes,

> We do not know how much of what we usually describe as "feminine characteristics" are really "masculine," and how much "masculinity" is common to both sexes. Our hazards are often wildly off the mark. We do not even know—though we theorise and penalise with ferocious confidence—whether the "normal" sexual relationship is homo- or bi- or heterosexual. We are content to make vast generalizations which quite often fit the facts well enough to be tolerable, but which—also quite often—inflict indescribable because indefinable suffering on those individuals who cannot without pain conform to our rough-and-ready attempt to make all men good and happy (192).

5. Significantly, one of the younger generation of writers whom Ellison Campbell encounters at the Merriam Society in 1929 is Winifred Holtby who, though only mentioned here (578) seems to promise a new standard of women's writing and to be one of those young women whom Campbell thinks able to "imagine that it was possible to marry and have children, and bring them up decently, and yet occupy a leading position in some art or profession." Although Holtby may have been able to imagine the combination, she never married, and if there could be said to be a person around

whom her life revolved, it was not a man but her friend Vera Brittain. Brittain's theory, however, was that Holtby's true love was Harry Pearson. In his recent narrative of the Catlin-Brittains, *Family Quartet*, Vera Brittain's son John Catlin says, "my mother felt strongly that Winifred's feelings for Harry were deeper than she [Holtby] realized . . . but her response came too late, so that what might have blossomed did not do so" (46). Like Brittain herself, Catlin implies that Holtby's "love" for Pearson argues against any sort of lesbian feelings between Holtby and Brittain. Interestingly enough, however, Catlin also hints, in his maddeningly oblique way, that Pearson may have been gay. He describes him as a "loner" and claims that it is "significant" that Pearson's "best friend" in India was T. E. Lawrence, "another, if more spectacular, loner" (47).

6. This comment makes clear, again, that in this text the feminist rhetoric applies only to middle- and upper-class women. At the same time, the trickle-down effect applies: with better conditions for upper-class women, the nurses and housemaids are better treated.

7. She had, admittedly, also a passionate friendship, possibly sexual, with a man, George Brett of Macmillan (her publishers). He, too, was married, and like Brittain's husband lived in the United States so was thus safely removed from her daily life.

8. The powerful attraction of a woman to an older woman, now dead, but with writing left behind is a popular theme in women's fiction. *The Heroes of Clone*, Mary Gordon's *In the Company of Women*, Amanda Cross's *Sweet Death, Kind Death* are other examples.

9. By "autobiographical project" I mean the three testaments and the diaries which are being published as "chronicles." None of these works is, strictly speaking, a traditional, formal autobiography.

List of Works Cited

Adam, Ruth. *I'm Not Complaining.* 1938. New York: The Dial Press, Virago Edition, 1984.

Ashton, Winifred. *Regiment of Women.* 1917. Westport, Connecticut: Greenwood Press, 1978.

Auerbach, Nina. *Communities of Women: An Idea in Fiction.* Cambridge: Harvard University Press, 1978.

Bailey, Hilary. *Vera Brittain.* Middlesex: Penguin Books, 1987.

Beauman, Nicola. *A Very Great Profession: The Woman's Novel 1914 – 1939.* London: Virago Press, 1983.

————. Introduction. *The Ladies of Lyndon* by Margaret Kennedy. London: Virago Press, 1981.

Bentley, Phyllis. *Inheritance.* New York: Grosset and Dunlap, 1932.

Berry, Paul, and Alan Bishop, eds. *Testament of a Generation: The Journalism of Vera Brittain and Winifred Holtby.* London: Virago Press, 1985.

Birley, Julia. Letter to the author, 12 January 1988.

Bishop, Alan, ed. *Chronicle of Friendship: Vera Brittain's Diary of the Thirties.* London: Gollancz, 1986.

"Bolshevism in Bagdad." Going-Down Play. MS. 1921. Somerville College Archives.

Brabazon, James. *Dorothy L. Sayers.* London: Gollancz, 1981.

Brittain, Vera. *Chronicle of Friendship*, see Bishop.

———. *Chronicle of Youth: The War Diary 1913–1917*. Ed. Alan Bishop with Terry Smart. New York: Morrow, 1982.

———. *The Dark Tide*. London: Grant Richards, 1923.

———. *Halcyon or The Future of Monogamy*. London: Kegan Paul, 1929.

———. *Honourable Estate*. New York: Macmillan, 1936.

———. *Lady into Woman*. New York: Macmillan, 1953.

———. *Not Without Honour*. London: Grant Richards, 1942.

———. *On Becoming a Writer*. London: Hutchison, 1947.

———. *Radclyffe Hall: A Case of Obscenity?* London: Femina Books, 1968.

———. *Testament of Experience*. 1957. New York: Seaview Books, 1981.

———. *Testament of Friendship: The Story of Winifred Holtby*. London: Macmillan, 1940.

———. *Testament of a Generation*, see Berry.

———. *Testament of Youth*. 1933. London: Virago Press, 1978.

———. *The Women at Oxford*. London: Harrap & Co., 1960.

———. *Women's Work in Modern England*. London: Noel Douglas, 1928.

Brittain, Vera, and Geoffrey Handley-Taylor, eds. *Selected Letters of Winifred Holtby and Vera Brittain 1920–1935*. London: Brown and Sons, 1960.

Brody, Miriam. "The Haunting of *Gaudy Night*: Misreading in a Work of Detective Fiction." *Style* 19 (Spring 1985): 94–116.

Brooks, Peter. *Reading for the Plot: Design and Intention in Narrative*. New York: Knopf, 1984.

Brownstein, Rachel. *Becoming a Heroine: Reading about Women in Novels*. New York: Viking Press, 1982.

Byrne, Muriel St. Clare, and Catherine Hope Mansfield. *Somerville College, 1879–1921*. Oxford: Oxford University Press, 1922.

Cadogan, Mary, and Patricia Craig. *Women and Children First: The Fiction of Two World Wars*. London: Gollancz, 1978.

Campbell, Sue Ellen. "The Detective Heroine and the Death of Her Hero: Dorothy Sayers to P. D. James." *Modern Fiction Studies* 29 (1983): 497–521.

Cary, Meredith. *Different Drummers: A Study of Cultural Alternatives in Fiction*, Metuchen, N.J.: The Scarecrow Press, 1984.

Catlin, John. *Family Quartet*. London: Hamish Hamilton, 1987.

Compton-Burnett, I. *Dolores.* 1911. London: Blackwood, 1971.

Cross, Amanda. *Sweet Death, Kind Death.* 1984. New York: Ballantine, 1985.

"A Day of Her Life at Oxford." By a Lady Undergraduate. *Murray's Magazine* 3 (May 1888): 678–688.

"A Day of His Life at Oxford." By an Undergraduate. *Murray's Magazine* 3 (May 1888): 664–677.

Delafield, E. M. *Diary of a Provincial Lady.* New York: Harper, 1931.

———. *A Good Man's Love.* New York: Harper, 1932.

de Villiers, Anne, Hazel Fox, and Pauline Adams. *Somerville College, Oxford, 1879–1979: A Century in Pictures.* Oxford: Somerville College, 1978.

DuPlessis, Rachel Blau. *Writing Beyond the Ending: Narrative Strategies of Twentieth-Century Women Writers.* Bloomington: Indiana University Press, 1985.

Ellmann, Mary. *Thinking About Women.* New York: Harcourt, Brace, and World, 1968.

Farnell, Vera. *A Somervillian Looks Back.* Oxford: Oxford University Press, 1948 (privately printed).

Feinstein, Elaine. Introduction. *Company Parade* by Storm Jameson. London: Virago, 1985.

The Fritillary. Publication of the Oxford women students. Various issues from 1912 through 1922. Somerville College and Lady Margaret Hall Archives.

Gaillard, Dawson. *Dorothy L. Sayers.* New York: Ungar, 1981.

Gilbert, Sandra M. "Soldier's Heart: Literary Men, Literary Women, and the Great War." In Higonnet et al., 197–226.

Gilbert, Sandra M., and Susan Gubar. *The Madwoman in the Attic: The Woman Writer and the Nineteenth-Century Literary Imagination.* New Haven: Yale University Press, 1979.

———. *No Man's Land: The Place of the Woman Writer in the Twentieth Century.* Vol. 1. New Haven: Yale University Press, 1988.

Grant, Joy. *Stella Benson: A Biography.* London: Macmillan, 1987.

Gregory, E. R. "Wilkie Collins and Dorothy L. Sayers." In Hannay, 51–64.

Hannay, Margaret P., ed. *As Her Wimsey Took Her: Critical Essays on the Work of Dorothy L. Sayers.* Kent, Ohio: Kent State University Press, 1979.

Heilbrun, Carolyn. "Biography Between the Lines." Rev. of *Dorothy L. Sayers: A Biography,* by James Brabazon and *Dorothy L.*

Sayers: A Literary Biography, by Ralph E. Hone, *American Scholar* 51 (1982): 552–561.

———. Introduction. *Testament of Experience* by Vera Brittain. New York: Seaview, 1981.

———. Introduction. *Testament of Friendship* by Vera Brittain. New York: Wideview, 1981.

———. "Sayers, Lord Peter and God." In *Lord Peter*, ed. James Sandoe. New York: Harper and Row, 1972, rpt. from *The American Scholar* 37 (Spring 1968).

Higonnet, Margaret Randolph, Jane Jenson, Sonya Michel, and Margaret Collins Weitz, eds. *Behind the Lines: Gender and the Two World Wars.* New Haven: Yale University Press, 1987.

Hitchman, Janet. *Such a Strange Lady.* New York: Avon, 1976.

Hobhouse, Christopher. *Oxford: As it was and as it is today.* London: B. T. Batsford, 1939.

Holtby, Winifred. *The Astonishing Island.* London: Lovat Dickson, 1933.

———. *The Crowded Street.* 1924. London: Virago Press, 1981.

———. *The Land of Green Ginger.* 1928. Chicago: Cassandra Editions, 1977.

———. *Letters to a Friend.* Ed. Alice Holtby and Jean McWilliam. New York: Macmillan, 1938.

———. *Mandoa, Mandoa!* 1933. London: Virago Press, 1982.

———. *Poor Caroline.* New York: Robert M. McBridge, 1931.

———. *South Riding: An English Landscape.* 1936. London: The Reprint Society, 1949.

———. *Virginia Woolf: A Critical Memoir.* 1932. Chicago: Cassandra Editions, 1978.

———. *Women and a Changing Civilization.* 1935. Chicago: Cassandra Editions, 1978.

Hone, Ralph E. *Dorothy L. Sayers: A Literary Biography.* Kent, Ohio: Kent State University Press, 1979.

Horowitz, Helen Lefkowitz. *Alma Mater: Design and Experience in the Women's Colleges from Their 19th-Century Beginnings to the 1930s.* New York: Knopf, 1984.

The Isis. Publication of Oxford Students. Various issues from 1912 to 1922. The Bodleian Library.

Jaeger, Muriel. *Experimental Lives: From Cato to George Sand.* London: G. Bell and Sons, 1932.

————. *The Man with Six Senses*. London: The Hogarth Press, 1927.

————. *The Question Mark*. New York: Macmillan, 1926.

————. *Shepherd's Trade*. Ilfracombe: Arthur H. Stockwell, 1965.

Jameson, Storm. *Company Parade*. 1934. London: Virago Press, 1985.

Kennedy, Margaret. *The Constant Nymph*. 1924. London: Virago Press, 1983.

————. *The Heroes of Clone*. 1947. London: Hutchison Library Services, 1974.

————. *The Ladies of Lyndon*. 1923. New York: Dial Press, 1981.

————. Letters to Flora Forster. Jan. 30 (1919) and Feb. 23 (1920). Somerville College Archives.

————. *The Midas Touch*. New York: Random House, 1939.

————. *Not in the Calendar: The Story of a Friendship*. London: Macmillan, 1964.

————. *Together and Apart*. 1936. London: Virago Press, 1981.

————. *Where Stands a Wingèd Sentry*. New Haven: Yale University Press, 1941.

————. *Women at Work*. London: Macmillan, 1966.

Kolodny, Annette. "Turning the Lens on 'The Panther Captivity': A Feminist Exercise in Practical Criticism." *Critical Inquiry* 8 (1981): 329–345.

Layton, Lynne. "Vera Brittain's Testament(s)." In Higonnet et al., 70–83.

Log Book. MS. Somerville College Archives.

Longford, Christine. *Making Conversation*. London: Gollancz, 1931.

Macaulay, Rose. *Dangerous Ages*. London: Collins, 1921.

————. *Potterism: A Tragi-Farcical Tract*. London: Collins, n.d. (1922).

————. *Told by an Idiot*. London: Collins, 1923.

Maio, Kathleen L. "Unnatural Woman: A Feminist Study of Dorothy L. Sayers." Ph.D. Diss., Goddard/Cambridge Graduate Center, 1975.

Mann, Jessica. *Deadlier than the Male: An Investigation into Feminine Crime Writing*. London: David and Charles, 1981.

Martin, Jane Roland. *Reclaiming a Conversation: The Ideal of the Educated Woman*. New Haven: Yale University Press, 1985.

Mellown, Muriel. "One Woman's Way to Peace: The Development of Vera Brittain's Pacificism." *Frontiers* 8 (1985): 1–6.

————. "Reflections on Feminism and Pacificism in the Novels of Vera Brittain." *Tulsa Studies in Women's Literature* 2 (Fall 1983): 215–228.

————. "Vera Brittain: Feminist in a New Age." In Spender, *Feminist Theorists*, 314–333.

Merry, Bruce. "Dorothy L. Sayers: Mystery and Demystification." In Bernard Benstock, ed. *Art in Crime Writing: Essays on Detective Fiction.* New York: St. Martin's Press, 1983, 18–32.

Mitchison, Naomi. *Memoirs of a Spacewoman.* 1976. London: The Women's Press, 1985.

Moi, Toril. *Sexual/Textual Politics: Feminist Literary Theory.* New York: Methuen, 1985.

Morris, Jan. *The Oxford Book of Oxford.* 1978. Oxford: Oxford University Press, 1984.

Morris, Virginia B. "Arsenic and Blue Lace: Sayers' Criminal Women." *Modern Fiction Studies* 29 (1983): 485–495.

Oxford Magazine. Various issues from 1912 through 1924. The Bodleian Library.

Oxford Poetry 1920. Oxford: Blackwell, 1920.

Pickering, Jean. "On the Battlefield: Vera Brittain's *Testament of Youth.*" *Women's Studies* 13 (1986): 75–85.

"Pied Pipings or The Innocents Abroad: A Modern Fairy Play." Going-Down Play. MS. 1915. Somerville College Archives.

Powell, Violet. *The Constant Novelist: A Study of Margaret Kennedy.* London: Heinemann, 1983.

Reid, Hilda. *Ashley Hamel.* Toronto: Macmillan, 1939.

————. *Phillida or The Reluctant Adventurer.* London: Chatto and Winhus, 1928.

Rintala, Marvin. "Chronicler of a Generation: Vera Brittain's Testament." *Journal of Political and Military Sociology* 12 (Spring 1984): 23–35.

Roberts, Denys Kilham, ed. *Titles to Fame.* New York: Thos. Nelson, 1937.

Rogers, Annie M. A. H. *Degrees by Degrees.* Oxford: Oxford University Press, 1938.

Rosowski, Susan J. "The Novel of Awakening." In *The Voyage In: Fictions of Female Development,* ed. Elizabeth Abel, Marianne Hirsch, and Elizabeth Langland. London: University Presses of New England, 1983.

Sackville-West, V. *The Edwardians.* New York: Doubleday, Doran and Co., 1930.

Sayers, Dorothy L. *Busman's Honeymoon.* 1937. New York: Avon, 1968.

————. *Even the Parrot: Exemplary Conversations for Enlightened Children.* London: Methuen, 1944.

————. *The Five Red Herrings.* New York: Harper, 1931.

————. *Gaudy Night.* 1936. New York: Avon, 1968.

————. *Have His Carcase.* 1932. New York: Avon, 1968.

————. "The Importance of Being Vulgar." Untitled, unpublished MS. Marion E. Wade Collection. Wheaton College, Illinois.

————. "The Incredible Elopement of Lord Peter Wimsey." *Hangman's Holiday.* New York: Harcourt, 1933. Rpt. in *Lord Peter,* ed. James Sandoe. New York: Harper and Row, 1972.

————. Letters to "Tony." Marion E. Wade Collection. Wheaton College, Illinois.

————. *Murder Must Advertise.* 1933. New York: Avon, 1967.

————. *The Nine Tailors.* 1934. New York: Harbrace Paper, 1962.

————. *Opus I.* Oxford: Blackwell, 1916.

————. "The Profession of Murder." Untitled, unpublished MS. Marion E. Wade Collection. Wheaton College, Illinois.

————. Speech given at Oxford proposing a toast to the University of Oxford. Untitled, unpublished MS. Marion E. Wade Collection. Wheaton College, Illinois.

————. *Strong Poison.* 1930. New York: Avon, 1967.

————. *Unnatural Death.* 1927. New York: Avon, 1964.

————. *The Unpleasantness at the Bellona Club.* 1928. New York: Avon, 1963.

————. *Unpopular Opinions.* New York: Harcourt, 1947.

————. *Whose Body?* 1923. New York: Avon, 1961.

Scott, Joan W. "Rewriting History." In Higonnet et al., 21–30.

Sedgwick, Eve Kosofsky. *Between Men: English Literature and Male Homosocial Desire.* New York: Columbia University Press, 1985.

Simmons, Christina. "Companionate Marriage and the Lesbian Threat." *Frontiers* 4, 3 (1979): 54–59.

Slung, Michelle. *Crime on Her Mind.* New York: Penguin Books, 1977.

Smith, Constance Babington. *Rose Macaulay.* London: Collins, 1972.

Solomon, Barbara Miller. *In the Company of Educated Women: A History of Women and Higher Education in America.* New Haven: Yale University Press, 1985.

Spender, Dale, ed. *Feminist Theorists: Three Centuries of Key Woman Thinkers.* New York: Random House, 1983.

———. *Women of Ideas (and What Men Have Done to Them).* Boston: Ark Paperbacks, 1983.

Spender, Dale, and Elizabeth Sarah, eds. *Learning to Lose: Sexism and Education.* London: The Women's Press, 1980.

Spurling, Hilary. *Ivy: The Life of I. Compton-Burnett.* New York: Knopf, 1984.

Strachey, Ray. *The Cause: A Short History of the Women's Movement in Great Britain.* 1928. London: Virago Press, 1979.

"Talking of Dorothy Sayers." *Dorothy L. Sayers Historical and Literary Society Publication.* 1979.

Tey, Josephine. *Miss Pym Disposes.* New York: The Macmillan Company, 1947.

Vicinus, Martha. "Distance and Desire: English Boarding-School Friendships." *Signs* 9 (1984): 600–622.

———. *Independent Women: Work and Community for Single Women 1850–1920.* Chicago: University of Chicago Press, 1985.

———. "'One Life to Stand Beside Me': Emotional Conflicts in First Generation College Women in England." *Feminist Studies* 8 (1982): 603–629.

Waley, Margaret H. *Winifred Holtby: A Short Life.* Unpublished, 1976. At Somerville College.

Wallace, Doreen. *Barnham Rectory.* London: Collins, 1934.

———. *Carlotta Green.* London: Collins, 1944.

———. *Daughters.* London: Collins, 1955.

———. *Elegy.* London: Collins, 1970.

———. *Even Such Is Time.* London: Collins, 1934.

———. *The Faithful Compass.* London: Collins, 1937.

———. *God's Tenth.* New York: Harper, 1933. Published in Britain as *The Portion of the Levites.*

———. *Going to the Sea.* London: Collins, 1936.

———. *In a Green Shade.* London: Lutterworth Press, 1950.

———. *Land from the Waters.* London: Collins, 1944.

———. Letter to the author, 27 November 1987.

———. *Latter Howe.* New York: The Macmillan Co., 1935.

———. *A Little Learning.* London: Ernest Benn, n.d. (1931).

————. *The Spring Returns.* London: Collins, 1940.

————. *So Long to Learn.* New York: The Macmillan Co., 1936.

————. *The Time of Wild Roses.* London: Collins, 1938.

————. *Woman with a Mirror.* London: Collins, 1963.

West, Rebecca. *Return of the Soldier.* New York: Garden City Publishers, Inc., 1918.

Woolf, Virginia. *A Room of One's Own.* 1929. New York: Harcourt (Harvest), 1957.

Index

Spender, Stephen, 21
Spurling, Hilary, *Ivy: The Life of I. Compton-Burnett*, 228n2, 233n5
Strachey, Ray, *The Cause: A Short History of the Women's Movement in Great Britain*, 41
Symons, Julian, 232n1

Tennyson, Alfred Lord, *The Princess*, 230n10
Tey, Josephine, *Miss Pym Disposes*, 233n5
Thatcher, Margaret, 229n9
Thomas, Margaret, 14, 50, 227n1, 228n5
Tony. *See* Godfrey, Catherine

Vicinus, Martha: "Distance and Desire," 38, 143; *Independent Women*, 49, 229n8; "One Life to Stand Beside Me," 40
Virgil, 105, 107; *The Aeneid*, 90

Waley, Margaret H., *Winifred Holtby*, 35, 58, 59
Wallace, Doreen, 2, 5, 8, 12, 128–147, 149, 151, 226, 230n3; *Barnham Rectory*, 130, 139, 142; *Carlotta Green*, 142; *Daughters*, 139, 141–142, 143; *Elegy*, 129, 142; *Esques*, 56; *Even Such Is Time*, 137, 139–

140, 147; *The Faithful Compass*, 139; *God's Tenth*, 133, 136, 137, 138, 139, 140–141, 146; *Going to the Sea*, 130, 137, 138, 142; "Going to the Sea," 142; *In a Green Shade*, 56, 57, 128, 144–145, 146, 147; *Land from the Waters*, 128–129, 130, 136, 145, 146; "Last Love," 130, 137, 138; *Latter Howe*, 136, 139, 142, 146; *A Little Learning*, 1, 57, 61, 130–136, 138, 139, 142–143; *The Spring Returns*, 137, 138; *So Long to Learn*, 136; *The Time of Wild Roses*, 112, 137, 139, 143; *Woman with a Mirror*, 136, 139, 140, 143–144
Wells, H. G., *The Time Machine*, 110
Wentworth, Patricia, 9, 107
West, Rebecca, 9, 227n1
Williams, Shirley, 229–230n9
women's suffrage, 18, 29, 41, 44, 50, 180, 211, 212, 213, 214, 236n3
Woolf, Virginia, 6, 7, 9, 11, 12, 128, 146, 192, 225–226, 228n2; *Night and Day*, 175, 176, 199; *A Room of One's Own*, 14, 15–16
Wordsworth, Miss, 29
World War I: education and, 214; "the new woman" and, 216, 217, 236n3; suffrage and, 214; sexuality and, 214, 215